Stanley Cavell and
Philosophy as Translation

Stanley Cavell and Philosophy as Translation

The Truth Is Translated

Edited by Paul Standish and Naoko Saito

ROWMAN & LITTLEFIELD
INTERNATIONAL

London • New York

Published by Rowman & Littlefield International, Ltd.
Unit A, Whitacre Mews, 26-34 Stannary Street, London SE11 4AB
www.rowmaninternational.com

Rowman & Littlefield International, Ltd. is an affiliate of Rowman & Littlefield
4501 Forbes Boulevard, Suite 200, Lanham, Maryland 20706, USA
With additional offices in Boulder, New York, Toronto (Canada), and London (UK)
www.rowman.com

British Library Cataloguing in Publication Information Available
A catalogue record for this book is available from the British Library

ISBN: HB 978-1-7866-0289-3

Library of Congress Cataloging-in-Publication Data Available

ISBN 978-1-78660-289-3 (cloth : alk. paper)
ISBN 978-1-78660-291-6 (electronic)

∞ ™ The paper used in this publication meets the minimum requirements of American
National Standard for Information Sciences Permanence of Paper for Printed Library
Materials, ANSI/NISO Z39.48-1992.

Printed in the United States of America

To Stanley Cavell and Cathleen Cavell

The volatile truth of our words should continually betray the inadequacy of the residual statement. Their truth is *translated*: its literal monument alone remains.

—Thoreau, *Walden*

Contents

Introduction

Paul Standish and Naoko Saito

The theme of this book is translation. Its main concerns, however, are not primarily with translation as conventionally understood; rather it explores the idea of translation as a philosophical and educational theme and as a substantive feature of philosophy of certain kinds, especially in relation to the work of Stanley Cavell. Let us try to say why it is important to do this.

In 1971 Cavell wrote what he calls his "little book on *Walden*,"[1] a text that in some respects constitutes a microcosm of his work. The book was written in a period of some six weeks, in the summer of that year, and in a sense of shame, at a time when the Vietnam War was nearing its denouement. This was also something like a midpoint in the sixteen years it took Cavell to complete *The Claim of Reason*.[2] With a philosopher so complex and intertextual as Cavell, there is no obvious starting point, but in some respects *The Senses of Walden* provides a fruitful way into his thought. That book's emphasis on language, and on the movement of thought that takes place within language, reflects ways in which Henry David Thoreau himself puts words to work or, better, reveals the dynamism that inheres in them. This is explicitly linked to translation. A remark by Thoreau, late in *Walden*, contributes part of the title of our book and indicates its orientation: "The volatile truth of our words should continually betray the inadequacy of the residual statement. Their truth is *translated*: its literal monument alone remains."[3]

But Thoreau's words are cryptic, and they stand in need of some expansion. The words say something of the distance between the settlement or fixation of thought in words, and the dynamic and sometimes elusive nature of meaning; in a sense, they juxtapose being against becoming. They anticipate thoughts that become current in philosophy a century later. One might think of the "literal monument" as something like the signifier in its relation-

ship to the signified, or of Ludwig Wittgenstein's pondering of this relationship in such remarks as "Every sign *by itself* seems dead. *What* gives it
life?—In use it is *alive*. Is life breathed into it there?—Or is the *use* its life?"[4]
An adjacent thought, developed still more richly, is to be found in the
contrast Emmanuel Levinas draws, in *Otherwise than Being*, between *le dire*
and *le dit* (the saying and the said).[5] For Levinas, our lives risk succumbing
to a fixity of thought in which the relation to the other is arrested. For
Thoreau, to hold too fast to the crystallization of thought in words may be to
achieve a false security and to cling to false necessities. To see the truth as
tied to a dynamism, and in circumstances where, of necessity, not everything
can be simply shown, is to realize a certain volatility, which is at the same
time the element within which culture and creativity are possible—precisely
the conditions of human being. This dynamism in meaning illustrates that the
qualities found in translation as conventionally understood are in fact there
already within language itself: Hence, translation needs to be understood as
being at work not only inter- but also intra-lingually.

But can we focus this better? Translation is always in danger of becoming
a somewhat vague metaphor for transformation or change of one kind or
another, and this book does indeed address questions of transformation. But
the danger can be resisted and a more serious point made. It is an important
aspect of our position—and by no means an original one, of course—that the
movement of meaning in translation from one language to another (the ordinary sense of translation) can be seen as part of the movement of meaning
within language more generally. The present collection discusses translation,
then, not simply as a matter of interlinguistic conversion: Philosophical discussion of translation is likely to be of little interest if it is taken primarily as
a metaphor for transformations of one kind or another; it will be of significant, but limited, interest if it is taken as a topic for direct analysis, as in the
work of Willard van Orman Quine, for example. But for present purposes it
will be more accurate and pertinent to see it neither as a metaphor nor as a
clearly circumscribed topic but as a metonym of our lives. To the extent that
language is constitutive of reality, this movement of meaning is inherent in
that reality. It is a legitimate step from here to see that movement of meaning
as the very means and substance of human transformation of various kinds. A
conception of education that was insensitive to this would, we believe, be
significantly deficient, as would any conception of human nature that denied
these facts. But let us take these thoughts forward with more specific remarks
about Cavell.

Cavell claims that "Thoreau's book on *Walden* can be taken as a whole to
be precisely about the problem of translation, call it the transfiguration from
one form of life to another."[6] In his earlier work, *The Senses of Walden*
(1992), he refers to Thoreau's passage on truth as itself being translated.[7]
This remark also stands in need of further explanation, however, for without

it the danger just acknowledged presents itself again. What is apparent is that Cavell cannot be talking primarily about interlingual translation as conventionally understood. Here the emphasis is plainly on something more fundamental about language itself, on something inherent in meaning and, hence, in the meaningfulness and sense that can be given, to a human life or to the world. At the same time, Cavell's manifest attention to the nature of expression and to the forms that this takes in structuring our world should make clear that this is by no means to regard translation as a metaphor for more specific forms of transformation: What is at stake is the condition for human life as a whole—for human beings as linguistic beings. The religious inflection that is given by the word "transfiguration" implies nothing otherworldly but a dimension of ordinary human experience. This is Cavell's sense of the sublime in the ordinary, or transcendence down. [8] Thus translation in these senses is a quality that is internal to Cavell's ordinary language philosophy, which is associated, obviously, with J. L. Austin and, less obviously, with Wittgenstein. This is a quality that is hidden from view where philosophy proceeds with too great a confidence in the machinery of rational scrutiny and reasoned argument, of the kind that is found in parts of its mainstream. The reference to the change from one form of life to another is a clear acknowledgment of Thoreau's anticipation, as was indicated above, of the insights of Wittgenstein's later work, just as it is suggestive of the antifoundationalism of American philosophy in general. Translation is a window through which to see an encounter between Wittgenstein and American transcendentalism.

The qualities of language identified above are of particular significance with regard to education, taking this not as the preserve of institutions such as schools and colleges but as a crucial feature of human life as a whole. Cavell has had little to say about educational institutions, [9] but he has frequently remarked that he has been struck by the recurrence of education as a preoccupation in his writings. This is perhaps especially evident in his writings on film and literature, and the title *Cities of Words: Pedagogical Letters on the Moral Life* [10] makes this explicit. But it is there also, as indicated above, in his reception of ordinary language philosophy and of the later Wittgenstein. In an earlier collection, *Stanley Cavell and the Education of Grownups*, [11] we took up this theme especially in the light of a now famous passage in *The Claim of Reason*. There the argument of part 1 of the book builds to a kind of crescendo, emphasizing life and culture as processes of transformation with language and meaning at their heart. Cavell writes:

> What I require is a convening of my culture's criteria, in order to confront them with my words and life as I pursue them and as I may imagine them; and at the same time to confront my words and life as I pursue them with the life my culture's words may imagine for me: to confront the culture with itself

along the lines in which it meets in me. . . . This seems to me a task that
warrants the name of philosophy. It is also the description of something we
might call education. In the face of the questions posed in Augustine, Luther,
Rousseau, Thoreau . . . we are children; we do not know how to go on with
them, what ground we may occupy. In this light philosophy becomes the
education of grownups. It is as though it must seek perspective upon a natural
fact which is all but inevitably misinterpreted—that at an early point in a life a
normal body reaches its full strength and height. Why do we take it that
because we must then put away childish things, we must put away the prospect
of growth and the memory of childhood? The anxiety in teaching, in serious
communication, is that I myself require education. And for grownups this is
not natural growth but change. Conversion is a turning of our natural reactions;
so it is symbolized as rebirth. [12]

Experience of translation, turning our natural reactions, can denaturalize the
idea of language, such that the complacency of taking language to be a tool
of communication begins to be dispelled. To speak of the lines along which
is to have recourse not so much to a conventional verbal formula as to the
lines of words, their phrasing—where lines do not merely cross in conversation, in a straight-line communication, as is often imagined, but sometimes
veer off and pick up speed as with the swerving, the *clinamen*, of thought. In
translation, thought comes off its tracks. Such an idea of translation, we want
to say, is internal to Cavell's conception of philosophy as the education of
grownups. [13]

The present book is a development from that earlier work, with some of
the same contributors involved, but including others whose work has focused
more specifically and substantially on translation. Our discussions cast new
light on Cavell's pursuit of ordinary language philosophy, in which the idea
of translation appears in his work both as a substantive feature and as itself
thematized: Cavell here takes up ideas that are more or less explicit in the
work of Emerson and Thoreau. He also draws out aspects of Austin's writing
that have sometimes not been appreciated in the mainstream reception of
ordinary language philosophy, especially where its main value has been tak-
en to be as a corrective to infelicities in expression and as a supplement to
conceptual analysis. In such a reception the work is in effect grafted onto
philosophy-as-usual, and its radicality is missed. The thematization of translation is a means of elaborating this greater significance.

Cavell's work has also been misunderstood, as has that of Emerson and
Thoreau before him, through its incorporation into a conception of American
philosophy as pragmatism. Pragmatism coincides with these strains of
thought in some respects, but our purpose will in part be to show, especially
with regard to language and translation, the divergence between the pragmatism of John Dewey and William James, for example, and the transcendentalism associated with Emerson, Thoreau, and Cavell. There have long been

questions regarding the reception of American philosophy beyond the shores of the United States, and this has obvious implications for cross-cultural understanding. Our project is, by design, located outside or on the borders of American tradition in order to raise these questions of ownership and appropriation in a new way—and from non-American perspectives.[14] This critical engagement and exploration of these problems, we believe, *is* translation embodied in our ways of reading and writing: Such criticism enhances the reach of American philosophy while at the same time problematizing its identity as "American" philosophy—destabilizing the border between pragmatism and American transcendentalism, as we further explain below.

In the light of this, the book puts Cavell's thought with regard to translation in dialogue not only with the pragmatism of, in particular, James and Dewey but also with Giorgio Agamben, Paul Celan, Jacques Derrida, and Gilles Deleuze—connections that prompt questions of translation between languages, and about the nature of the truth to which expression aspires, in especially significant ways. It is important here that we draw on recent work, to which our authors have contributed, on "untranslatables" in philosophy—including such terms as *Bildung, ressentiment*, and care. We consider the life-long preoccupation with translation, both professional and poetic, in Celan and its examination by Derrida. Likewise, we ponder over Martin Heidegger's dwelling on questions of translation in his appropriation of Eastern thought—a preoccupation in Heidegger that itself has been subjected to criticism by Cavell.[15]

The inescapably political aspect of these matters is developed also in two further ways. First, there are the obvious questions of political domination, colonization, suppression, and restriction of language, whether by law, education, or commerce. Such matters are pervasive in *The Senses of Walden* and are prominent in the Cavell-inspired anthropological work of Veena Das, as they are in Cavell's own writings about film, where boundaries of class, gender, and race are to the fore.[16] Second, the political (understood, of course, in wider terms than, say, the party-political) is already at issue, as Cavell shows, in language's wording of the world—in the way our city is a city of words. The fact that the wording so described is fundamentally political can easily be obscured by too strong an emphasis on the overtly political. The essays in the collection help to show how this is so.

Translation exposes aspects of language that can easily be ignored, renewing the sense of the proximity and inseparability of language and thought. The ancient quarrel between philosophy and literature was an early expression of a self-understanding of philosophy that has, in some quarters at least, survived the centuries. The linguistic turn in twentieth-century thought brought about a revolution in significant respects, but there is a sense in which the implications of this are still to be pursued; there is a sense in which, with the contemporary reassertion of scientific naturalism, they are now being newly denied. Yet to further this line of thought is not to collapse philosophy and literature. It is rather to recognize that the relationship between them remains in need of continual rearticulation. The question at the close of *The Claim of Reason*, "But can philosophy become literature and still know itself?" expresses this ongoing need.[17] We place our book within the continuing approach to this question.

One reason that practices of translation cannot be seen in purely technical terms is that translation relates to the nature of judgment. To translate from one language is not to correlate the terms of the source and target languages with a third, more or less stable object of reference, for such objects must themselves come to light, and hence be conceived, according to the systems of difference afforded by particular natural languages. So translation necessarily works with incommensurability, and it is precisely the continual need to decide between different possible terms but in the absence of any stable referent that opens the space of judgment. Translation provides a space for judgment *par excellence*. No algorithm answers the translator's problems, and hence the exercise of judgment here is in some ways exemplary for our moral lives. But there is something more than this, too. The translator faced with the difficulty of translating a phrase finds certain possibilities presenting themselves.[18] These different phrases are what occurs to her most readily. Then, through reflecting on the inadequacies of each, on why each does not get the sense right, and on the different ways they go wrong, she may find that a further phrase comes to mind, and so on. The point is that this "coming to mind" occurs where this new space between possibilities opens up. Translation produces a new experience of thought, and the thought of something new. This is not simply the result of the exercise of judgment. At least that phrase, "exercise of judgment," is apt to fall short. It involves, rather, a kind of self-criticism and receptiveness of the imagination, our words always being tested in the eyes of others in the language community. This is the renewal of the "father tongue," in Thoreau's provocative phrase.[19]

The reconceptualizing of language to which these thoughts lead helps in understanding ways in which the child's acquisition of language is typically misconceived: It is understood within the purview of developmental psychology. What this misses, in its preoccupation with competence and instrumental purpose, is the significance of finding one's own voice—the stakes of which come to light in various forms of expressiveness and inexpressiveness, and in the recurrent faltering and breakdown of language, including the sense of what is beyond expression that language makes possible. Thoughts are not, on the whole, packaged into words, for it is words, as we have seen, that lay the way for thoughts. Translation, then, far from a merely technical matter, is at work in human being, and it is the means of humanization: Through translation our imagination and experience are humanized.

Our approach to this, in the chapters that follow, has been to begin by making apparent the general landscape of the book. We do this not in a systematic manner but rather by way of a series of chapters that work with the key ideas that concern us. This landscape extends across the territory of translation as internal to the nature of language, of translation as generative of human transformation, and of what we shall call the *immigrancy of the self*. Hence, the first four chapters—by Naoko Saito, Sandra Laugier, Vincent Colapietro, and Paul Standish—all deal directly with Cavell's philosophy in the light of the idea of philosophy as translation.

Following this, chapters by Joris Vlieghe, Ian Munday, Sami Pihlström, Megan Laverty, and Claudia Ruitenberg turn these lines of thought toward more specific matters, of practical significance for human life and education. It is important that such matters—questions of education, in particular—prove significant philosophically in that they lead to responses in which the blurred boundary between pragmatism and Cavell's American transcendentalism becomes more clearly accentuated. Moreover, there is within these chapters something of a challenge to Cavell's idea of translation and to the main current of thought in this book. The dynamic, dialogical aspect that this adds extends the parameters within which we address our topic.

The closing parts of the book, with further chapters by Saito and Standish, return to the landscape within which we started. This time, however, the idea of philosophy as translation is explored in relation to themes of philosophy as autobiography (with its implications for skepticism), in relation to Cavell's own experience and in the light of an idea of the immigrancy of the self.

The chapters that are included in this book are the outcome of an international project funded by Kyoto University (with Naoko Saito as principal investigator), under the aegis of the Supporting Program for Interaction-based Initiative Team Studies (SPIRITS), and with the title "Philosophy as Translation and Understanding Other Cultures" (2013–2017). Authors included in this volume are international members of this project, and the work presented here has been developed through a series of conferences and symposia—in Helsinki (November 17–18, 2014, in collaboration with Helsinki Collegium for Advanced Studies at the University of Helsinki) and in London (February 14–15, 2015, in collaboration with the UCL Centre for Philosophy of Education). We would like to thank Yusuke Arai (College of Law, Nihon University) for his work in making this publication possible by co-organizing the SPIRITS project and for his contribution to the convening of multiple meetings, including two conferences, during his term of office at Kyoto University. We would also like to thank Sarah Campbell and Isobel Cowper-Coles of Rowman and Littlefield International for their interest, thoughtfulness, and efficiency in bringing this text to publication, and Will True, our production editor, for his patience and attention to detail.

NOTES

1. Stanley Cavell, *The Senses of Walden* (Chicago: University of Chicago Press, 1992).
2. Stanley Cavell, *The Claim of Reason: Wittgenstein, Skepticism, Morality, and Tragedy* (Oxford: Oxford University Press, 1979).
3. Henry D. Thoreau, *Walden and Resistance to Civil Government*, ed. William Rossi (New York: W. W. Norton & Company, 1992), 216.
4. Ludwig Wittgenstein, *Philosophical Investigations*, ed. G. E. M. Anscombe and R. Rhees (Oxford: Blackwell, 1953), para. 432.
5. Emmanuel Levinas, *Otherwise Than Being or Beyond Essence*, trans. Alphonso Lingis (Dordrecht and Boston, MA: Kluwer Academic Publishers, 1978).
6. Stanley Cavell, "*Walden* in Tokyo," in *Walden in Tokyo: Stanley Cavell and the Thought of Other Cultures*, ed. Paul Standish and Naoko Saito (manuscript under review).
7. Cavell, *Senses*, 27.
8. Paul Standish, "Pure Experience and Transcendence Down," in *Education and the Kyoto School of Philosophy: Pedagogy for Human Transformation*, ed. Paul Standish and Naoko Saito (Dordrecht: Springer, 2012), 19–26.
9. See Stanley Cavell, *Themes Out of School: Effects and Causes* (Chicago: University of Chicago Press, 1984).
10. Stanley Cavell, *Cities of Words: Pedagogical Letters on a Register of the Moral Life* (Cambridge, MA: Harvard University Press, 2004).
11. Naoko Saito and Paul Standish, eds. *Stanley Cavell and the Education of Grownups* (New York: Fordham University Press, 2012).
12. Cavell, *Claim,* 125.
13. Saito and Standish, *Stanley Cavell and the Education of Grownups*.
14. David LaRocca and Ricardo Miguel-Alfonso's edited collection, *A Power to Translate the World: New Essays on Emerson and International Culture* (Hanover, NH: Dartmouth College Press, 2015), is particularly pertinent here
15. Cavell, "*Walden* in Tokyo."
16. See, for example, Cavell's readings of *Gaslight* and *Stella Dallas* in *Contesting Tears: The Hollywood Melodrama of the Unknown Woman* (Chicago: Chicago University Press, 1996).
17. Cavell, *Claim*, 496.
18. See Paul Standish, "Social Justice in Translation: Subjectivity, Identity, and Occidentalism," *Educational Studies in Japan: International Yearbook*, No. 6 (2011): 69–79.
19. Henry David Thoreau, *Walden and Resistance to Civil Government*, ed. Williiam Rossi (New York: W. W. Norton & Company, 1992), 69.

BIBLIOGRAPHY

Cavell, Stanley. *The Claim of Reason: Wittgenstein, Skepticism, Morality, and Tragedy*. Oxford: Oxford University Press, 1979.
———. *Themes Out of School: Effects and Causes*. Chicago: University of Chicago Press, 1984.
———. *The Senses of Walden*. Chicago: University of Chicago Press, 1992.
———. *Contesting Tears: The Hollywood Melodrama of the Unknown Woman*. Chicago: Chicago University Press, 1996.
———. *Cities of Words: Pedagogical Letters on a Register of the Moral Life*. Cambridge, MA: Harvard University Press, 2004.
———. "*Walden* in Tokyo." In Walden *in Tokyo: Stanley Cavell and the Thought of Other Cultures*, edited by Paul Standish and Naoko Saito (manuscript under review).
LaRocca, David, and Ricardo Miguel-Alfonso, eds. *A Power to Translate the World: New Essays on Emerson and International Culture*. Hanover, NH: Dartmouth College Press, 2015.

Levinas, Emmanuel. *Otherwise Than Being or Beyond Essence*. Translated by Alphonso Lingis. Dordrecht and Boston, MA: Kluwer Academic Publishers, 1978.

Saito, Naoko, and Paul Standish, eds. *Stanley Cavell and the Education of Grownups*. New York: Fordham University Press, 2012.

Standish, Paul. "Social Justice in Translation: Subjectivity, Identity, and Occidentalism." *Educational Studies in Japan: International Yearbook*. No. 6 (2011): 69–79.

———. "Pure Experience and Transcendence Down." In *Education and the Kyoto School of Philosophy: Pedagogy for Human Transformation*, edited by Paul Standish and Naoko Saito. Dordrecht: Springer, 2012: 19–26.

Thoreau, Henry D. *Walden and Resistance to Civil Government*. Edited by William Rossi. New York: W. W. Norton & Company, 1992.

Wittgenstein, Ludwig. *Philosophical Investigations*. Edited by G. E. M. Anscombe and R. Rhees. Oxford: Blackwell, 1953.

Chapter One

Philosophy as Translation and the Realism of the Obscure

Naoko Saito

The American philosophy that runs from Ralph Waldo Emerson to John Dewey, and then to Hilary Putnam, Richard Rorty, and Stanley Cavell in the twentieth and twenty-first centuries, shares the common idea of philosophy for life: It returns philosophy to the ordinary. Philosophy "must learn to reawaken," as Thoreau says, by "an infinite expectation of the dawn."[1] It is this sense of the dawn ever to be celebrated, I shall argue, that permeates the texture of the philosophies of these American thinkers. This does not, however, mean to present a unifying view of "American philosophy," but rather tries to elucidate its internal gaps, tension, and deviation, especially between Dewey's pragmatism and Emerson's and Thoreau's transcendentalism (via Cavell).

Within this general scheme, this chapter in particular will highlight the distinctive role of Cavell in renewing the dawn of American philosophy. Cavell is known to be a philosopher of ordinary language: returning language back to the ordinary. Putnam, who otherwise highly appreciates Cavell's work, has made the following remark: "My criticism would be that Cavell depoliticizes transcendentalism [of Emerson and Thoreau]. Remember that transcendentalism was an anti-slavery movement. It was anything but apolitical."[2] From more of an outsider's perspective, Michael Peters, in his essay "White Philosophy in/of America," identifies a failure in American philosophy, including Cavell's, in its social and political awareness, specifically in relation to questions of race.[3] The implication here is that Cavell is too personal or too subjective to be political, too private to be public, and too individualist to be social. In reality, however, Cavell's whole endeavor in his language philosophy is to demonstrate that the fact "that language can be-

11

come private needs to be acknowledged," and that "to make language public is a responsibility in each of us": and, further, that "language is not, as such, either public or private."[4] With Emerson and Thoreau, Cavell performs his antifoundationalist mode of thinking, following Emerson's remark: "The inmost in due time becomes the outmost."[5] In his apparently paradoxical combination of perfectionism and antifoundationalism, Cavell's mode of thinking and language exceeds Dewey's pragmatism. His American philosophy, the dawn still to come, discloses a chasm between pragmatism and transcendentalism—an internal tension within American philosophy that in itself is a dynamic source of re-creation of American philosophy, whose dawn still to come.

With this basic stance, this chapter tries to show how unique Cavell's rereading of Thoreau is in the light of ordinary language philosophy, and to introduce a perspective of "translation" as a helpful entry into his ordinary language philosophy, by reviving the latter's significance not only for personal transformation and perfection, but also for cultural renewal. After introducing Cavell's idea of philosophy as translation, I shall focus particularly on the notion of what might be called the *realism of the obscure*—a worldview that is elucidated in his rereading of Thoreau. I shall try to show that this distinctive realism is inseparable from Cavell's stance toward skepticism and its concomitant theme of the loss of the self. In conclusion, I shall argue that through translation as an incessant process of human's reengagement with language (symbolized by Cavell's and Thoreau's idea of the father tongue), humans are always open to a new possibility of and hope for rebirth and conversion when they are undergoing crisis. Such moments of self-transcendence are crucial components in one's understanding of *other* cultures.

THE ABSENCE OF THOREAU IN AMERICAN PHILOSOPHY

The literary redemption of language is at the same time a philosophical redemption; the establishment of American literature undertaken in *Walden* requires not only the writing of a scripture and an epic, but a work of philosophy. . . . The changes require have to be directed to the fact that is not only philosophers who have interpreted the world, but all men; that all men labor under a mistake—call it a false consciousness; and that those who learn true labor are going to be able to do something about this because they are the inheritors of philosophy, in a position to put philosophy's brags and hopes for humanity, its humanism, into practice.[6]

The importance of me of not losing my perception of Thoreau's philosophicality, the perception, let's call it, of an American difference in philosophy (something not equivalent to what one would mean, if anything, by "an American philosophy"), is my sense of the ease with which this difference is neglected within the institutions of philosophical education, so that the writing of Emerson and of Thoreau is persistently perceived as philosophically primitive or amateurish. This is painful enough if strangers accept it, but wrenching when it causes us to mistake ourselves, for then we stand to lose the America that is in search of itself.[7]

Thoreau's voice has been neglected in America and in American philosophy. This might be called the phenomenon of the *absence of Thoreau* in American philosophy. Dewey's silence about Thoreau is symbolic; Rorty and Putnam scarcely mention Thoreau. For Cavell this absence itself prompts questions concerning the philosopher's self-knowledge[8] and about the suppression of the voice of American transcendentalism by American culture itself.[9] For Cavell, the absence of Thoreau in philosophy in general and in American philosophy is the manifestation of America's "refusal to discover America" as Thoreau with Emerson perceive the "state of unawakenedness, or spiritual imprisonment. . . in an American way and place."[10] Cavell reclaims the voice of Thoreau as a philosopher who responds to America's own skepticism.

Cavell, through his experiment in reading Thoreau's *Walden* (1845) in his book, *The Senses of Walden* (1992), elucidates this blindness to and the suppression of voice in American philosophy. "Thoreau . . . takes his *Walden* as revealing the ways America fails to become itself, say to find its language."[11] The whole of *Walden* is a "work of philosophy" and it is a "text about crisis and transformation, or metamorphosis."[12] The original portion of the book was written in the summer of 1971 with his (as an American) sense of shame toward the debased state of America during the time of Vietnam War. This has not only literary and philosophical implications, but it also has political implications.[13] By shifting the framework of interpreting Thoreau's "private sea" (*Walden*, 214) as personal, private, or individualistic, Cavell's rereading of Thoreau enables us to find in *Walden* the running thread in American philosophy of "democracy [as] a way of life."[14] Cavell does not depoliticize transcendentalism; rather, transcendentalism permeates the political dimension and this requires self-transcendence via language.

In contrast to a stereotypical reading of Thoreau's *Walden* as a eulogy to nature or an environmentalist manifesto, or as the evocation of some kind of mystic experience in the woods, Cavell reads the book through something more like ordinary language philosophy. Following Ludwig Wittgenstein's idea of "leading words back from their metaphysical to their everyday use,"[15] Cavell says that "Emerson's and Thoreau's transcendentalism underwrites the philosophy of ordinary language."[16] Returning language back to the ordinary does not mean to replace philosophy's language by mundane ordinary words; rather, it means to find something uncommon in the common by being reengaged with language. Participation in language community means to "offer [one's] assertion as exemplary in some way, testing this against the responses of others, and testing her own responses against what those others themselves say."[17]

PHILOSOPHY AS TRANSLATION

The idea of translation, or to put it more correctly, of *philosophy as translation* helps us enter into Cavell's ordinary language philosophy. In this, the idea of translation plays a crucial role, internal to the very nature of language, as the way in which we engage in the world, and how it involves the whole process of human transformation. By elucidating this inseparable relationship between ordinary language and translation, Cavell's rereading of Thoreau's *Walden* illustrates not only the nature of language as translation but also the life of human beings as always being translated (and hence, in immigrancy): "The self is always to be found" (*Senses*, 52). He does this by representing Thoreau as a mediator who stands on "tiptoe" between borders.

> Heaven is under our feet as well as our heads. (*Walden*, 188; *Senses*, 101)

> In any weather, at any hour of the day or night, I have been anxious to improve the nick of time, and notch it on my stick too to stand on the meeting of two eternities, the past and future, which is precisely the present moment; to toe that line. (*Walden*, 11; *Senses*, 9)

Thoreau lives here and now on an intersection between the natural, the spiritual, and the political dimensions of human life, and between the past and the future. This makes him a translator who lives on borders, in transience, while at the same time attesting to the transfiguration of life.[18] Cavell is in tune with this sense of translation that permeates *Walden* as follows: "Thoreau's book on *Walden* can be taken as a whole to be precisely about the problem of translation, call it the transfiguration from one form of life to another."[19] Translation is a perspective through which to elucidate the antifoundationalist and perfectionist thought of Cavell and Thoreau. Cavell shows that translation is not simply an interaction between different language systems; rather, as part of language's intrinsic nature, translation permeates our life as a form of human *transformation*. Via language we are open to the possibility of undergoing the experience of transcendence in the ordinary.

Thoreau himself expresses this sense of translation with this phrasing: Truth refuses to be finally fixed; it is "instantly *translated*" (*Walden*, 217; *Senses*, 27). His antirepresentationalist and antifoundationalist view of language is characterized by transitivity and volatility. The idea of translation is most distinctively captured by Thoreau and Cavell's idea of the "father tongue"—"a reserved and select expression, too significant to be heard by the ear, which we must be born again in order to speak" (*Walden*, 69; *Senses*,

15). Reengagement with the father tongue is a way of sustaining the space of what Cavell calls "the daily, insistent split in the self that being human cannot . . . escape."[20] While Cavell says that the father and the mother are united (*Senses*, 16), their relationship is neither reciprocal nor complementary nor symmetrical. There is no "pure" original state in which they are united in a perfect fit. Rather, it symbolizes our dual relation to language.

We must relinquish any idea that translation is to be taken as a metaphor; rather, it is a "metonym" of our lives.[21] Undergoing the experience of translation means to experience the strange in the familiar. Again, Cavell captures this sense as below: "I consider that it is an essential moment in the work of philosophy to make human existence, or show it to be, strange to itself."[22] The scenes of translation in *Walden* that are revivified by Cavell's words convey to the reader (whose language is translated in the process of reading *Walden* with Cavell as a translator) that the act of reading and writing is to be engaged in the transient phenomenon of life in resistance to stability and fixation.

A symbolic image that captures this antifoundationalist sense is the idea of *bottom* or, to put it more correctly, the sense of *bottomlessness* in *Walden*: "While men believe in the infinite some ponds will be thought to be bottomless" (*Walden,* 190). "There is a solid bottom everywhere" (*Walden*, 220; *Senses*, 76). In the process of translation, it is the responsibility of a reader (or a translator) to weigh toward this and to find where to stand—to "stand on tiptoe" as if alert on a precarious border (*Walden*, 71). In Thoreau's idea of bottomlessness, this is not the complete negation of the ground or fixation. The task of Thoreau as a translator is to respond to this question: "How are we going to weigh toward [a solid bottom], arrive at confident conclusions from which we can reverse direction, spring an arch, choose our lives, and go about our business?" (*Senses*, 6). In *Walden* and *The Senses of Walden*, words are not mere words but are inseparable from the work of "*placing* ourselves in the world" (*Senses*, 53). In order to have "no particular home, but [to be] equally at home everywhere," one must acquire the art of *sauntering*, as a "*Sainte-Terre*," being *sans terre*, "without land."[23] Thoreau is "at home" at Walden Pond, but only in the sense that "he learned there how to sojourn, i.e., spend his day" (*Senses*, 52).

THE REALISM OF THE OBSCURE

In the process of translation attested in *Walden*, the inner and the outer are always in translation. Thoreau quotes from the poem of William Habington: "Direct you eye right inward, and you'll find a thousand regions in your mind yet undiscovered" (quoted in *Walden*, 213). He also quotes a maxim of "outward and visible sign of an inward and spiritual grace" (*Walden*, 47;

Senses, 91). Cavell pays particular attention to this relationship between the inner and the outer and says that the task of Thoreau as a "watchman of the private sea" is to be alert to one's relation to "*outward* condition or circumstances in this world" (*Senses*, 55).[24] The inward and the outward, however, never close their chasm. The relationship is not that of unification, but is always to be achieved as that of "neighboring": "Unity between these aspects is viewed not as a mutual absorption, but as a perpetual nextness, an act of neighboring or befriending" (*Senses,* 108). Undergoing this sense of gap within and without the self is the very experience of translation. A translator must keep standing on border between the inner and the outer always with the sense of the vague, the ambiguous, or in Cavell's words, "being on some boundary or threshold, as between the impossible and the possible."[25] Thoreau as a translator stands on a border between the heaven and the earth, the inner and the outer: "The self is always to be found" (*Senses,* 53). The experience of translation is to keep carrying the fated duality and gap of the self and between selves and the self and the world. This is how he was "at home" in Walden, and yet learning "how to sojourn" (*Senses,* 52).

It is the idea of obscurity that has crucial relevance to the idea of translation and the way of living on a "threshold."

> I desire to speak somewhere without bound; like a man in a waking moment, to men in their waking moments. For I am convinced that I cannot exaggerate enough even to lay the foundation of a true expression. . . . In view of the future or possible, we should live quite laxly and undefined in front, our outlines dim and misty on that side; as our shadows reveal an insensible perspiration toward the sun. The volatile truth of our words should continually betray the inadequacy of the residual statement. Their truth is instantly *translated*; its literal monument alone remains. The words which express our faith and piety are not definite; yet they are significant and fragrant like frankincense to superior natures. (*Walden*, 216–17)

The experience of translation accompanies and requires the sense of the obscure, the indefinite, and yet, paradoxically that is the condition of achieving a "true" expression.

Indeed the obscure is an essential component of Thoreau's realism. Thoreau's *Walden* is filled with realistic observation of the facts of nature and daily life. It is permeated by a sense of embodiment, his feet gravitating toward the ground. His realism, however, is not a matter of the exact representation of a "reality out there." A symbolic image that permeates *Walden* and *The Senses of Walden* is that of the obscure.

> You will pardon some obscurities, for there are more secrets in my trade than in most men's. (*Walden*, 11)

I do not suppose that I have attained to obscurity. . . . The purity men love is like the mists which envelop the earth, and not like the azure ether beyond. (*Walden*, 217)

Realism in Thoreau's *Walden* might be called the *realism of the obscure*—of a reality of the world that cannot be fully illuminated under light. The state of purity is to be obtained through obscurity: The obscure is the condition for achieving the rigor of thinking.

Ourselves in translation can only speak to the other as a "kindred from a distant land" (*Walden*, 1; *Senses*, 54)—the other never to be fully grasped. And yet, it is only through the process of translation that one can learn to be neighbor with the other. The gist of translation is captured by Cavell's remark: "What is most intimate is what is furthest away; the realization of 'our infinite relations,' our kinships, is an endless realization of our separateness" (*Senses*, 54).

THE TRUTH OF SKEPTICISM

The realism of the obscure takes us also into questions of skepticism—a fated human condition that originates in loss and separation from the world and others. This is at the heart of translation. Cavell tells us that Thoreau responds to a question of skepticism, the "scandal of skepticism," left unanswered by Kant (*Senses,* 106–7). Thoreau recovers the worlds as real. "His difference from Kant on this point is that these *a priori* conditions are not themselves knowable *a priori*, but are to be discovered experimentally" (*Senses*, 95). Thoreau's experimental and scientific spirit seems to foreshadow something of Dewey's pragmatism; and yet what Thoreau has in mind is a matter less of action than of passion—that we suffer what happens to us, and simultaneously that the universe answer to our conceptions (*Senses,* 112). Phenomenological reencounter with the world and the objects around us requires us to reword the world (*Senses,* 64) through a "redemption of language," bringing it back to the ordinary (*Senses,* 92). This is at the heart of Cavell's idea of the "truth of skepticism"—an idea that "our primary relation to the world is not one of *knowing* it" (*Senses,* 106–7, italics added). Cavell's articulation of the "truth of skepticism" is accompanied by his quest for remarriage with the world, which involves human transformation and translation. Remarriage with the world is not as, say, unifying as is Dewey's interaction, which is characterized by exchange, mutuality, and equilibrium.

Against the (western) philosophical quest for clarity, Cavell's worldview is permeated by the Wittgensteinian sense of the obscure and the transient (the ungraspable). Interpreting Emerson's response in his own effort to respond to the question René Descartes has left, Cavell writes:

The beauty of the answer lies in its weakness (you may say it emptiness)—indeed, in two weaknesses. First, it does not prejudge what the I or self or mind or soul may turn out to be, but only specifies a condition that whatever it is must meet. Second, the proof only works in the moment of its giving, for what I prove is the existence only of a creature who *can* enact its existence, as exemplified in actually giving the proof, not one who at all times does in fact enact it. The transience of the existence it proves and the transience of its manner of poof seem in the spirit of the *Meditations*, including Descartes's proofs for God; this transience would be the moral of Descartes's insistence on the presence of clear and distinct ideas as essential to, let me say, philosophical knowledge. Only in the vanishing presence of such ideas does proof take effect.[26]

It is this unresolvable sense of anxiety and groundlessness that separates Cavell and Thoreau's realism of the obscure from Deweyan pragmatism, whose inclination is always to move from uncertainty toward certainty. Cavell expresses this sense of groundlessness as "uncanny homeliness."[27] It is the idea of the ordinary and yet with a sense of strangeness as a part of the familiar. This again separates Cavell, Emerson, and Thoreau from the sense of the ordinary that is more commonly associated with pragmatism. In the former, uppermost on the agenda is the need to find a measure of life where there is no "fixed and immovable fulcrum."[28]

REBIRTH: TRANSLATION AS TRANSFORMATION, TRANSLATION AS TRANSCENDENCE

Loss and separation from the world is the condition for humans to leap further. Here comes another imaginary of translation: transformation and rebirth. With the metaphors of shedding "false skin" (*Walden*, 16) (or in Cavell's rephrasing, "cast[ing] off like a skin" [*Senses*, 59]) and of the birds' molting season, along with the images of morning and awakening, Cavell and Thoreau elucidate the occasions of rebirth and transformation. Transformation is not something at which one can aim at will; rather, like the animals in the wood, it needs to be *awaited* (*Senses*, 58). Equally, transformation in *Walden*, unlike the experience of religious conversion, is not simply beyond human control: It requires human labor, our conscious reengagement with language as "the father tongue requires rebirth" (ibid.). Translation is filled with apparent paradoxes. True expression is something both to be awaited and to be sought. The foundation of language, though newly created, is not conceived out of thin air: Our words must be "yarded"; and it is only from within such limits that one can become "*extra-vagant*," that is to say, wander beyond bounds (*Walden*, 216). Rebirth of the self is a matter of repossessing our own words, of "replacing" them where we stand (*Senses*, 92). This is to regain the answerability of the self to the self and to the world (*Senses,* 109).

Such "answerability," however, can never be the full solution of a problem, for, as Emerson says, "there is always a residuum unknown, unanalyzable."[29]

These strains of imagery invoked by translation invite us to a kind of self-transformation. Self-possession requires dispossession, losing of the self. We need to undergo "strangeness" to suffer from what happens to us (*Senses*, 60). Hence, passion, passivity, and receptivity are key terms in Cavell's recounting of Thoreau's words in *Walden*. In translation, we learn to be "beside ourselves in a sane sense" (*Walden*, 91; *Senses*, 102). In English, to "be beside oneself" is an idiomatic phrase that means primarily to be crazy, to be mad, or at least to be overcome. But here the phrase is qualified almost paradoxically ("in a sane sense") so that the madness is tempered or balanced. What is emphasized is that we must be taken outside ourselves, which is to say out of any complacent settled view of the world. This doubling, as Cavell puts it, is "the spiritual breakthrough from yearning and patience which releases its writher's capacity for action" (*Senses*, 102).

The success of translation hinges on regaining new interest and trust in the world, learning to trust ourselves to the world, and celebrating the rebirth of our words. A key to transcendence is *leaving* and *abandoning*. "The way of life is wonderful; it is by abandonment."[30] Human beings, as grownups, have a capacity to leave in "anticipation" (*Senses*, 110), with the conviction that "*we* can turn" (*Senses*, 97). The metaphor of melting ice at Walden in the early spring expresses this critical turning point as that of "the learning of resolution" (*Senses*, 99); here the implicit contrast is with the solution of problems. We might call this their attaining of a "pure" (or purer) state through the obscure. Our "renewed innocence" (*Walden*, 209) is not a pure, original infant state to return. This is, in Cavell's words, the state of the "eventual ordinary," the "actual ordinary" transformed,[31] where we are re-married with the world as our own and come back home again. Yet again, this is not the end state; the self is "knotted" to the next, further state.[32]

We regain our power as "the result of rising" only *through* and *after* we expand our circles (*Senses*, 136). This may be a frightening experience, and yet fear is the source of happiness and hope, the very precondition of regaining our tongue, the father tongue.

UNDERSTANDING OTHER CULTURES

Could a greater miracle take place than for us to look through each other's eyes for an instant?[33]

Does mutual profit here really mean hitting a home run rather than simply getting to first base?[34]

Philosophy as translation thus shows us that the life of humans is always being translated, transformed, and transcended; our selves are always on the way, with the gap and chasm never to be filled. Such translation already does and always will operate in the apparently trifling, accidental scenes of the ordinary. The gift of translation is for us to be able to undergo the moment of crisis—crisis of the loss of and separation from the world—and to celebrate the moment of miracle "for us to look through each other's eyes for an instant." The miracle of neighboring with the other is contingent to our incessant labor.

Self-transcendence through translation is a crucial component in understanding our own and other cultures. This is not a matter of the mutual understanding of a "different" culture but rather, of the understanding of *other* cultures—others not only outside, but also inside ourselves. Continuing reconstruction of the neighboring relationship with the other requires a conversion in understanding other cultures: Our reengagement with language is always already involved in our relation to our cultures, inside and outside. This requires an endless endeavor of perfecting one's own culture in encountering the other—to keep moving on to the "first base" rather than "hitting a home run." This implies neither the cosmopolitan fusing of the boundaries of different cultures nor the romanticization of the unknowable other. What is tested here is how each one of us can transcend borders: how the truth is translated while we ourselves are being translated. Our "home base" is kept destabilized and transformed. This is accompanied by internal transformation. The internal conversion is the condition of creating the public and criticism of culture from within.

Cavell's metaphor of hitting a single instead of a home run is a contemporary idiomatic expression of his Emersonian moral perfectionism, the idea of perfection without final perfectibility. Understanding other cultures is the experience not of closing the gap but of living with others in distance: "For the child to grow he requires family and familiarity, but for a grownup to grow he requires strangeness and transformation, i.e., birth" (*Senses*, 60).

Such internal transformation is at the heart of Cavell's idea of "education of grownups."[35] We as grownups are encouraged to create something new from within the constraints of our mother tongue and test it in conversation. Philosophy as translation does not drive us to relativism—to the idea that anything goes. Rather Cavell's antifoundationalist view of language reminds us of the constraints of the language community to which we are fated. Only from within such limits can we learn to acquire the language of "*extravagance,*" a risk-taking language, in which bounds can be transcended. It demands the rigor of teachers and students in their constant reconstructing of the criteria of language "to confront the culture with itself, along the lines in which it meets in me."[36] In this broader sense, translation is inseparable from cultural criticism.[37]

NOTES

1. Henry D. Thoreau, *Walden and Resistance to Civil Government*, ed. William Rossi (New York: W. W. Norton & Company, 1992), 61. Hereafter cited as *"Walden."*

2. Hilary Putnam, Naoko Saito, and Paul Standish, "Hilary Putnam Interviewed by Naoko Saito and Paul Standish," *Journal of Philosophy of Education* 48, no. 1 (February 2014): 19.

3. Michael Peters, "White Philosophy in/of America," in *My Teaching, My Philosophy: Kenneth Wain and the Lifelong Engagement with Education,* ed. John Baldacchino, Simone Galea, and Duncan P. Mercieca (New York: Peter Lang, 2014), 121. The question of race and the nature of this criticism is raised in Stanley Cavell and Paul Standish, "Stanley Cavell in Conversation with Paul Standish," *Journal of Philosophy of Education* 46, no. 2 (2012); see the main text and the endnotes.

4. Cavell and Standish, "Stanley Cavell in Conversation with Paul Standish," 157.

5. Ralph Waldo Emerson, *The Essential Writings of Ralph Waldo Emerson*, ed. Brooks Atkinson (New York: The Modern Library, 2000), 132.

6. Stanley Cavell, *The Senses of Walden* (Chicago: University of Chicago Press, 1992), 93; hereafter cited as *"Senses."*

7. Stanley Cavell, *Little Did I Know: Excerpts from Memory* (Cambridge, MA: The Belknap Press of Harvard University Press, 2010), 503.

8. Stanley Cavell, *The Claim of Reason: Wittgenstein, Skepticism, Morality, and Tragedy* (New York: Oxford University Press, 1979), 240.

9. Stanley Cavell, *"Walden* in Tokyo," in Walden *and Tokyo and the Thought of Other Cultures*, ed. Paul Standish and Naoko Saito (manuscript under review).

10. Stanley Cavell, *Philosophy the Day after Tomorrow* (Cambridge, MA: The Belknap Press of Harvard University Press, 2005), 220.

11. Cavell, *Philosophy the Day After Tomorrow*, 225.

12. Ibid., 216.

13. Paul Standish and Naoko Saito, "Stanley Cavell to *Woruden* no Sekai: Nihon no Dokusha he no Izanai" ("Stanley Cavell's *Walden*: An Introduction for the Japanese Reader"), in Stanley Cavell, *Sensu obu Woruden (The Senses of Walden)*, trans. Naoko Saito (Tokyo: Hosei University Press, 2005), 220: "This then is to see [a speaker's] autonomy as inevitably tied to the political (the creation of the *polis*)—as two sides, so it might be said, of the same coin—and to see it as inextricably tied to the conditions of response within which she finds herself. The political is to this extent internal, and literary activity conditions political participation."

14. John Dewey, "Creative Democracy: The Task Before Us" (1939), in *The Later Works of John Dewey*, vol. 14, ed. Jo Ann Boydston (Carbondale: Southern Illinois University Press, 1988), 226.

15. Cavell, *Philosophy the Day After Tomorrow*, 234.

16. Stanley Cavell, *Themes Out of School: Effects and Causes* (Chicago: University of Chicago Press, 1984), 32. He also says: "Thoreau is doing with our ordinary assertions what Wittgenstein does with our more patently philosophical assertions—bringing them back to a context in which they are alive" (*Senses*, 92).

17. Standish and Saito, "Stanley Cavell to *Woruden* no Sekai," 220.

18. Cavell pays attention to the fact that natural scenes and animals in the woods in *Walden* are described as those "awaiting transformation, moulting" (*Walden*, 58).

19. Cavell, *"Walden* in Tokyo."

20. Stanley Cavell, *Cities of Words: Pedagogical Letters on a Register of the Moral Life* (Cambridge, MA: The Belknap Press of Harvard University Press, 2004), 5.

21. Paul Standish, "Sophia Coppola's 'Valentine to Tokyo,'" paper presented at the 14th biennal meeting of the International Network of the Philosophers of Education, Cosenza, August 20, 2014.

22. Cavell, *"Walden* in Tokyo."

23. Henry D. Thoreau, *Great Short Works of Henry David Thoreau*, compilation, introduction, and notes by Wendell Glick (New York: Harper & Row Publishers, Inc., 1982), 295.

24. Cavell says: "The first step in attending to our education is to observe the strangeness of our lives, our estrangement from ourselves, the lack of necessity in what we profess to be

necessary. The second step is to grasp the true necessity of human strangeness as such, the opportunity of outwardness" (*Senses*, 55).

25. Cavell, "Walden in Tokyo."

26. Stanley Cavell, *In Quest of the Ordinary: Lines of Skepticism and Romanticism* (Chicago: University of Chicago Press, 1988), 109.

27. Ibid., 129.

28. Ibid., 111.

29. Emerson, *Essential Writings*, 254.

30. Ibid., 262.

31. Cavell and Standish, "Stanley Cavell in Conversation with Paul Standish," 166.

32. Stanley Cavell, *Conditions Handsome and Unhandsome: The Constitution of Emersonian Perfectionism* (Chicago: University of Chicago Press, 1990), 12.

33. *Walden*, quoted in Cavell, "*Walden* in Tokyo."

34. Cavell, "Walden in Tokyo."

35. Naoko Saito and Paul Standish, eds., *Stanley Cavell and the Education of Grownups* (New York: Fordham University Press, 2012).

36. Cavell, *The Claim of Reason*, 125.

37. Some of the ideas developed in this chapter are elaborated and extended in the following articles: Naoko Saito, "Gifts from a Foreign Land: *Lost in Translation* and the Understanding of Other Cultures," *Philosophy of Education* 2015: 436–44; "Philosophy as Translation and Understanding Other Cultures: Becoming a Global Citizen through Higher Education," *Educational Studies in Japan: International Yearbook* No. 9 (2015): 17–26.

BIBLIOGRAPHY

Cavell, Stanley. *The Claim of Reason: Wittgenstein, Skepticism, Morality, and Tragedy*. New York: Oxford University Press, 1979.

———. *Themes Out of School: Effects and Causes*. Chicago: University of Chicago Press, 1984.

———. *In Quest of the Ordinary: Lines of Skepticism and Romanticism*. Chicago: University of Chicago Press, 1988.

———. *Conditions Handsome and Unhandsome: The Constitution of Emersonian Perfectionism*. Chicago: University of Chicago Press, 1990.

———. *The Senses of Walden*. Chicago: University of Chicago Press, 1992.

———. *Cities of Words: Pedagogical Letters on a Register of the Moral Life*. Cambridge, MA: The Belknap Press of Harvard University Press, 2004.

———. *Philosophy the Day after Tomorrow*. Cambridge, MA: The Belknap Press of Harvard University Press, 2005.

———. *Little Did I Know: Excerpts from Memory*. Cambridge, MA: The Belknap Press of Harvard University Press, 2010.

———. "Walden in Tokyo." In *Walden in Tokyo and the Thought of Other Cultures*, edited by Paul Standish and Naoko Saito (manuscript under review).

Cavell, Stanley, and Paul Standish. "Stanley Cavell in Conversation with Paul Standish." *Journal of Philosophy of Education* 46, no. 2 (2012): 155–76.

Dewey, John. "Creative Democracy: The Task Before Us" (1939). In *The Later Works of John Dewey*, vol. 14, edited by Jo Ann Boydston, 224–30. Carbondale: Southern Illinois University Press, 1988.

Emerson, Ralph Waldo. *The Essential Writings of Ralph Waldo Emerson*. Edited by Brooks Atkinson. New York: The Modern Library, 2000.

Peters, Michael. "White Philosophy in/of America." In *My Teaching, My Philosophy: Kenneth Wain and the Lifelong Engagement with Education*, edited by John Baldacchino, Simone Galea, and Duncan P. Mercieca, 108–23. New York: Peter Lang, 2014.

Putnam, Hilary, Naoko Saito, and Paul Standish. "Hilary Putnam Interviewed by Naoko Saito and Paul Standish." *Journal of Philosophy of Education* 48, no. 1 (February 2014): 1–27.

Saito, Naoko. "Gifts from a Foreign Land: *Lost in Translation* and the Understanding of Other Cultures." *Philosophy of Education* 2015: 436–44.

———. "Philosophy as Translation and Understanding Other Cultures: Becoming a Global Citizen through Higher Education." *Educational Studies in Japan: International Yearbook* no. 9 (2015): 17–26.

Saito, Naoko, and Paul Standish, eds. *Stanley Cavell and the Education of Grownups*. New York: Fordham University Press, 2012.

Standish, Paul. "Sophia Coppola's 'Valentine to Tokyo.'" Paper presented at the 14th biennal meeting of the International Network of the Philosophers of Education, Cosenza, August 20, 2014.

Standish, Paul, and Naoko Saito. "Stanley Cavell to *Woruden* no Sekai: Nihon no Dokusha he no Izanai" ("Stanley Cavell's *Walden*: An Introduction for the Japanese Reader"). In Stanley Cavell, *Sensu obu Woruden* (*The Senses of Walden*). Translated by Naoko Saito. Tokyo: Hosei University Press, 2005.

Thoreau, Henry D. *Great Short Works of Henry David Thoreau*. Compilation, introduction, and notes by Wendell Glick. New York: Harper & Row, Publishers, Inc., 1982.

———. *Walden and Resistance to Civil Government*. Edited by William Rossi. New York: W. W. Norton & Company, 1992.

Chapter Two

Stanley Cavell, the Ordinary, and the Democratization of Culture(s)

Sandra Laugier

My thesis in this chapter and in my work on American philosophy is that the specific and contemporary theme of the ordinary sets off from America, and the transcendentalism of Emerson and Thoreau, in order to reinvent itself in Europe with ordinary language philosophy (OLP), and reappears in a transformed shape in America. But in order to understand this, it is necessary to perceive what Stanley Cavell, inspired by Ludwig Wittgenstein and Henry David Thoreau, calls "the uncanniness of the ordinary." What the ordinary is, and its relation to translation, is something I hope progressively to show.

In his foreword to the work of Veena Das, *Life and Words*, Cavell notes that the ordinary is our ordinary language insofar as we constantly render it foreign to ourselves, which invokes the Wittgensteinian image of the philosopher as explorer of a foreign tribe: It is we, this tribe, who are foreigners and strange to ourselves—"at home perhaps nowhere, perhaps anywhere." This intersection of the familiar and the strange, shared by anthropology, psychoanalysis, and philosophy, is the location of the ordinary: "Wittgenstein's anthropological perspective is one puzzled in principle by anything human beings say and do, hence perhaps, at a moment, by nothing."[1] The ordinary does not exactly mean the *common*. We no more know what is common than what is ordinary to us. It is not determined by a web of beliefs or shared dispositions. Common language nevertheless defines the ordinary: Between the ordinary (everyday, shared life) and ordinary language, between the proximity to ordinary life called for in American transcendentalism, in the cinema and literature that inherit it, and the OLP of Wittgenstein and J. L. Austin, the ordinary is the search for a new land to discover and explore, then to describe. The thought of the ordinary is experiential, improvisational; it demands new forms of attention to the human form of life.

"I ASK NOT FOR THE GREAT, THE REMOTE, THE ROMANTIC"

I will start from Concord, Massachusetts, where transcendentalism was born, and from the hypothesis of Cavell: that the distinctive feature of American thought, its capacity to begin philosophy again in America, is found in its invention of the ordinary. This new departure of philosophy—which has nothing of the clean slate about it, but rather, like the Hollywood remarriage comedies, has to do with a second chance[2]—is a reversal of philosophy's two inveterate tendencies: the denial of ordinary language and of our ordinariness in the philosophical pretension to go beyond them, to correct them, or again the philosophical pretension to know what we mean, what is common to us, universal. The call to the ordinary is traversed by the "uncanniness of the ordinary."[3]

It is from this perspective that it is necessary to register Cavell's return to Emerson and Thoreau. In a famous passage of "The American Scholar," Emerson, the founding father of American philosophy, asserts the intellectual independence of America, the appropriation of the ordinary in contrast to the sublimities inherited from Europe: "I ask not for the great, the remote, the romantic; what is doing in Italy or Arabia; what is Greek art or Provençal minstrelsy; I embrace the common, I explore and sit at the feet of the familiar, the low. Give me insight into today, and you may have the antique and future worlds."[4] Admittedly, recourse to the "common," to the "low," has existed for a long time in philosophy, and it plays a central role in English thought: Berkeley and Hume appeal to innate human understanding, as opposed to established philosophy. But there is a new accent on the ordinary here. It is not a matter of praising common sense but of bringing all thought back to the ordinary, to the categories of the ordinary—the low, the close at hand—which precisely stand in opposition to the great and the remote, and allow for the possibility of knowing "the meaning" of ordinary life: "What would we really know the meaning of? The meal in the firkin; the milk in the pan; the ballad in the street; the news of the boat; the glance of the eye; the form and the gait of the body." Emerson expresses here the demand for a distinctive American culture, as an alternative to European culture. Such a culture would be defined by this positive aspiration for the common. He anticipated the privileged objects of American cinema or those of photography, as though it were necessary to renounce "sophisticated" European art in order to envisage truly American ordinary art.

His list in "The American Scholar" of the matters whose "ultimate reason" he demands of students to know—is a list epitomizing what we may call the physiognomy of the ordinary, a form of what Kierkegaard calls the perception of the sublime in the everyday. It is a list, made three or four years before Daguerre will exhibit his copper plates in Paris, epitomizing the obsessions of photography.[5]

There is here an elaboration of a list of new categories, those of the ordinary, more precisely of the elements of a physiognomy, of a gait, or of a "look" of the ordinary, that philosophy but also cinema and photography to an equal degree would have to describe. It is as if the classic transcendental question has mutated: The question is no longer about knowing the "ultimate reason" of the phenomena of nature, but about establishing a connection to ordinary life and to its details, its particularities. For Emerson, this new approach, particularist and perceptual, is inseparable from a new relationship between classes, from a *democratization of perception* itself.

> One of these signs is the fact that the same movement which effected the elevation of what was called the lowest class in the state, assumed in literature a very marked and as benign an aspect. Instead of the sublime and beautiful, the near, the low, the common, was explored and poeticized. That which had been negligently trodden under foot by those who were harnessing and provisioning themselves for long journeys into far countries, is suddenly found to be richer than all foreign parts. The literature of the poor, the feelings of the child, the philosophy of the street, the meaning of household life, are the topics of the time.

The poor, the child, the street, the household: These are new objects that it will be necessary to *see*.

> In this he joins his thinking with the new poetry and art of his times, whose topics he characterizes as "the literature of the poor, the feelings of the child, the philosophy of the street, the meaning of the household life." I note that when he describes himself as asking "not for the great, the remote, the romantic," he is apparently not considering that the emphasis on the low and the near is exactly the opposite face of the romantic, the continued search for a new intimacy in the self's relation to its world.[6]

The search for the ordinary takes its meaning from the menace of skepticism—of the loss of or distance from the world. As he presents it at the beginning of "Experience," Emerson associates this loss with the failure of speech, which by definition renders it inadequate, or unhappy. It is this inadequacy, infelicity of language that in "Self-Reliance," Emerson calls the conformity of his contemporaries, and that Thoreau denounces as "quiet desperation": "Their every truth is not quite true. Their two is not the real two, their four not the real four; so that every word they say chagrins us, and we know not where to begin to set them right."[7] In their defense of the ordinary against the vain wish to conceptualize and grasp reality, Emerson and Thoreau are the precursors of OLP, recommending the attentive description of reality: being *next* to the world.

> The connection means that I see both developments—ordinary language philosophy and American transcendentalism—as responses to skepticism, to that anxiety about our human capacities as knowers. My route to the connection lay at once in my tracing both the ordinary language philosophy as well as the American transcendentalists to the Kantian insight that Reason dictates what we mean by a world. [8]

For Emerson, America must reinvent transcendental philosophy, while following its own methods, temperaments, and moods. It must then invent an access to the ordinary, this new nature—for which the categories of transcendental philosophy, the conceptual mode of access to nature developed by Europe, are inoperative.

Thoreau puts it nicely in *Walden*:

> It is time that we had uncommon schools, that we did not leave off our education when we begin to be men and women. It is time that villages were universities. Shall the world be confined to one Paris or one Oxford forever? Cannot students be boarded here and get a liberal education under the skies of Concord? [9]

This school of ordinary language will be found in Wittgenstein, but for Cavell, it signifies the importance of American thought. As Cavell says, "Words come to us from a distance; they were there before we were; we are born into them. Meaning them is accepting that fact of their condition" (Cavell, *Senses*, 64). The meaning of a word is its use: "We do not know what 'Walden' means if we do not know what Walden is" (Cavell, *Senses*, 27). So it is with all the words employed by Thoreau, to which he gives a new sense: morning (morning is when I am awakening and there is the dawn in me), the bottom of the pond (we do not know what the base is, or the foundation, so long as we have not probed, like Thoreau, the bottom of Walden Pond), the sun (a morning star).

"Discovering what is said to us, just like discovering what we say, is to discover the exact place of where it is said; to understand why it is said at this precise place, here and now" (Cavell, *Senses*, 34). It is the education, or the method of ordinary language to see why, when, we say what we say, and in which circumstances—because without its use a word is a "dead sign." [10] Everything is already in front of us, displayed before our eyes: We need to *see the visible*. Thoreau thus announces the project of the *Investigations*, which is to see the ordinary, which escaped us because it is near to us, beneath our eyes: "What we are supplying are really remarks on the natural history of human beings; we are not contributing curiosities, however, but observations which no one has doubted, but which have escaped remark only because they are always before our eyes."[11] One could return to a beautiful formulation of Foucault, where the important point is that he connects this ability to "see the visible" to OLP and its project of attending to ordinary usage to discover what is actually going on ("faire une analyse critique de la pensée à partir de la manière dont on dit les choses"): "We have long known that the role of philosophy is not to discover what is hidden, but to render visible what precisely is visible—which is to say, to make appear what is so close, so immediate, so intimately linked to ourselves that, as a consequence, we do not perceive it."[12] The ordinary exists within this characteristic difficulty of access to what is right before our eyes, and what one must learn to see. It is always an object of enquiry—this will be the approach of pragmatism—and an object of interrogation; it is never given. The low always has to be reached, in an inversion of the sublime. It is not a matter of correcting the heritage of European philosophy and of creating new categories; it is necessary to give another sense to the inherited words (such as "experience," "idea," "impression," "understanding," "reason," "necessity," and "condition"), to bring them back from the immanent to the common, or from the metaphysical to the ordinary. In the epigraph to "Experience," Emerson proposes his own version of the categories, with the list of "the lords of life": "The lords of life, the lords of life,— / I saw them pass, / In their own guise, / Like and unlike, / Portly and grim; / Use and Surprise, / Surface and Dream, / Succession swift, and Spectral Wrong."[13] At first glance, the lords of life resemble categories that control our life, our experience, and determine our access to the world, as with Immanuel Kant—those of causality, substance, or totality. But the list demonstrates that it cannot be these Kantian categories. By contrast, use, surprise, surface, dream, succession, evil, temperament—in Emerson there is the idea that a new list of concepts must be invented in order to describe the ordinary, the given, or, rather, the diverse materials that there are, "strewn along the ground." And it is a new ordinary man who will be needed to build or, as he says, "to domesticate" this: "This revolution is to be wrought by the gradual domestication of the idea of Culture. The main enterprise of the world for splendor, for extent, is the upbuilding of man. Here are the materials strewn along the ground."[14]

THE CATEGORIES OF THE ORDINARY, AND THE DEMOCRACY OF EXPERIENCE

If Emerson were satisfied with carrying on with the arrangement of the categories, and substituting for a traditional list (the European transcendental heritage) a modernized, Americanized list, the contribution would be weak.

To imagine categories of the ordinary alters the very idea of category. The idea of domestication of *culture* is not the idea of mastery of reality—because the ordinary is neither conceptualized nor grasped. It is not a matter of rewriting the list of categories, but of redefining their use: not as conceptual grasping of reality, but as neighboring the world. It is the recognition of reality as next to me, near or close, but also separated from me: as next door. This is the process of translating ourselves. Neighboring is a process of translation. The revolution achieved by Emerson consists less in a redefinition of categories than in a remodeling of what experience is, which continues from James to Dewey to Wittgenstein.

Hence, our relation to the world is no longer a matter of (actively) applying categories of understanding to experience but of (passively) watching the lords of life passing by in the course of experience. They will emerge from experience, suddenly appear—"I find them in my way"—as if the categories, instead of being imposed or posed, are simply to wait patiently and to be found: "Illusion, Temperament, Succession, Surface, Surprise, Reality, Subjectiveness—these are threads on the loom of time, these are the lords of life. I dare not assume to give their order, but I name them as I find them in my way."[15] Emerson subverts Kant's system. The lords of life do not control our perception, or our experience, they come out from it, like forms on a background: "I saw them pass."[16] The categories themselves are the object of exploration. Such is the intellectual revolution brought about by transcendentalism. The transcendental question no longer is, How do we know from experience? Rather, it is, How do we approach the world? How do we *have an experience*? This difficulty of approaching the world is expressed by Emerson in "Experience" with regard to the experience of grief, and is generalized to an experience of the world taken as a whole under the sign (the category) of loss. Skepticism is the inability to have an experience. We are not as much ignorant as *inexperienced*. William James will follow this thread of Emersonian thought (for example, in "The Will to Believe"), Dewey will follow it as well by proposing his own categories, and Wittgenstein uses it in his later writings.

In Emerson, experience cannot teach us anything, contrary to what a "paltry" empiricism tells us—not because it is insufficient, that we must go beyond it, as the traditional epistemology asserts, but because it does not touch us. Our attempts to master the world and things, in order to grasp them in all senses of the term (materially and conceptually) distance us from them. It is what Emerson describes in *Experience* as "the most unhandsome part of our condition,"[17] this fleeting reality slips between our fingers at the moment when—even *because*—we clutch at it: It is un*hand*some. It is our desire to grasp reality that causes us to lose it, keeps us from ordinary proximity with things, and cancels their availability or their attractiveness (the fact that they are at hand, handsome). Emerson transforms the Kantian synthesis, not by going the transcendental way but the opposite, down, toward immanence. This overcoming of synthesis by the low, and not by the high, is characteristic of Emerson and Thoreau. Emerson thus offers an ironic recapitulation of Cartesian and Kantian themes from the European theory of knowledge: "It is very unhappy, but too late to be helped, the discovery we have made, that we exist. That discovery is called the Fall of Man. Ever afterwards, we suspect our instruments. We have learned that we do not see directly, but mediately."[18] We need to give up on this "cognitive rapaciousness"—this unhandsome hand with its fingers that clutch and clench. Just like the criticism brought about by Wittgenstein in the *Blue Book* of the "craving for generality."[19] The attention to the particular that he demands goes against our tendency toward a comprehensive grasp: "We feel as if we had to *penetrate* phenomena: our investigation, however, is directed not toward phenomena, but, as one might say, toward the '*possibilities*' of phenomena."[20] When Wittgenstein specifies that our "grammatical" investigation is directed not toward phenomena but toward their possibilities, he intends to substitute for the categories an imaginative and improvised grammar of human concepts, a grammar of the particular. The difference with Kant is that, in Wittgenstein and Emerson, each word of ordinary language, each bit of ordinary experience, each aspect of the ordinary requires a deduction to know its use: Each one must be retraced in its application to the world, by the criteria of its application. A word, for Emerson and for Wittgenstein, must be stated in the particular context where it has a meaning, or else it is false (it sounds false), it "chagrins me." The series of lords again is not a renovated list of categories but a grammar of particular experience. The radical empiricism of Emerson consists in saying that speaking of the *given* is still too much. What interests him would be, we may say, the "found." "Finding as founding," Cavell puts it.[21]

The ordinary, then, is what escapes us, what is distant precisely because we seek to appropriate it to us rather than letting ourselves go to the things, and to insignificant encounters: "All our blows glance, all our hits are accidents. Our relations to each other are oblique and casual," writes Emerson.[22] This insistence on the accidental, the contingent, situates the ambiguity of Emerson. The casual is also misfortune, fatality—hence his pun on "casual" and "casualty." Our experiences may be both casual and catastrophic, and the casual structures ordinary experience, as the low and the near: "But perception is not whimsical, but fatal."[23] The conversion that philosophy requires is not the (transcendental) passage toward another world. The new America is here, in front of me. And it is only in this ordinary world that I can *change*, metamorphose myself. As Emerson writes, "Why not realize your world? But far be from me the despair which prejudges the law by a paltry empiricism. . . . There is victory yet for justice; and the true romance which the world exists to realize, will be the transformation of genius into practical power."[24] To realize the world, Emerson transforms and de-sublimes the transcendental, bringing the categories back to the ordinary, realizing the "possibility" of "true romance," realizing genius into practical power. There are no longer two worlds but only one, which always and ordinarily remains for us to discover and to describe. Starting off is what counts, being always ready to go, not attachment, identity, or rootedness, which are synonymous with being stationed or with clutching, with clenching the nation or oneself. This pluralism of cultures is central to the ordinary: "But in truth all is now to be begun, and every new mind ought to take the attitude of Columbus, launch out from the gaping loiterers on the shore, and sail west for a new world."[25] The pioneer is an exemplary figure of this impulse to set off. The pioneer (like Will Hunting at the end of Gus Van Sant's film) moves toward the West, which is also the East where the sun rises, since we now know that the Earth is round and that the sun "is but a morning star," as Thoreau puts it in the last sentence of *Walden*.

THE IMPORTANCE OF IMPORTANCE

By claiming the ordinary, Emerson calls for a revolution ("Here are the materials strewn along the ground"). The American hope becomes that of the construction, *Bildung* for a new human being and culture, who will be "domesticated," which is the opposite of oppressed and enslaved: the domestic person is the one who comes to harmonize inner and outer, public voice and private voice, without renouncing one or the other. The construction of American democracy is the invention of an ordinary human: "the upbuilding of man." Public expression is then founded on self-reliance, which is not trust in a pre-given self (philosophy of the ordinary is not a philosophy of subjectivity) but trust in one's shared experience. Culture is this building and *Bildung* of democracy. Trust in one's experience: This defines the recourse to practice, in a genuinely empirical move. One could explore the political implications of this trust.

Cavell has applied it in the first place to film and to what it teaches us. In *Pursuits of Happiness*, he examines the act of "checking one's experience," which is to say, of examining one's own experience, of "let[ting] the object or the work of your interest teach you how to consider it"—to educate one's experience, so as to be made educable by it. To be interested in film as work of thought means to be interested in our experience. That means a displacement of the object of the investigation, from the object to the experience I have of the object, "the interest that I bring to my own experience"—a reliance on the experience of the object, in order to find the right words to describe and express it. For Cavell, it is the viewing (repeated and common) of films that leads to trusting one's own experience, and to acquiring at the same time an authority over it. "[It] is a conceptual as much as an experiential undertaking. . . . I think of this as checking one's experience."[26]

Cavell returns then to "the empiricism practiced by Emerson and Thoreau."[27] Empiricism reread thus defines the paradoxical link between experience and trust: It is necessary to educate one's experience in order to trust it. Here is a new reversal of the Kantian inheritance: not to surpass experience via theory, go in reverse from what is, in philosophy, the standard process of knowledge; to surpass theory via experience. The trust in self is defined by the ordinary and expressive authority one has over one's experience: "Without this trust in one's experience, expressed as a willingness to find words for it, . . . one is without authority in one's own experience."[28] Trust consists of discovering in oneself (in one's "constitution," says Emerson, in the political and subjective sense) the capacity to *have* an experience, and to express it.

To have an experience means to perceive what is important, what matters. What interests Cavell in film is the way our experience makes what counts emerge, be seen. Cavell is interested in the development of a capacity to see the importance, the appearance, and the significance of things (places, people, motifs):

> The moral I draw is this: the question what becomes of objects when they are filmed and screened—like the question what becomes of particular people, and specific locales, and subjects and motifs when they are filmed by individual makers of film—has only one source of data for its answer, namely the appearance and significance of just those objects and people that are in fact to be found in the succession of films, or passages of films, that matter to us.[29]

What defines importance is the capacity to "express their appearances, and define those significances, and articulate the nature of this mattering."[30] As Cavell explains,

> If it is part of the grain of film to magnify the feeling and meaning of a moment, it is equally part of it to counter this tendency, and instead to acknowledge the fateful fact of a human life that the significance of its moments is ordinarily not given with the moments as they are lived, so that to determine the significant crossroads of a life may be the work of a lifetime.[31]

So how are we to recover this elusive ordinary life? How are we to know what is important without being focused on only the pertinent? To realize what one wants to say, to be precisely expressed, would be to manage to put the phrase into context. To take up an expression of Wittgenstein, it would be to restore the phrase to its country of origin, its "natural environment." This is the task Wittgenstein assigns to OLP: "To bring words back from their metaphysical to their everyday use."[32] But in the ordinary there is nothing to recover. Cavell says of Thoreau, "Walden was always gone, from the beginning of the words of *Walden*."[33] The only assurance registered in the use of my speech is that of abandonment, of the departure that one constantly finds in American thought—of departure, of the road.

It is in American film that an access or mode of approach to this ordinary is constituted. The cinema for Cavell is not viewed as an aesthetic object, but as ordinary practice, repeatable, integrated with our lives. The talking movie is a moving projection on the screen of ordinary conversation and expression. The link to the ordinary that cinema maintains is visible in scenes of classic Hollywood movies where the heroes share daily moments, for example, when Clark Gable and Claudette Colbert mimic a domestic squabble in *It Happened One Night*, or the apocalyptic scene of breakfast preparation by Katharine Hepburn in *Woman of the Year*. The uncanniness of the ordinary emerges in classic films such as *It's a Wonderful Life* (Frank Capra, 1946), where the hero (James Stewart) faces a world in which he does not exist. Film presents us a world from which we are necessarily absent. It reproduces the distance of the world itself, which involves our fundamental foreignness and separateness to it.

The next stop along the ordinary's transatlantic circuit is thus Great Britain and OLP. The exploration of uses is an inventory of our forms of life: for Austin, we examine "what we would say when"—"which words to employ in which situations," what is fitting to the circumstances or allows one to act on them. Austin makes clear: "We are not looking merely at words, but also at the realities we use the words to talk about. We are using our sharpened awareness of words to sharpen our perception, though not as the final arbiter of, the phenomena."[34] The language of description is then a tool for focusing and attentiveness, associated with agreement and with the perception of the important detail.

Very important here is the transition made by Cavell from the question of common language to that of the form of life in language, which is not only the sharing of social structures but of all that constitutes the fabric of human existences and activities. The theme of the ordinary introduces skepticism into practice: Certainty, or trust in what we do (play, argue, value, promise), models itself on the trust that we have in our shared uses of language and our capacity for using it appropriately. The enigma of speaking the same language—the uncanniness of the use of ordinary language—is the possibility for me of speaking in the name of others, and vice versa. It is not enough to invoke commonness; it remains to be known what authorizes me to speak, what is the real strength of the agreement. "It is," Wittgenstein writes, "what human beings say that is true and false; and they agree in the language they use. That is not agreement in opinions but in form of life."[35] It is crucial for Cavell that Wittgenstein says that we agree *in* and not *on* language. That means that language precedes this agreement as much as it is produced by use.

We learn and teach words in certain contexts, and then we are expected, and expect others, to be able to project them into further contexts. Nothing insures that this projection will take place (in particular, not the grasping of universals nor the grasping of books of rules) [...]. It is a vision as simple as it is difficult, and as difficult as it is (and because it is) terrifying.[36]

A ROMANTICISM OF DEMOCRACY

To reinsert the human voice in philosophical thinking[37] and to draw out the ethical and political consequences of this reinsertion has been a goal of Cavell's work. In *The World Viewed,* he writes:

> This romanticism reasserts that, in whatever locale I find myself, I am to locate myself. It speaks of terror, but suggests elation—for the shaking of sentiment never got us home, nor the shiver of the picturesque. The faith of this romanticism, overcoming the old, is that we can still be moved to move, that we are free, if we will, to step upon our transport.[38]

For him, the challenge, and aim, of OLP is to understand that language is *spoken*, pronounced by a human voice within a form of life, and then to move from the question of the common usage of language to the less-explored question of the relationship between an individual speaker and his or her community. For Cavell, this implies a redefinition of subjectivity in language, on the basis of the rightness or fit of agreements in language. The quest for this "rightness," *pitch*, for an absolute expression that adjusts the inner with the outer—combines language and politics, and defines romanticism, its legacy in America according to Cavell, Emerson, and Thoreau: a democratic romanticism of democracy that fulfills the romantic dream of reappropriating the ordinary world through individual expression and ordinary language.

> To speak of our subjectivity as the route back to our conviction in reality is to speak of romanticism. Perhaps romanticism can be understood as the natural struggle between the representation and the acknowledgment of our subjectivity (between the acting out and the facing off of ourselves, as psycho-analysts would more or less say). Hence Kant, and Hegel; hence Blake secreting the world he believes in; hence Wordsworth competing with the history of poetry by writing out himself, writing himself back into the world.[39]

The question of description and description's adequacy to its object turns out to be the question of expressive rightness. To thus go from truth to expression is indeed to follow the romantic project of reappropriating the world through subjective exploration—here, through the quest for voice. Such romanticism appears in *The Claim of Reason*, where Cavell takes up the question of expression. To bear expression is to acknowledge that your expressions in fact express you, that they are yours, that you are in them. This means allowing yourself to be comprehended, something you can always deny. Not to deny it is, I would like to say, to acknowledge your body, and the body of your expressions, to be yours, you on earth, all there will ever *be* of you. [40]

To so acknowledge means to accept expression as identically inner (it expresses me) *and* outer (it exposes me). Subjectivity is thus defined in its movement to reappropriate its voice, which is also a way of approaching reality. The inability to be the subject of one's words—e.g., to be able to speak the common language—is the political *and* romantic version of skepticism, which can be countered by reappropriating the ordinary world through our language practices. [41] Cavell demonstrates the fragility and profundity of our language agreements and our forms of life, thus pointing to another romantic dimension of OLP: The fact that our ordinary language is based on nothing but itself is not only a source of disquiet about the validity of what we do and say, it is the revelation of a truth about ourselves. "I" am the only possible source of such validity. And in the constant quest for a voice, for the right tone, there is a simultaneously subjective and collective requirement: "to believe your own thought, to believe that what is true for you in your private heart is true for all men—that is genius. Speak your latent conviction, and it shall be the universal sense; for the inmost in due time becomes the outmost." [42] For Cavell, true morality lies in "finding one's voice," in hitting on the appropriate expression for a certain situation (a theme in Austin). This requires both an individual constitution ("the only right is what is after my constitution") and a shared one, a political Constitution that allows each person to find expression, to be expressed by the common, and to accept expressing the common. Democracy is what gives me a political voice and what can take this voice away from me; it may also deceive and betray me to the point that I no longer want to speak for it or let it speak for me, *in my name*. My participation is constantly in question, in *conversation*. But if I refuse consent, I do not thereby withdraw from the community: Withdrawal, dissonance, retreat into the unknown are all inherent to my belonging to or desire for community.

> Human beings do not naturally desire isolation and incomprehension, but union or reunion, call it community. It is in faithfulness to that desire that one declares oneself unknown. (And of course the faithfulness, the desire, and the declaration may all be based on illusion. The conceptual connection, however, would remain as real as ever.) [43]

It is *me*, my voice, that determines my agreement, and not the other way around. I determine my consent to or refusal of society, and this is what makes my choice a potentially revolutionary one. It is here and now—daily, ordinarily—that my consent to my society is settled. Democracy must include actions and expressions that radically call the institutions of the social game into question—not out of tolerance or "openness," but out of perfectionism.

Here we rediscover the aim of democracy: to achieve expression. For Wittgenstein and Emerson, what is private is merely what refuses expression: the private is inexpressiveness, conformity. For Cavell, the accord that allows my private voice to be truly expressive is based purely on the particular validity of voice: my individual voice stakes its claim as is—a "universal voice." *Claim* is what a voice does when it bases itself on nothing other than itself in order to simultaneously establish universal consent and a relationship to the reality; Cavell and Emerson ask us to formulate such claiming as the principle of our democratic practices. This reinscription of the subjective at the heart of the political is also the form given here to political romanticism, which defines the principle of democracy as each individual's right to assess his or her needs and happiness: "Suppose that romanticism can be thought of as the discovery, or one rediscovery, of the subjective; the subjective as the exceptional; or the discovery of freedom as a state in which each subject claims its right to recognition, or acknowledgment; the right to name and assess its own satisfaction."[44] The quest for voice and rightness is thus a constant rejection of conformity—including conformity to the moral and political principles one holds, including *conformity to oneself.* This points to one aspect of the principle of democracy: the *pursuit of happiness* that is both a political and a romantic pursuit. *To mean what one says* is to know oneself, others, and the world—that is, the ordinary world, the one in which romanticism *finds* itself.

The critique of conformity defines the condition of ordinary democratic morality and the necessity of dissent for anyone who wishes to know what he or she means. The ideal political conversation—the conversation of democracy—is a circulation of words in which no voice is minor and no one is without voice. Claim and dissent are neither excesses nor constraints of democracy; they define the very nature of true democratic conversation. This tradition of dissent is rooted in the American tradition and has developed over the course of America's many contemporary social and political movements. It combines consent and disobedience, as if the original dream of America, the principles of the founding fathers, could be realized through internal dissent.

This discovery of individuality in expression also defines ordinary romanticism, and Thoreau and Emerson inherit both from Samuel Coleridge and William Wordsworth and from the spirit of the American Revolution. We should note that this romanticism, like all true romanticism is a post-romanticism, just as for Cavell, the modern is always postmodern, aiming beyond itself. Cavell, like Emerson and Thoreau does not refer to the picturesque, the trembling of affect, or the exaltation of the self, proper to "old Europe" to define ordinary romanticism—"I ask not for the great, the remote, the romantic."[45] His romanticism is a romanticism of the ordinary. Emerson writes: "This revolution is to be wrought by the gradual domestication of the idea of Culture. The main enterprise of the world for splendor, for extent, is the upbuilding of a man. Here are the materials strewn along the ground."[46]

CULTURE, THE ORDINARY, AND HUMANIZING THE WORLD

This ordinary romanticism shares a principle with today's Occupy and civil disobedience movements. If we are to progress toward the human and attain the ordinary world and adequate expression, self-reliance compels us to seek neither subjective confidence nor contact with ourselves, but rather our capacity to be expressive, to be *public*. It is by claiming myself that my obscurity, my opacity to myself, becomes political and my confidence in myself becomes confidence in *us*, in a plural self, selves—*because* I give myself to be heard by others. We must discover ourselves; that is, we must first make ourselves obscure to ourselves. Thoreau seeks obscurity in order to reach true clarity: "I do not suppose that I have attained to obscurity, but I should be proud if no more fatal fault were found with my pages on this score than was found with the Walden ice."[47] Thoreau advocates accepting one's obscurity to oneself, and within this obscure claim to oneself, which is a constant repetition of revolution, we hear the common voice of plural selves raised even at the cost of dissonance, isolation, and the unknown. Thoreau sees this claim as the antidote to people's "lives of quiet desperation." Here again is the goal of politics: to locate in ourselves and in others the words that "chagrin us"[48] in the strong sense, and dispossess us of our voices and our world. This is again the perfectionist claim, immanent to and inherent in democratic life. The romanticism expressed here is a democratic romanticism, a romanticism of the banal, in a sense; a deeply realistic and pragmatic romanticism.

> The wish to be extraordinary, exceptional, unique, thus reveals the wish to be ordinary, everyday. So both the wish for the exceptional and for the everyday are foci of romanticism. One can think of romanticism as the discovery that the everyday is an exceptional achievement. Call it the achievement of the human.[49]

At the end of "Experience," Emerson announces "the transformation of genius into practical power," calling this "true romance."[50] Cavell identifies the romantic quest with *the quest for the ordinary*: However, clearly there is something vexed about a passionate desire to be ordinary, and this is a significant risk run by political romanticism: "Think of the spectacle of the likes of Rousseau and Thoreau and Kierkegaard and Tolstoy and Wittgenstein going around hoping to be ordinary, preaching the everyday as the locale of the sublime!"[51] For Cavell, romanticism discovered the "fact of adolescence," that is, "the task of wanting and choosing adulthood, along with the impossibility of this task";[52] for Kant, skepticism is the philosophical version of adolescence—thinking that has not yet reached the age of "mature and male judgment."

The new romantic confidence in oneself and in ourselves makes it possible to find in each individual and in the ordinary the resources to rediscover the human. Emerson's return to the ordinary when he travels to Europe is highly significant; there, he rediscovers ancient splendors while denouncing the romantic illusion of the grandeur of a distant and somehow authentic art. The romantic reappropriation of antiquity can occur only in fragments and reproductions. In a passage from the journal he kept during his stay in Rome in the spring of 1833, Emerson writes of spotting, in a "wilderness of marble," the Torso of Belvedere, celebrated by Michelangelo and Johann Winckelmann, and compares it to a veteran of the Revolutionary War: "Here too was the Torso Hercules, as familiar to the eyes as some old revolutionary cripple."[53] The romantic use of citation and the constant, fragmented returns to European heritage in Emerson and Thoreau thus stem from a claim that is at once inseparably romantic *and* realist, ordinary because revolutionary. The remark above reveals all the profound and ancient practice of making moldings or engravings of masterpieces of ancient sculpture—in short, the practice of reproduction, the only channel open to the American Scholar whose advent Emerson calls for. It is both a naturalization of the artistic fragment and a reminder of the constant presence of survivors from the founding of the nation, colossal even when crippled. This brings us back once again to the revolution (both past and future) that Emerson calls for at the end of "Experience": "Here are the materials strewn along the ground."

Emerson doubles and naturalizes "ground" with "materials"—the ground is not a base on which to construct philosophy, Culture, or revolution, but rather is the very *material* of the ground. This brings to mind the ability to occupy ground, to reappropriate the land (the land beneath our feet) that today's movements deploy and that we see at work in political romanticism, which has taken on a new form in ecological struggles and in the idea of the "global": This is the idea of a democratized earth defined by its occupation, including mobile, circulatory forms of occupation. Cavell writes:

> The idea of "ground" itself is one among the materials from which, in progressing with Culture we are to make something further, more human. Then further, in Emerson's saying "Here are materials strewn," I gather a reference to the men and women there are scattered (that is, as yet unsocial) along the ground, from which men and women are to be upbuilded.[54]

There never was any first America, any wild, untouched land, any romantic wilderness. Thoreau had already said as much at Walden: "Walden was always gone, from the beginning of the words of *Walden*. . . . The first man and woman are no longer there."[55] The nostalgia for an original purity of nature and of the human is the last illusion that cinema must strip us of, while at the same time teaching us the miracle of this degraded world whose very imperfection and finitude carries us: "We want to walk: so we need friction!"[56]

For there is but one world; as one slogan puts it, "There is no Planet B." There is only the ordinary world: "Heaven is under our feet as well as over our heads."[57] The ordinary world is not everything there is in the world. Here is the description of the ordinary world by Cavell, as early as *Must We Mean What We Say?*

> What they had not realized was what they were saying, or, what they were *really* saying, and so had not known *what they meant*. To this extent, they had not known themselves, and not known the world. I mean, of course, the ordinary world. That may not be all there is, but it is important enough: morality is that world, and so are force and love; so is art and a part of knowledge (the part which is about the world); and so is religion (wherever God is).[58]

The choice of finitude "means the acknowledgment of the existence of finite others, which is to say, the choice of community."[59] The impossibility here lies in the fact that these choices about community have been handed down to us by the past and they demand conformity. "So romantics dream of revolution, and break their hearts."[60] Beyond sentimentalism, romanticism in politics lies in human claims made even in the face of loss. The claim of today's revolts and occupations is a new collective *cogito* that demands and produces proof of the existence of the human. These movements reflect "the apprehension that human subjectivity, the concept of human selfhood, is threatened; that it must be found and may be lost; that if one's existence is to be proven it can be proven only from oneself; and that upon that proof turns what proof there is in the continued existence of the human as such."[61] The new romantic confidence in oneself and in ourselves makes it possible to find in each individual and in the ordinary the practices and resources to reclaim the human. This ordinary world is what I would like to define as our uncommon translatable *culture*.

NOTES

1. Stanley Cavell, "Foreword," in *Life and Words: Violence and the Descent into the Ordinary*, by Veena Das (Berkeley and Los Angeles: University of California Press, 2007), vii.

2. Stanley Cavell, *Pursuits of Happiness: The Hollywood Comedy of Remarriage* (Cambridge, MA: Harvard University Press, 1981).

3. Cavell, *Pursuits of Happiness*.

4. Ralph Waldo Emerson, "The American Scholar," 1837, in *The Essential Writings of Ralph Waldo Emerson*, ed. Brooks Atkinson (New York: Modern Library, 2000), 56.

5. Stanley Cavell, *The Senses of Walden*, expanded ed. (Chicago: University of Chicago Press, 1992), 149–50.

6. Stanley Cavell, *The Senses of Walden* (San Francisco: North Point Press, 1972), 149–50.

7. Ralph Waldo Emerson, "Self-Reliance," in *The Essential Writings of Ralph Waldo Emerson*, ed. Brooks Atkinson (New York: Modern Library, 2000), 136.

8. Stanley Cavell, *In Quest of the Ordinary: Lines of Skepticism and Romanticism* (Chicago: University of Chicago Press, 1988), 4.

9. Henry D. Thoreau, *Walden: A Fully Annotated Edition*, ed. Jeffrey S. Cramer (New Haven, CT: Yale University Press, 2004).

10. Ludwig Wittgenstein, *The Blue and Brown Books*, ed. R. Rhees (Oxford: Blackwell, 1958, second ed. 1969), 3.

11. Ludwig Wittgenstein, *Philosophical Investigations: The English Text of the Third Edition*, trans. G. E. M. Anscombe (Englewood Cliffs, NJ: Prentice Hall, 2000), §415.

12. Michel Foucault, "La philosophie analytique de la politique," in *Dits et écrits*, vol. 3, 1994 [1978], 540–41.

13. Emerson, *The Essential Writings of Ralph Waldo Emerson*.

14. Emerson, "The American Scholar," 562.

15. Emerson, *The Essential Writings of Ralph Waldo Emerson*.

16. Emerson, *The Essential Writings of Ralph Waldo Emerson*, 7.

17. Emerson, *The Essential Writings of Ralph Waldo Emerson*, 81.

18. Emerson, *The Essential Writings of Ralph Waldo Emerson*.

19. Wittgenstein, *The Blue and Brown Books*.

20. Wittgenstein, *Investigations*, §90.

21. Stanley Cavell, *This New Yet Unapproachable America: Lectures after Emerson after Wittgenstein* (Albuquerque, NM: Living Batch Press, 1989).

22. Emerson, *The Essential Writings of Ralph Waldo Emerson*, 94.

23. *The Essential Writings of Ralph Waldo Emerson*, 81.

24. Emerson, "Self-Reliance," 106.

25. Emerson, "The Senses and the Soul," in *Essays: First and Second Series* (New York: Library of America, 1990).

26. Cavell, *Pursuits*, 18.

27. Cavell, *Pursuits*, 18.

28. Cavell, *Pursuits*, 19.

29. Cavell, "What Becomes of Things of Film," in *Themes out of School: Effects and Causes* (San Francisco: North Point Press, 1988), 182–83.

30. Cavell, "What Becomes of Things of Film," 183.

31. Cavell, "The Thought of Movies," in *Themes out of School: Effects and Causes* (San Francisco: North Point Press, 1988), 11.

32. Wittgenstein, *Investigations*, §116.

33. Cavell, *Senses*.

34. J. L. Austin, *Philosophical Papers* (Oxford; New York: Clarendon Press; Oxford University Press, 1962), 182.

35. Wittgenstein, *Investigations*, §241.

36. Stanley Cavell, *Must We Mean What We Say? A Book of Essays* (Cambridge: Cambridge University Press, 1976), 52.

37. Stanley Cavell, *Contesting Tears: The Hollywood Melodrama of the Unknown Woman* (Chicago: University of Chicago Press, 1996), 63.

38. Stanley Cavell, *The World Viewed: Reflections on the Ontology of Film*, enlarged ed. (Cambridge, MA; London: Viking Press, 1971), 114.

39. Cavell, *The World Viewed*, 22.

40. Stanley Cavell, *The Claim of Reason: Wittgenstein, Skepticism, Morality, and Tragedy* (Oxford: Oxford University Press, 1979), 383.

41. Cavell, *In Quest of the Ordinary*.

42. Emerson, *Essential Writings*, 132.
43. Cavell, *The Claim of Reason*, 463.
44. Cavell, *The World Viewed*, 466.
45. Emerson, *Essential Writings*, 57.
46. Emerson, *Essential Writings*, 55–56.
47. Thoreau, *Walden*, 316.
48. Emerson, *Essential Writings*, 137.
49. Cavell, *The Claim of Reason*, 463.
50. Emerson, *Essential Writings*, 326.
51. Cavell, *The Claim of Reason*,464.
52. Cavell, *The Claim of Reason*, 464.
53. Ralph Waldo Emerson, *Emerson in His Journals* (Cambridge, MA: Harvard University Press, 1984), 100.
54. Cavell, *This New Yet Unapproachable America*, 9.
55. Cavell, *Senses*, 119.
56. Wittgenstein, *Investigations*, §107.
57. Thoreau, *Walden*, 92.
58. Cavell, *Must We Mean*, 40.
59. Cavell, *The Claim of Reason*, op. cit., 463.
60. Cavell, *The Claim of Reason*, 463.
61. Cavell, *The Claim of Reason*, 465.

BIBLIOGRAPHY

Austin, J. L. *Philosophical Papers*. Oxford; New York: Clarendon Press; Oxford University Press, 1962.
Cavell, Stanley. *The World Viewed: Reflections on the Ontology of Film*. Enlarged edition. Cambridge, MA; London: Viking Press, 1971.
———. *Must We Mean What We Say? A Book of Essays*. Cambridge; New York: Cambridge University Press, 1976.
———. *The Claim of Reason: Wittgenstein, Skepticism, Morality, and Tragedy*. Oxford; New York: Clarendon Press; Oxford University Press, 1979.
———. *Pursuits of Happiness: The Hollywood Comedy of Remarriage*. Cambridge, MA: Harvard University Press, 1981.
———. *In Quest of the Ordinary: Lines of Skepticism and Romanticism*. Chicago: University of Chicago Press, 1988.
———. *Themes out of School: Effects and Causes*. San Francisco: North Point Press, 1988.
———. *This New Yet Unapproachable America: Lectures after Emerson after Wittgenstein*. Albuquerque, NM: Living Batch Press, 1989.
———. *Conditions Handsome and Unhandsome: The Constitution of Emersonian Perfectionism*. La Salle, IL; Chicago: Open Court; University of Chicago Press, 1990.
———. *The Senses of Walden*. Expanded edition. Chicago: University of Chicago Press, 1992.
———. *Contesting Tears: The Hollywood Melodrama of the Unknown Woman*. Chicago: University of Chicago Press, 1996.
———. "Foreword." In *Life and Words: Violence and the Descent into the Ordinary*, by Veena Das. Berkeley and Los Angeles: University of California Press, 2007.
Das, Veena. *Life and Words: Violence and the Descent into the Ordinary*. Berkeley and Los Angeles: University of California Press, 2007.
Emerson, Ralph Waldo. *Emerson in His Journals*. Cambridge, MA: Harvard University Press, 1984.
———. *Essays: First and Second Series*. New York: Library of America, 1990.
———. *The Essential Writings of Ralph Waldo Emerson*. Edited by Brooks Atkinson. New York: Modern Library, 2000.
Foucault, Michel. "La philosophie analytique de la politique," in *Dits et écrits*, vol. 3. 1994 [1978].

Malick, Terrence. *To the Wonder*. Brothers K Productions; Magnolia Pictures, 2013.

Thoreau, Henry David. *Walden: A Fully Annotated Edition*. Edited by Jeffrey S. Cramer. New Haven, CT: Yale University Press, 2004.

Wittgenstein, Ludwig. *The Blue and Brown Books*. Edited by R. Rhees. Oxford: Blackwell, 1958; second edition 1969.

———. *Philosophical Investigations: The English Text of the Third Edition*. Translated by G. E. M. Anscombe. Englewood Cliffs, NJ: Prentice Hall, 2000.

Chapter Three

Speaking Out of a Sense of Our Impoverishment

Vincent Colapietro

> We stand waiting, empty—knowing, possibly, that we can be full, surrounded by mighty symbols which are not symbols to us, but prose and trivial toys. Then cometh the god and converts the statues into fiery men, and by a flash of his eyes burns up the veil which shrouded all things, and the meaning of the very furniture, of cup and saucer, of chair and clock and tester, is manifest. [1]
> —R. W. Emerson, "Circles" [2]

At the outset of his *Philosophical Investigations* Ludwig Wittgenstein asserts, "Explanations come to an end somewhere." [3] So, too, do justifications. [4] Somewhat later in the *Investigations* Wittgenstein observes, "If I have exhausted the justifications I have reached bedrock, and my spade is turned. Then I am inclined to say: 'This is simply what I do.'" [5] Ralph Waldo Emerson, one of Stanley Cavell's other philosophical inspirations, is, if anything, even more emphatic about this: "I shun father and mother and wife and brother when my genius calls me. I would write on the lintels of the doorpost, *Whim*. I hope it is somewhat better than whim at last, but we cannot spend the day in explanation"—or justification. [6]

This text is of course a pivot around which Cavell's thought turns (e.g., *Conditions Handsome and Unhandsome*; also "What's the Use of Calling Emerson a Pragmatist?"). In his interpretation of this passage, Cavell takes great pains to imagine the *tone* in which this deceptively simple utterance resounds in Wittgenstein's own later thought. [7] It is, in Cavell's ears, anything but the tone of triumphalism or even confidence. Rather, it is one of doubt and almost certainly one of impoverishment: It is indeed the tone audible when one is *at a loss* regarding what to say in justification of one's own practice. In the context of initiation or apprenticeship, the expert or even

45

simply the competent practitioner might be disposed to say, "This is simply what *we* do" or, more authoritatively, "This is how it is done" (the latter being an utterance in which the effacement of the personal operates to intensify the authority of some implicit "we"). But, for Wittgenstein and Cavell, the scene of inheritance or initiation should be one of invitation, not a site of imposition, much less bullying (e.g., *This New Yet Unapproachable America*). Expert or merely competent practitioners cannot but be taken as an exemplars or representatives of the undertaking or tradition in question. Indeed, they can hardly avoid taking themselves to be such. For the sake of facilitating their role as initiators into the practice, however, this facet of their persona might be deliberately suppressed ("Then I am inclined to say: 'This is simply what I do'"). The tone of this utterance bespeaks a sense of finitude, in particular, the disconcerting absence of an incontestable foundation for even our most assured explanations and justifications. It in effect is that of confessing or acknowledging that one is bereft of such warrants for one's practices and utterances.

Yet what richness accrues to our utterances when we cultivate the capacity to speak out of a sense of our own impoverishment, linguistic and otherwise![8] In turn, what impoverishment befalls us when we rest assured of our own incalculable inheritance and thus wealth! Emersonian self-trust is, at bottom, inseparable from a Cavellian mistrust of the various registers of the triumphalist tone, including that of American pragmatism. Even so, there is at least this kinship between Cavell, on the one hand, and Charles Peirce, William James, and John Dewey, on the other: the necessity to translate our words into experience, also to approach our experience as a drive toward expression,[9] as nothing less than a demand to search for just the right words, the most apt metaphors. Insofar as we presume unreflectively that the words ready to hand are sufficient to the task, we denigrate both experience and language. Insofar as we speak out of a sense of our own lack, perhaps experiential but certainly linguistic, we are in effect poets, wrestling with language as a result of wrestling with experience. The aim of this chapter is to explore this process of translation especially in light of our experience of impoverishment, that of being time and again at a loss of what to say, even how to feel.

The recursive movement of thought and indeed experience[10] exhibits itself here, often quite dramatically. This movement circles back on itself, nowhere more notably than consciousness becoming conscious it itself.[11] But the more specific forms of recursive movements are the more important and instructive ones. For instance, we might become contemptuous of our tendency to be contemptuous of others, or angry at our uncontrolled and uncontrollable irascibility. In "Experience," to consider an especially poignant example, Emerson grieves that grief has nothing to teach him. Even in our most devastating losses, we are thrown back on ourselves and, in the process, made acutely aware of our sense of being at a loss as to know what this loss is or means ("In the death of my son, now more than two years ago, I seem to have lost a beautiful estate—no more. I cannot get it nearer to me. . . . I grieve that grief can teach me nothing, nor carry me one step into real nature.")[12] The meaning of our losses drives home not so much a loss of meaning as a loss of confidence in knowing how to name, much less measure, their character and depth. "Of course, our justification of our modes and criteria of justification seems itself to generate an infinite regress." So, too, we might have an impoverishing (not merely impoverished, but truly impoverishing) view of our poverty as well as wealth. Whatever else philosophy as the education of grownups might be, it is, for some groups at least, the cultivation of our ability to speak out of a sense of our impoverishment. Somewhat paradoxically, this demands greater self-trust than virtually any other endeavor, since time and again we are thrown back on ourselves, on our resources, with no assurance that we are intelligible, even to ourselves. This is, at least, the phenomenon I want to explore here.

MEDIATION, REFLEXIVITY, AND SOCIALITY

To speak out of a sense of our own impoverishment means speaking with genuine humility. Such humility is anything but self-abasement. Indeed, self-abasement precludes such humility. There is however a deep but often overlooked link between humility and courage. Much arrogance is rooted in anxiety and insecurity, whereas genuine humility traces its root to that confidence in oneself identified by Emerson as *self-trust*. The identity of the self in whom one is entitled to place one's trust is far from evident. The self of Emersonian self-reliance or self-trust is not anyone given, but someone forged in the crucible of adversity. The Over-Soul is and is not the readily identifiable self who bears such proper names as "Ludwig" or "Ralph" or "Stanley." Whatever else one might say about this identity, one must say that it is not the insular self, the self completely closed in upon itself. Put positively, it is the participatory self, the one whose boundaries are continually being redrawn in ever more inclusive or expansive circles.

> Our life is an apprenticeship to the truth that around every circle another can be drawn; that there is no end in nature, but every end is a beginning; that there is always another dawn risen on midnoon; and under every deep a lower deep opens.[13]

As a consequence of such circles being enclosed in ever wider ones,[14] the self is exposed to others in a way that beings other than finite, social, reflexive selves simply are not. Indeed, to be a self designates as much as anything else a zone of hazard, because it is a site where the drama of being confronted by and engaged with others unfolds. Insofar as the finite self is finite, it is fragmentary, bounded, limited, conditioned; but insofar as the self is truly a self, s/he is in principle boundless. This means that such a self is self-conditioned or self-determined. Such a self becomes a self by enacting its birthright, its right to define itself in its own manner. While this carries the risk of unintelligibility, it holds the promise of autonomy. It is a boot-strap autonomy.

In any event, reflexivity is on this account a hallmark of selfhood. While in certain respects reflexivity is closely allied to privacy, it is not to be taken as the equivalent of an inner sphere inaccessible to all but the reflexive self. Indeed, its origin, functions, and transformations need to be seen in conjunction with sociality (or participation).

What emerges from these considerations is a portrait of the self in which an ongoing process of variable mediation shows itself to be constitutive of the self. The relationship of the self to itself is mediated by its relationship to others. In turn, the relationship of the self to others is mediated by its relationship to itself. At every turn the self is threatened by its entanglements with others; so too its relationships to others are themselves threatened by its absorption in itself, also the pathologies so often defining the relationship of the self to itself.

Whatever else it might be, translation is a process of mediation in which this dialectic of self and other unfolds. The self and other *as given*, however, need to be questioned. The extent to which self and other are constituted in and through processes of mediation makes it necessary to conceive of the process as primordial, the figures of self and other as derivative. Experience provides grounds for identification and, indeed, reidentification. The import of experience is manifest: Antecedently fixed identities are illusions to be exposed and exploded. In contrast, experientially emergent ones are, however precarious and provisional, the only identities obtainable by the human animal in its fateful struggles with its historical inheritances. Here the antecedently fixed is usurped by the historically emergent, the self-same illusion in its Protean disguises by the self-altering truth in its elusive guises.

BEING AT A LOSS

"Philosophy begins," Cavell suggests, "in loss, in finding oneself at a loss, as Wittgenstein more or less says."[15] To begin anywhere else is, he insists, quite simply to fail as a philosopher, to avoid the task at hand: "Philosophy that does not so begin is so much talk."[16] It is so much idle chatter, in one of its most deplorable forms, so much fashionable chitchat. Of utmost importance, we must appreciate: "Loss is *as such* not to be overcome, it is interminable, for every new finding may incur a loss." The *experience* of loss is, however, not anything to be abjectly accepted; rather it imposes an impossible task—a recovery from loss, an *ongoing* struggle against the insidious seductions of fatal muses or murderous sirens. Understood in this sense, the "recovery of loss is, in Emerson, as in Sigmund Freud and in Wittgenstein, a finding of the world, a returning of it, to it." It is hardly an exaggeration to insist that what is at stake here is nothing less than the world. What enables us to return to what we have always already lost is paradoxically is bound up with avowing a sense of loss. That is, the recovery from loss is only possible through an acknowledgment of loss, such acknowledgment being itself never anything more than a series of insights obtained through a *process* of mourning (grief-work). That is, the price of such recovery "is necessarily to give up something, to let go of something, *to suffer one's poverty*" (emphasis added). The resolute avowal to let go, to suffer one's poverty, is a necessary step toward the enriching poverty of that condition signaled by the epigram with which we opened these reflections: "We stand waiting, empty."

The loss in which philosophy begins, however, can take any number of forms. For the wealth of one's inheritance (or experience) might be overwhelming, so much so that one is at a loss about what to do with such wealth. In this context, at any rate, loss does not designate the abstract unavailability of resources; rather it signifies the disconcerting lack of personal command over whatever resources we happen to possess (often handsomely possess).[17] In other words, it designates powerlessness, the *in*capacity to make use of what is ready to hand. In its more extreme forms, this incapacity is rooted in deadness, being dead to oneself and the world. The recovery of the world is, accordingly, that of one's self, hence, of one's vitality, purpose, energy: "Never mind the ridicule, never mind the defeat; *up again, old heart!*"[18]

In a fuller account, I would need to consider what Emerson argues in "Wealth" and, indeed, other writings on this and allied topics. Allow me to try very briefly showing how my emphasis on a sense of loss is congruent with his pronouncements on wealth. Very briefly, however, let us consider "Fate," since the movement of his thought in this essay illuminates the dialectic of fate and freedom, and this dialectic might in turn help illuminate the dialectic of loss and inheritance, or closely allied to this, that of poverty and riches.

In "Fate" Emerson so compellingly makes the case for the accidentally and externally conditioned character of human existence that no space appears to be left for freedom (or self-determination). But at a critical juncture he stresses, "Fate against Fate is only parrying and defence; there are also the noble creative forces. The reverence of Thought takes man ought of servitude into freedom."[19] "This beatitude [the perception of the inward eye of the Unity in life] dips from on high down to us, and we see. It is not in us so much as we are in it. If the air comes to our lungs, we breathe and live; if not, we die. If the light comes to our eyes, we see; else not. And if truth come to our mind we suddenly expand to its dimensions, as if we grew to worlds."[20]

This ultimately leads to the realization that "nature makes every creature do its own work and get its living [or being]. . . . The planet makes itself. The animal cell makes itself. . . . As soon as there is life, there is self-direction and absorbing and using of material. Life is freedom—life in the direct ratio of its amount."[21] "Do you suppose that he [the living person] is contained in his skin—this reaching, radiating, jaculating fellow? The smallest candle fills a mile with its ray, and the papillæ of a man run out to every star."[22] Constraints can be enabling as well as limiting, while external and accidental conditions can be critical for the self-direction and self-definition of at least living, conscious beings.

The dialectic of impoverishment and wealth is analogous to that of fate and freedom. Just as our fate does not destroy the possibility of our freedom but secures its attainment, poverty properly understood is not the opposite of wealth but a condition for its appropriation, enlargement, and indeed enjoyment. Properly used, wealth does not free us from labor but makes the labor of appropriation all the more necessary and difficult. Insofar as we presume our wealth is our *exclusive* possession, we are unwittingly impoverished, perhaps fatally so. Insofar as we *use* our wealth as a resource to exercise and expand our spiritual power, we are truly rich. But the use of wealth as such a resource flows from our sense of radical impoverishment, not that of accidental entitlement. "As long as our civilization is one of property, of fences, of exclusiveness, it will be mocked by delusions. Our riches will leave us sick. . . . Only that good profits which we can taste with all doors open, and which serves all men."[23]

Several important objections might be raised here, not least of all the possibility of idealizing material circumstances of a dehumanizing character. So, too, one might object that the approach being advocated here uncritically endorses the perspective of privilege from which matters appear in this light. Of course, poverty either leaves some of us sicker than we need to be or without the resources to regain our health. Such objections are hardly ones escaping Emerson's notice, also hardly ones exposing him as utterly bereft of any resources to meet them. This is all the truer of Cavell. The capacity to meet these objections insures that Emerson's insight is hardly discredited: Our wealth is impoverishing if it is merely ours. Our wealth is indeed a means for the exercise of *our* power, but the possessive here points to the complex relationship between the first-person singular and plural (the intricate dynamic between "I" and "we"). As Georg Hegel noted, there is no "I" without "we," but any "we" can maintain itself only by assuming the form of a singular agent (that is, the status of an "I"). In this as in so many other respects, Emerson is clearly one of Hegel's progeny.

In the writings of Hegel[24] no less than in those of the pragmatists, also in the texts of Emerson, the name for the process in which human consciousness assumes its divergent shapes is *experience*. Experience plays an unquestionably central if somewhat implicit, at least undertheorized, role in Cavell's writings. This is as it should be. The point of his writings is not to provide a theoretical account of experience but to stage dramatic inducements to experience the impasses, aporias, breakthroughs, reversals, and much else characteristic of the course of experience. To read an author like Hegel, Emerson, or Cavell, as they intend us to read their texts, is to live through the experience of thought in a singular and typically memorable way. It is not so much a case of translating their words into our experience as it is having our experience translated into their utterances so that we begin to be in a position to have our own experience, to attain the resolute will to refuse ceding our defining experiences to any cultural authorities. "If I am to possess my own experience I cannot afford," Cavell insists, "to cede it to my culture as that culture stands. I must find ways to insist upon it, if I find it unheard, ways to let the culture confront itself fin me, driving me some distance to distraction"[25]—hence, some distance from myself. The injunction is biblical (e.g., Matthew 10:39), but the appropriation of the injunction by Emerson and Cavell entails not so much a rejection of this scriptural context as a creative appropriation in a secular yet spiritual manner of this existential imperative (one must lose one's life in order to possess it).

EXPERIENCE AS ENCOUNTER, ENGAGEMENT, AND ENTANGLEMENT

As prominent as it is in Cavell's writings, his use of experience tends to be, remarkably, unarticulated or undertheorized.[26] The work of gathering the senses in which he uses this term is, however, not only a rewarding but also a necessary task. He might have distilled, for his readers, the significance of this term, but they are far better off for engaging in the work of distilling the variable meanings of this elusive word. Let me suggest that, as the result of my engagement with Cavell's writings (i.e., my *experience* of his texts), I am disposed to foreground experience as encounter and engagement, hence as drama.

Carrying forward Emerson's preoccupation with "conformity" (i.e., our proclivity for self-betrayal and self-negation), Cavell is anxious about our tendency to cede our own experience to others, thereby in effect negating that experience in the very act of ceding it.[27] This prompts him to cultivate "aversion to ourselves in our conformity."[28] Indeed, much of his aversive thought is a conscientious effort to counteract this prevalent tendency.

Here it is instructive to recall a passage from *Philosophy the Day after Tomorrow*. Cavell asks, "Can I, must I, leave it to, say, literature, or history, or anthropology, to articulate and preserve the richness of my experience for me? Are their authorities in position to word my impressions that are essentially different from my capacities as a participant of a human culture?"[29] "To cede my understanding of my experience, trivial and crucial, to them would require, from my point of view," he adds, "a massive effort of discounting."[30] It is hardly an exaggeration to suggest that to cede one's understanding of one's own experience turns out effectively to entail nothing less than the *negation* of that experience.[31]

Having experience in the relevant sense, then, involves, at the very least, cultivating perception. Gliding ghostlike through nature here stands in marked contrast to moving *perceptively* through the world.[32] In *Art as Experience*, Dewey distinguishes between recognition and perception.[33] It is one thing for me to recognize you, quite another to perceive you. Recognition can be virtually immediate, whereas perception in his sense must be indefinitely protracted. Of course, the immediacy or spontaneity of recognition, in this restricted sense, is almost always the result of mediation, very often that of a protracted, at least involved, process.[34] The immediacy with which we *recognize* the letters of the alphabet conceals a prehistory in which we struggled to correlate shapes and sounds. For the purpose of using these shapes and sounds *artfully*, however, it may be advantageous for the literary artist to recover an acute sense of this forgotten struggle, perhaps even to cultivate a form of aphasia. The poet tends to be after all the one who most appreciates the degree to which the most adequate utterances fall short of truly adequate expression. "Not half bad" is more likely the self-praise voiced here. In other words, poets write out of a sense of their own impoverishment. The struggle here with language, experience, and the world at once disclosed and distorted in experience is, for the poet, what crafting sounds and shapes into poetry is. In brief, this struggle *is* poetry, at least poetry in the making. If it is the case that what we confront are not things but things in the making, how much more so is this true regarding poetry?

The context for introducing this distinction is of course important. That context is aesthetics or, more precisely, the necessary or "organic" conjunction of artful execution and aesthetic perception. "The process of art in production is," Dewey insists, "related to the esthetic in perception organically."[35] An artful performance or production *is* artful insofar as it is inaugurated, guided, and consummated by aesthetic perception or experience. "Until the artist is satisfied in perception with what he is doing, he continues shaping and reshaping. The making comes to an end when its result is experienced [by the artist] as good—and that experience comes not by mere intellectual and outside judgment but in direct experience."[36] For example, the painter steps back from the canvas, endeavors to perceive what is actually there, and *in light of that perception* most likely returns to the task of painting, until that time when the painter experiences the work as fulfilled and fulfilling. The task of adequately perceiving one's own work, as it turns out, is far more difficult than especially novices appreciate. The ability to get outside of their own presumptions and preconceptions in order to get inside their own work is, in a sense, the decisive moment in their artistic development. Critical distance and innermost alliance with the initially inchoate impulses of one's aesthetic endeavors are, as it turns out, of a piece.

The salience of this distinction is, however, not confined to the context in which Dewey introduces the distinction. The work of the artist is indeed rooted in perception. But that of virtually every other human persona, in any imaginable context, also is rooted in perception. For example, the art of pedagogy is unquestionably one in which the perceptiveness of teachers is critical—better, vital. The difference between a dead and deadening time, on the one hand, and a lively and enlivening one, on the other, turns as much as anything on the perceptiveness of the participants. This demands breaking through the hardened crust of our inherited conventions.[37] Familiarity breeds credulity more often than contempt.[38] The extremely delicate balance of keenly alert attention and seemingly indifferent orientation is, in most circumstances, the ideal one. The apparent indifference or even distractedness alone allows the other the freedom to be. In such contexts it is imperative to do what it proves so difficult, so often, actually and resolutely to do: to be one of those whom James describes in this fashion:

> They do not close their hand on their possessions. When they profess a willingness that certain persons should be free they mean it not as most of us do—with a mental reservation, as that the freedom should be well employed and other humbug—but in all sincerity, and calling for no guarantee against abuse which, when it happens [as it inevitably does], they accept without complaint or embitterment as part of the chances of the game. They let their bird fly with no string tied to its leg.[39]

The courage, humility, and forbearance required to let others go on in their way is indeed rare.

EXPERIENCE AS TRANSLATION

Any number of metaphors have proven themselves to be apt for characterizing experience. No single metaphor by itself however could ever be adequate. In a very late typescript, Dewey explicitly resists translating the stream of consciousness into the flux of experience, though his resistance is nuanced:

> Experience is no stream, even though the stream of feelings and ideas that flow upon its surface is the part which philosophers most love to traverse. Experience includes the enduring banks of natural constitution and acquired habits as well as the stream. The flying moment is sustained by an atmosphere that does not fly, even when it most vibrates.[40]

At this point—one, of course, *in medias res*—I would like to propose another metaphor. Experience is itself *a process of translation*, one wherein present situations are often automatically translated into past ones, so that the uniqueness of the present, the defining contours and textures of our everyday engagements and endeavors, tends to be lost. The recovery of the ordinary might then be imagined as a deliberate attempt to counteract this inevitable tendency.

To translate experience itself into a process of translation enables us to approach what the psychoanalytic theorist Christopher Bollas so tellingly identifies as the work of experience from an illuminating angle.[41] The *work* of experience is that of translation. For the immediately urgent and narrowly practical demands of countless situations, our rough-and-ready translations are "good enough." But human beings are, to a far greater extent than we appreciate, the victims of our success as experiential translators. The wealth of experience upon which we are able to draw in our everyday lives tends to be impoverishing, whereas only a sense of impoverishment promises to position us in such a way as to garner the richness of *this* moment. Little words often have tremendous import. "What did you do today?" "I *just* went to class and then met a friend to discuss a draft of an essay he's working on." How great a denigration of the everyday is implied in that seemingly innocent adverb *just* (and how significant is it that it is an adverb, a modifier of a verb, i.e., an action)! The judgment is unmistakable: nothing much, if at all, is to be told, hence nothing to be translated. The denigration of the everyday in effect relieves us of any felt need to take up the task of experiential translation. In general, however, the work of experience is in no small measure that of translating, more often than not, translating one phase of experience into another. Here as much as anywhere else, the presumption of equivalence needs to be contested. How can I carry forward the past into the present in such a way that the jagged edges of distinct phases are not so smoothed down as to lose their cutting edge?

The poet of the quotidian is not necessarily anyone other than an imaginative individual who can translate the present situation into the truly singular occasion it inherently is. "We cannot shake off the lethargy now at noonday. Sleeps lingers all our lifetime about our eyes, as night hovers all day in the boughs of the fir-tree."[42]

The "quality of the imagination is to flow, not to freeze."[43] This is nowhere more imperative but also nowhere more difficult than in the work of experience, at least when this work is envisioned as a process of translation. Rough equivalences are to be seen for what they are, the inevitable residuum[44] a symbol of both an inexhaustible wealth and an invincible poverty. There is always more here than our translations can articulate. A sense of impoverishment, of "ever not quite" almost always haunts us. The residuum indicates that there is all too much here for us to handle, at least artfully or poetically. We are never fully equipped to handle the seemingly trivial disclosures of even our most commonplace experiences. "The sea, the mountain-ridge, Niagara, and every flower-bed . . . super-exist, in pre-cantations, which sail like odors in the air, and when any man goes by with ear sufficiently fine, he overhears them and endeavors to write down the notes without diluting or depraving them."[45] Therein lies the challenge to—and, hence, the task of—the poet of the quotidian, regardless of the medium: to translate our experiences "without diluting or depraving them." But our dilutions can be so extreme and our depravations so thoroughgoing that these dilutions amount to nothing less than negations and these depravations to nothing less than desecrations. The recovery of the everyday is, at bottom, a discovery of the sacred in the moments of transitions[46]—the only moments that actually are. "Nothing is secure but life, transition."[47] The wealth underwriting our sense of security is, alas, the source of our impoverishment, while an exhilarating sense of our invincible poverty alone encourages us to seek the sacred in the fleeting and significance in the transitional. "People wish to be settled; [but] only as far as they are unsettled[48] is there any hope for them."[49] The inevitable form of human experience is fixation. The Emersonian reformation encompasses strategies of unsettlement, disruption, interruption, and allied processes of experiential re-translation. In his translation of Emerson, beginning with an unattributed quotation, James writes of his own inspiration (i.e., Emerson): "The day is good . . . in which we have the most perceptions.[50][51] There are times when the cawing of a crow, a weed, a snowflake, or a farmer planting in his field become symbols to the intellect of truths equal to those which the most majestic phenomena can open."[52]

Hence, the somnambulism for which we have traded our lives calls for, from Emerson's own perspective, a reassessment. Recall that in "Experience" he claims, "Our life is not so much threatened as our perception."[53] But, from his vantage point, this amounts to nothing less than a threat to those lives, not necessarily our physical lives but our spiritual ones. Our spiritual lives are, however, nothing but our physical lives caught up in processes of translation, not least of all those involving the translation of different phases of experience into one another, but also those involving translating experience into some mode of symbolization. "The use of symbols," Emerson contends, "has a certain power of emancipation and exhilaration for all men."[54] This is especially true when symbols are used to translate not other symbols but experiences. In any event, the transitions, transformations, and indeed transfigurations resulting from these translations alone enable us to cast off our sleepwalking selves.[55]

CONCLUSION

But what would prompt us to undertake such an arduous, uncertain, and so often frustrating task? My answer to this question—what is likely to prompt us to undertake this task *is* more than anything else our willingness and ability to speak out of a sense of our own impoverishment—is one to which readers are now invited to respond. Initiation into a culture is most humane and effective when it is overwhelmingly the result of acts of uncoerced acceptance, the acceptance of the invitations of parents, teachers, and others who are for any number of reasons cast into the role of representing that culture. What justifies, say, our use of words or what underwrites our explanations cannot be anything to which we can univocally and uncontroversially point. We are ourselves the pointers. That to which we point can at best be glimpsed while we are in transit. As it turns out, we are always in transit, however we appear to be fixed to some place. Moreover, that to which we in our very being point is never anything we can hold securely in our hands—or, of greater import, in our minds, or our utterances.

Our inheritances here are of the utmost relevance. But their wealth and poverty is nowhere more evident than in the grace with which we go on—or in our stuckness, our inability to go on in innovative and effective ways, most distressingly, to go on in any fashion at all. The self-trust rooted in a sense of the poverty of our inheritances optimally means (to paraphrase the conclusion of Emerson's "Experience") translating our whimsical genius into practical power.[56] This and this alone is "the true romance" for which the quotidian world exists. In turn, this romance helps us to discern the shape of the drama for which *we* exist. The translation of experience into words can be an enhancement of both our words and our experience, but only if it is at the same time an exercise of our power, an exercise in which a genius uncertain of its warrant trusts a power unmeasured in its force. That is, such translation must be animated and guided by a sense of loss, a refusal to cover over the disconcerting fate of being at a loss to know what to say or how to act.[57] Stanley Cavell's literary corpus bears eloquent witness to the possibility and power of such translation. It is in effect an invitation to readers to undertake for themselves the arduous yet often exhilarating task of owning up to the disclosures and dramas of their own experience. Readers can of course decline the invitation. They can even do so by dismissing the endeavor: That is simply what *he* does (what he happens to do) and, thus, there is no necessity for me to do so as well. He has said as much in his invocation of Wittgenstein's famous confession.[58] But what are we doing when we decline such invitations? This question is itself an invitation, an invitation to take both Cavell and ourselves more seriously than most of us habitually do. It reveals us to be already engaged in the task of translating our experience and indeed having our selves always already been translated by others in ways both stultifying and enlivening, both obfuscating and clarifying. The disclosures, disruptions, impasses, confusions, and intimations of our experience drive us to take up this task of translating anew, for ourselves, though always *with* others.

NOTES

1. Note that these are examples of everyday objects ("tester" here almost certainly designates a canopy over a bed), and this is in this context, of course, of the utmost significance.

2. "Circles," in *Emerson: Selected Essays*, ed. Larzer Ziff (New York: Penguin Books, 1982), 231.

3. *Philosophical Investigations*, trans. G. E. M. Anscombe (Malden, MA: Blackwell Publishing, 2001), #1.

4. *On Certainty,* trans. Denis Paul and G. E. M. Anscombe (San Francisco: Harper & Row, 1972), #192.

5. *Philosophical Investigations*, #217.

6. "Self-Reliance," in *Selected Essays*, 179.

7. In "The Social Value of the College-Bred," a talk originally given at Radcliff College in 1907, reprinted in *The Moral Equivalent of War and Other Essays*, ed. John K. Roth (New York: Harper & Row, 1971). William James acknowledges, "'Tone,' to be sure is a terribly vague word to use, but there is no other, and this whole meditation [on the higher education of women] is over questions of tone. By their tone are all things human either lost or saved." See *The Works of William James*, ed. Frederick H. Burghardt (Cambridge, MA: Harvard University Press, 1975). As an interpreter of philosophical texts but also as an author of ones singularly in his own name, Cavell is acutely attuned to tone. In practice, he in effect honors the insight that all things human are lost or saved by their tone.

8. I am sensitive to the possibility that there are gender and quite likely other biases built into my celebration of the need to speak out of a sense of one's own poverty. The need for women might be just the opposite, since it might be to speak out of an unabashed sense of their own experiential wealth, the very act of speaking being crucial for working toward a just sense of this experiential wealth.

9. John E. Smith, *Experience and God* (New York: Fordham University Press, 1995), 13. See also Vincent Colapietro, "Transition, Transmutation, and Transfiguration: Notes for a Poetics of Experience," in *Thinking with Whitehead and the Pragmatists*, ed. Brian G. Henning, William T. Myers, and Joseph D. John (Lanham, MD: Lexington Books, 2015), 209–26.

10. For some thinkers at least, thought inevitably becomes a focus of thought; they cannot help but think about thinking. So, too, experience is not infrequently turned back on itself, occasionally in such a manner that reflexive experience becomes a familiar form of our everyday encounters. Subjects of experience become absorbed in their own processes of encounter and engagement, so much so that their encounters and engagements with others often involve effacement of others.

11. "It is very unhappy, but too late to be helped, the discovery we have made that we exist. That discovery is called the Fall of Man. Ever afterwards we suspect our instruments [including our own consciousness and rationality]. We have learned that we do not see directly, but mediately, and that we have no means of correcting these colored and distorting lenses which we are, or of computing the amount of their errors" (*Selected Essays*, 304). Such suspicion is, given the traumas generative of self-consciousness, inescapable and, in a sense, ineradicable. But this makes self-trust and indeed self-affirmation necessary, not impossible. If self-trust in the Emersonian sense was easy, it would be far more commonplace. If it was impossible, it would not be discernible anywhere. Its arresting presence cannot be gainsaid, just as its rarity must be admitted.

12. "Experience," in *Selected Essays*, 288.

13. Emerson, "Circles," in *Selected Essays*, 225. See Walter Benn Michaels, "*Walden*'s False Bottoms," *Glyph* 1 (1977): 132–49.

14. A different but related point is made by means of another metaphor: "Every spirit makes its house; but afterwards the house confines the spirit" ("Fate," in *Selected Essays*, 365). As a result spirit must exile itself from its home—or wither and die. That is, a larger circle must be drawn around the increasingly confining and stifling one.

15. *This New Yet Unapproachable America* (Chicago: University of Chicago Press, 2013), 114.

16. Ibid.

17. It is partly the recovery and enhancement of one's power. The concluding sentence of Emerson's "Experience" is, after all, "the true romance which the world exists to realize will be the transformation of [personal] genius into practical power" (311). The recovery of the world is as much as anything else the recollection that *this* is romance for which the world exists, at least as far as we are concerned when we are healthy or alive. For an insightful reading of Emerson on power, see Cornel West, *The American Evasion of Philosophy: A Genealogy of Pragmatism* (Madison, WI: University of Wisconsin Press, 1989), 13–25.

18. "Experience," in *Selected Essays*, 310–11 (emphasis added).

19. "Fate," in *Selected Essays*, 375.

20. Ibid., 375–76.

21. Ibid., 383.

22. Ibid., 384.

23. "Montaigne," in *Selected Essays*, 359.

24. In the preface to *The Phenomenology of Spirit*, Hegel notes: "We learn by experience that we meant something other than we meant to mean; and [this discovery,] this correction of our meaning compels our knowledge to go back to the proposition, and understand it in some other way" (G. W. F. Hegel, *Phenomenology of Spirit*, trans. A. V. Miller [Oxford: Oxford University Press, 1977], 39). Only thus can we go on (cf. Wittgenstein, *Philosophical Investigations*; also Cavell).

25. Cavell, *Philosophy the Day after Tomorrow* (Cambridge, MA: The Belknap Press of Harvard University Press, 2005), 82.

26. The theme of experience "missed or lost" is an increasingly prominent one in Cavell's writings (e.g., *Philosophy the Day after Tomorrow,* 9). "Experience missed, in certain of the forms in which philosophy has interested itself in this condition, is," he emphasizes, "a theme developing itself through various of my intellectual turns in recent years" (10). It is however especially experience *ceded*, ceded to some authority because a lack of self-trust, that concerns Cavell.

27. Cf. Vincent Colapietro, "Experience Ceded and Negated," *Journal of Speculative Philosophy* 22, no. 2 (2008): 118–26.

28. Stanley Cavell, *Conditions Handsome and Unhandsome* (Chicago: University of Chicago Press, 1990), 58.

29. Cavell, *Philosophy the Day after Tomorrow*, 2–3.

30. Ibid., 3.

31. Colapietro, "Experience Ceded and Negated."

32. E.g., Emerson's "Experience," in *Selected Essays*, 286.

33. *Art as Experience: The Later Works of John Dewey*, volume 10, ed. Jo Ann Boydston (Carbondale, IL: Southern Illinois Press, 2008), 60.

34. "'Intuition' is that meeting of the old and the new in which the readjustment involved in every form of consciousness is effectively suddenly [or spontaneously] by means of a quick and unexpected harmony which in its bright abruptness is like a flash of revelation; although in fact it is prepared for by long and slow inculcation" (*Art as Experience*, 270). In the language of Hegel, this would make such "intuitions" mediated immediacies.

35. *Art as Experience*, 56.

36. Ibid.

37. John Dewey, *Human Nature and Conduct: The Later Works of John Dewey*, volume 14, ed. Jo Ann Boydston (Carbondale, IL: Southern Illinois Press, 1983), 118. See also Richard Rorty, "Introduction," in *The Later Works of John Dewey*, volume 8, ed. Jo Ann Boydston (Carbondale, IL: Southern Illinois Press, 1986), ix.

38. John Dewey, "The Need for a Recovery of Philosophy," in *The Middle Works of John Dewey*, volume 10, ed. Jo Ann Boydston (Carbondale, IL: Southern Illinois Press, 1980), 23.

39. William James, quoted in Ralph Barton Perry, *The Thought and Character of William James*, volume 2 (Boston: Little, Brown & Co., 1935), 269.

40. *The Later Works of John Dewey*, volume 1, ed. Jo Ann Boydston (Carbondale, IL: Southern Illinois Press, 1981), 370.

41. To be precise, he uses the expression, as the subtitle to *Cracking Up* (New York: Hill & Wang, 1995), "the work of unconscious experience." Of course, Stanley Cavell is a philosopher for whom the Freudian unconscious is not anything to be slighted, much less ridiculed. Human experience involves, for Cavell and indeed Emerson no less than Freud and Bollas, unconscious communication. As Bollas puts it, "unconscious communication between two people is not necessarily about lucid, effective, and memorable understandings of one another; rather, it is a way of life. . . . One person's direct effect on the other—unconscious to unconscious—cannot be witnessed by consciousness. It is a discordant symphonic movement of a reciprocally infinite fall of one self into another. There are harmonic duets, that is for sure: two people sharing mental processes and ills. But the effect of one person upon another is ordinarily too idiosyncratic to be comprehended" (28).

42. "Experience," in *Selected Essays*, 286.

43. "The Poet," in *Selected Essays*, 279.

44. "The philosophy of six thousand years has not searched the chambers and magazines of the soul. In its experiments there has always remained, in the last analysis, a residuum it could not resolve. Man is a stream whose source is hidden. Our being is descended into us from where we know not whence" ("The Over-Soul," in *Selected Essays*, 206; cf. 217)

45. Emerson, "The Poet," in *Selected Essays*, 273.

46. Emerson, "Circles," in *Selected Essays*, 237.

47. Ibid.

48. This is unmistakably audible in one of the most famous quotations from this eminently quotable author: "Do not set the least value on what I do, or the least discredit on what I do not, as if I pretended to settle any thing as true or false. I unsettle all things. No facts are to me sacred, none are profane; I simply experiment, an endless seeker with no Past at my back" ("Circles," in *Selected Essays*, 236). One way to read the concluding self-characterization (I am "an endless seeker *with no Past at my back*") is however to suggest that Emerson is a traveler with a past by his side. Such a past is not anything upon which he can fall back, as refuge or fortress (he would be forced, at least disposed, to say in countless circumstances, "This is imply what *I* do," not "This is what my inheritance unquestionably authorizes me to do"). It would nonetheless be a traveling companion, an inescapable one (sometimes a nuisance, sometimes a resource, all too often a fatal distraction). See Bollas on nostalgia (*Cracking Up*).

49. Emerson, "The Poet," in *Selected Essays*, 237.

50. Emerson, "Inspiration" in *Letters and Social Aims*, volume 8 of *The Complete Works* (New York: Houghton, Mifflin, 1904), 296.

51. In his homage to Emerson on the centenary of his forbearer's birth, James identifies one side of Emerson's genius as following this directive: "Let me mind my own charge, then, walk alone, consult the sky, the field and forest, sedulously waiting every morning for the news concerning the structure of the universe which the good Spirit will give me" (William James, "Address at the Emerson Centenary in Concord," in *William James: The Essential Writings*, 288). He is however quick to note: "This was the first half of Emerson, but only half: for genius, as he said, is insatiate with expression, and truth has to be clad in the right verbal garment. The form of the garment was so vital with Emerson that it is impossible to separate it from the matter" (ibid). In sum, the "duty of spiritual seeing and reporting determined," James judged, "the whole tenor of his life" (ibid.).

52. William James, "Address," 288.

53. Emerson, "Experience," in *Selected Essays*, 286.

54. "The Poet," in *Selected Essays*, 276.

55. Colapietro, "Transition, Transmutation, and Transfiguration."

56. The lines being in part paraphrased here are of course these: "Never mind the ridicule, never mind the defeat, up again, old heart!—it [the solitude to which every man and woman is

always returning] seems to say,—there is victory yet for all justice; and the true romance which the world exists to realize will be the transformation of genius into practical power" (*Selected Essays*, 310–11). It seems relevant to recall an equally famous passage from William James's *The Varieties of Religious Experience*, one in which he unabashedly confessed, "I am leaning only upon mankind's common instinct for reality, which in point of fact has always held the world to be essentially a theatre for heroism. In heroism, we feel, life's supreme mystery is hidden." To put it otherwise, a life without courage would be one without truth, humility, patience, forbearance, and indeed integrity. The translation of our experience into the utterances of us is paradoxically one of the principal means by which we can attain a critical distance from, and take fuller possession of, that experience. This is an act; better, it is a performative utterance in which the translating is an instance of doing. It is at the very least a provisional avowal in a dramatic context.

57. See once again Cavell, *This New Yet Unapproachable America*, 114.

58. Wittgenstein, *Philosophical Investigations*, #217.

Chapter Four

Rebuking Hopelessness

Paul Standish

I take the philosophical interest of translation to depend upon something other than its being taken as a metaphor—a metaphor for various kinds of transformation. The interest stems in large measure from the ways in which the practicalities and problems of translation, as commonly understood, reveal, writ large, more general aspects of language and meaning, and of so much else that rests on them.[1] These problems are particularly acute or intense in the translation of poetry from one language to another. Hence, much of my discussion is going to relate to someone who was a professional translator and a poet, and whose translations of poetry from a number of languages are extensive—none other than Paul Celan. But I want to begin elsewhere.

PATIENCE AND EXHAUSTION

On the last pages of *A Pitch of Philosophy* Stanley Cavell makes three dedications, which he presents in reverse order to the chapters to which they refer. The last of these runs as follows:

> The first chapter is dedicated to the memory of Yochanan Budick, a friend to me, to Cathleen, to Benjamin, and to David, each differently. His life in Jerusalem and his death there are bound up for me with the all but unbearable significance of the place. I end by quoting, in translation, the first paragraph of a story carried by the Jerusalem papers on the day of Yochanan's funeral. In identifying him as the subject of the story I am revealing nothing unknown to the hundreds of people who attended the funeral. "The lives of two Jerusalemites and a woman from Ramallah were saved yesterday thanks to organ donations by a fifteen-year-old boy, who died the day before at Hadassah Ein Kerem Hospital after a serious head injury." On one real, ordinary day in

Jerusalem, whatever else was happening, the end of the days of a young man
of that city, a Jew, provided continuation to the days of, among others, an Arab
woman from Ramallah. It rebukes hopelessness. [2]

This is a moving statement, not least its closing line, from which my title is
taken. It expresses simultaneously a kind of incredulity at the loss of this, but
also an acknowledgment of something supererogatory in the releasing of the
body parts for the transplants, something that, in crossing ancient yet still
urgent political divisions, exceeds any economies of obligation and satisfaction. Emily Budick's "Sense and Sensibility: Stanley Cavell's Philosophy of
Moral Manners," which considers further Cavell's dedication to her son,
notes that his book concludes with the words "rebuking hopelessness." She
points out that, like Ralph Waldo Emerson's term "admonition," the word
"rebuke" prescribes no moral directive or meaning: "Rather, like the term
'aversion' in Emerson's idea that 'self-reliance' is the 'aversion' of 'conformity,' the words turn us away from preconceived or predetermined notions
and toward personal, private, independent thought and decision-making." [3]
The event of Yochanan's death, the interruption it brings about, is an event in
virtue of the narratives that frame it, including Cavell's in this dedication;
and these narratives in turn depend upon a kind of reception. There is an
internal relation between the concepts of event, narrative, address, and reception. Cavell's motif for this is the faculty of hearing, and he speaks of "the
trauma of the birth of culture within oneself." [4]

In prefacing the chapter in question, Cavell emphasizes a conviction that
echoes Emerson's claim that "the deeper the scholar dives into his privatest,
secretest presentiment, to his wonder he finds this is the most acceptable,
most public, and universally true." [5] The vision is of an education for philosophy that lays the way for the recognition that "we live lives simultaneously of
absolute separateness and endless commonness, of banality and sublimity." [6]
In the second chapter of this same book Cavell will go on to articulate a
further conviction to the effect that, whatever the connections of his own
preoccupations with those of Jacques Derrida, the distance between them,
especially over the idea of the ordinary, is real enough: Cavell takes Ludwig
Wittgenstein and J. L. Austin as exposing the harm in philosophy's bewitch-
ment by the metaphysical voice as the suffocation of the ordinary voice; the
irony of Derrida's work, by contrast, is that it contributes to the continuation
of philosophy's flight from the ordinary. A salient passage in respect of these
matters, directed against a different kind of reader but reprising, through its
imagery, the intertwining of separateness and commonality, banality and
sublimity, is to be found in Cavell's remarks about responses to Wittgenstein's turning of the spade ("If I have exhausted the justifications I have
reached bedrock, and my spade is turned. Then I am inclined to say: 'This is
what I do,'" #217). What Cavell brings to this passage in this essay, signifi-

cantly in his coupling of it with Henry David Thoreau's hoeing of his bean-
field, is his sense of the "nervous laughter or outright contempt"[7] that a
certain autobiographical or literary reading of the turned spade might exact:
nervousness about the literary because of the ancient worry about words'
turning and re-turning of our thoughts; nervousness about the autobiographical because this signals a weakening of the disciplinary hold of community,
which gives way to an affirmation of community's dependence upon voice,
upon my being "inclined to say," upon the account I am inclined to give in
my words and work. Cavell has elaborated on the idea of inclination in "The
Argument of the Ordinary," while here he finds it figured in the hunching of
the body over the spade.[8] Unapologetic in the face of the nervousness, he
now goes on provocatively to say,

> Things get worse. My way of taking this passage shows it, more particularly,
> as a comment on a certain style of writing—evidently that of the Investigations
> in which it appears—since the implement is, to speak with due banality, mas-
> culine, but the gesture (of waiting, putting one's self or body, on the line that
> way) is feminine; so that patience, and a recognition of rebuff and exhaustion
> also become earmarks of the writing of this pedagogy, simultaneously with
> what Thoreau calls the labor of his hands only.[9]

That hope implies waiting and patience, putting oneself on the line and the
risk of rebuff, and that all this can be exhausted provides me with an entry
into what follows. For this is a case in which hope is tested to the extreme.

HOPE FOR A WORD

It seems that Paul Celan became aware of Martin Heidegger's work through
his relationship with Ingeborg Bachmann in the late 1940s. She was in the
course of writing a dissertation on Heidegger that addressed the vexed question of the extent of the Nazi connections in his thought. Almost in spite of
himself, so it seems, Celan became interested in the substance of Heidegger's
philosophy, and this was sustained for the rest of his life. Heidegger, for his
part, became aware of Celan's writings, perhaps through the growing interest
there was among literary circles in the Germany of the 1950s; indeed during
this time Celan was much in demand as a speaker at poetry readings.
Through two decades there was an exchange of letters between the two men,
not frequent but cautious, tentative but sustained, and both showed not only
respect but some affinity with the other's work. This was a mutual recognition that drew Celan to Heidegger with a mixture of fascination and abhor-
rence. In 1967 they met. Celan had been invited to speak at the University of
Freiburg, where he drew a crowd of over one thousand. By arrangement he
met Heidegger at the start of the evening, and the next day he visited him in

the mountain hut that was Heidegger's preferred home. From there the two men went for a walk on the moor for some ninety minutes. The poem *Todt-nauberg* records this encounter.[10]

Heidegger remarked to Hans-Georg Gadamer that he was impressed by Celan's knowledge of the plants of the forest—better than Heidegger's own! And the poem starts with two plant names: *Arnica* and *Augentrost* (arnica and eyebright). What follows reads like a set of notes—field-notes perhaps or a diary entry—recording different aspects of the visit: the drink from the well, the signing of, and entry in, the visitors' book, the woodland turf, the two men, metamorphosed as two wild orchids, the driver taking them through the woods, the log paths, and the surrounding wetness. A string of notes in a single sentence with no main verb. Marks etching a line down the page.

A second look takes us deeper. Because of their supposed medicinal properties, the two plants named at the start already signal much more: Arnica is used in the relief of pain, while eyebright gets its name from its benefits in the treatment of poor eyesight. So it is a need to relieve pain and (for at least someone) to see more clearly that have, it seems, led Celan to this hut. The signing of the visitors' book, with the parenthesis of the question, "Whose name did it take in before mine?" recalls the thought that Celan is signing his name somewhere beneath those of Heidegger's youthful Nazi friends who had been invited to this retreat decades before. While Celan had the day before declined to be photographed with Heidegger, he does now inscribe his own words into that book, writing a line about hope for a "thinker's" word in "the heart" ("thinker," a word so freighted for Heidegger). But this expression is itself interrupted, and the anticipated "word" is preceded and qualified by the hiatus of "undelayed coming", a bracketed expression stretched between lines: the word is broken, detaching the negative prefix ("un-") and leaving it suspended, hyphenated, as a line by itself. And then the text falls gradually away, back into the woodland landscape, with its two men, identified equally as *Orchis* and *Orchis*, two orchids, upright and un-bending towards the other—disinclined, as it might inadequately be said; yet where the Greek etymology of the term in question connects semantically with *testes* in Latin and, hence, with "testimony" and "witness."

As if this were not enough, we can go to a third stage and draw from the substantial commentary the poem has prompted. Perhaps one of the most searching exhumations of this text is the one offered in the 1980s by Pierre Joris. Space allows me to excerpt only a part of his analysis.[11] One word that draws Joris's attention particularly in the poem is *Waldwasen*, which might, at first glance, stand for "those bucolic meadows where poets and philoso-phers can sport and relax and chat." But this is not, in fact, such a common word. Is it then erudite or "poetic," preferred to the more obvious *Waldwie-sen*? Is it preferred because of its rhyming with the "a"-sound in "Arnika,

Augentrost"? But a *Wase* is, first of all, a piece of sod together with the plants that grow in it. Celan has in mind not just the grassy surface, then, but something, it seems, that goes deeper. Further, as Joris tells us, in northern Germany, the term *Wasen* is used to mean turf or peat, which is known both for its use in making a fire but also for its extraordinary preservative qualities, preserving things, bodies, even from the prehistoric past. What might have been a romantic glade has already become *unheimlich*, which in Heideggerian thought is disturbed still further if we think of the proximity of *Wasen* to *Wesen* (essence), a key lexical site for this philosopher. But still there is more. What is also suggested is that the land that the two men walk across is that of the *Wasenmeister*, of the knacker who guts and buries the dead livestock; thus, we are in the "knacker's yard" or, one might say, the "killing fields." The walk, Joris suggests, is over a cemetery in Celan's poetic thought, the "all-pervasive topos" of his work. And here Celan has come to see Heidegger in the hope of a word—a word of apology or explanation: for the destruction, like cattle, of the Jewish people. Joris falters, troubled by the thought that he has gone too far in translation. But then, he explains, his "eye fell on yet another '*Wase*,' a word current in northern Germany, and used to describe a bundle of dead wood, the etymology of which Grimm leads back through French '*faisceau*' to Latin '*fasces*,' the curator's bundle of rods, which became the symbol of, and gave the word for, 'fascism.'" In his preface to his book on Heidegger, George Steiner writes of the way that, over a sustained period, Heidegger and Celan were present to one another. But he takes the meeting in 1967 to have ended in "a numbing, soul-lacerating deception."[12] In spite of its apparently casual recording of details, one can find in the structure of the poem a movement of seismic scale. With each line the tremors intensify until one reaches the word "word," the middle point and epicenter of the poem. What more central site can there be for a poet and translator? And for a philosopher for whom language is the house of being, what more pointed challenge could there be? Three years after the events recorded in the poem, Paul Celan committed suicide.

REVISITING TODTNAUBERG

The signature of *Todtnauberg*[13] has an indelibility that renders the poem inseparable from Celan's own life. How can the poem be read—how can it be a poem—other than in autobiographical, confessional terms? And yet matters should not be left there. As James Lyon has shown, Celan's reports of his meeting with Heidegger seem to have been by no means as decisively negative as Steiner's comment and the above reading would suggest. On January 30, 1968, Heidegger sent him a copy of *Wegmarken* (*Track Markings*), his most recent work, and in that year and the year to follow, Celan

embarked on a rereading of *Was Heisst Denken?* (*What Is Called Thinking?*).
In June 1968 Celan stayed with Gerhard Neumann, the driver referred to in
the poem, and spent several days with Heidegger. During these months Celan
made remarks to the effect both that Heidegger had "recaptured for language
its 'limpidity'"[14] and that "you (by your stance) have decisively weakened
that which is poetic and, I venture to surmise, that which is thinking, in the
serious will to responsibility of both."[15] On March 19, 1970, less than a
month before his suicide, Celan traveled to Germany to give what was to be
his final poetry readings, and in the course of this four-day visit he met
Heidegger at least twice. Bruised by what he perceived to be the response to
his first reading, he was heartened in the second by the attentiveness of
Heidegger's response. But it was by then clear that these fluctuations of
mood were part of a deeper condition that had burdened him for many years.
At the final reading, Heidegger had presented Celan with two gifts—a copy
of his *On the Matter of Thinking* and a recent bilingual, French-German
edition of his "Art and Space," with the dedications "in gratitude for the
reading" and "upon meeting again." But he remarked privately: "Celan is
ill—incurably."[16]

If I am right that *Todtnauberg* exists as a poem in a way that is inseparable from the event it records and from the lives of those brought together in
this encounter, this complication of the subsequent history renders its interpretation less clear or stable, even given the scrupulousness and tenacity of
Joris's investigation. Celan's psychological instability becomes present in
the problems of interpretative response, defying any aspiration for closure.
And that instability was plainly provoked by an acquaintance with poles of
experience, in a way of which he was himself only too aware. The relation to
such poles is there in his poetics and in his account of what language might
be. Consider then the following. Toward the end of *The Meridian*, his speech
on the occasion of the award of the Georg Büchner prize, a text in his
dialogue with Heidegger continues to be present; Celan speaks of

> language become reality, language set free under the sign of an individuation
> which is radical, yet at the same time remains mindful of the boundaries
> established for it by language. This as-always of the poem can, to be sure, only
> be found in the poem of that person who does not forget that he speaks from
> under the angle of inclination of his existence, the angle of inclination of his
> position among all living creatures.[17]

Celan's "angle of inclination" speaks deftly against the neuter, impersonal,
pagan voice of Heidegger's "Language speaks." It shows the partiality of the
human and the essential place in language of the address. "Ladies and gentle-
men," he continues,

I find something which offers me some consolation for having traveled the impossible path, this path of the impossible, in your presence. I find something which binds and which, like the poem, leads to an encounter. I find something, like language, abstract, yet earthy, terrestrial, something circular, which traverses both poles and returns to itself, thereby—I am happy to report—even crossing the tropics and tropes. I find . . . a meridian. [18]

In failing to realize language as address, the neutered, impersonal vision fails also to see the place in human experience of the encounter. This is not only the most obvious matter of the encounter between people, the potential intensity of which is witnessed in *Todtnauberg*; it is also the encounter constituted by the poem itself, insofar as the poem is itself an address.

Poetry cannot be other than as address. In Celan's work this is accentuated by the recurrence of *Du*, the intimate address to the other person, which occurs around thirteen hundred times in his work.

MEANING, TRANSLATION, BEARING WITNESS

The excuse, if one is needed, for dwelling in this way, for the purpose of this book, on one poem by Paul Celan, with this English version by John Felstiner, and with this commentary by Pierre Joris, is that all three are poet-translators for whom the question of translation is philosophical if nothing else. Their interest in poetry is in part provoked by the fact, as we saw at the start, that poetry accentuates and brings into view problems of meaning—or, perhaps better, aspects of the nature of meaning—that are there in language as a whole. The task of the translator reveals a space for judgment that is there in our ordinary experience, words, and thought. Language occurs not in an abstract realm but in the address of the other and the event of encounter. And words inevitably produce something new in, and of, the world. The thought I am trying to hold onto here is that in its address to the other the poem also opens the space of hope. Even the writing of a poem of despair is also, qua address, some minimal expression of hope.

Before the final section of this discussion, I want to make a short detour via some writings of Derrida in response to Celan, whose work he had studied for some years before he realized that they were working in the same institution. The particular text I shall refer to is written in part in tribute to Gadamer, and in it Derrida considers Celan's poem *Grosse Glühende Wölbung* ("Vast Glowing Vault"), dwelling in particular on its last line: "Die Welt ist fort, ich muß dich tragen" ("The world is lost. I must carry you").The world is lost in the sense that its sense seems always to have fallen away, to be something from which we are already severed, something already lost, something that has slipped through our grasp; it is as if experience were not enough to satisfy us. The world stands in need of a renewal at our hands, which is to say, through the words we bring to it. The sense of *tragen* as "carry" or "bear" implies also the carrying of a child, as if the responsibility of words made us pregnant with possibility, charged with producing something new. It orients us to what comes, which suggests a kind of receptivity, and to what is to come, which opens the field of hope. But this carrying should also be "addressed to the dead, to the survivor or to the specter, in an experience that consists in carrying the other in oneself, as one bears mourning—and melancholy."[19] Such a way of thinking would be tied to singularity and to the production of narrative, which in turn would become an event. Budick draws attention to the ways that "storytelling functions as philosophical investigation for Cavell in relation to the problem of moral perfectionism within the context of culture." This no doubt is true, but the point being made here with this detour via Derrida is, I think, of a more pervasive kind. Without pursuing this further now, I shall conclude this chapter by drawing attention to what I take to be contiguities in the discussion above with key elements in Cavell's thought. Let me say, though, that I see only limited interest in the finding of similarities. The test of value must be more to do with how far what is said can move thought forward, and here especially in relation to the idea of philosophy as translation. Thoreau's claim that the truth is translated, with which Cavell plainly indicates an affinity, cries out for further development, and I hope what I say here can contribute to this.

CONTIGUITIES WITH CAVELL

There are multiple themes in Cavell that extend these thoughts, and it is impossible here to acknowledge them all. Yet one particular line of thought beckons for further expression in this context. The connection I want to press is precisely with the meridian, the vertical longitudinal line running from north to south, and from pole to pole. Celan's enigmatic title for his speech upon receiving the Büchner Prize might be read as expressive of his own condition—of this and so much more. The meridian, otherwise the line of midday, which occurs in the north and in the south and at the equator too, is the line of high sun, as high as it gets for the particular time of year. It suggests the high point in the tensions under which Celan lived.

These tensions are epitomized by his relationship with Heidegger, who, on the one hand, stood out for him as a thinker above others, with insights regarding language not unlike his own, and who, on the other, was so fatefully compromised by connection with unspeakable horror. This bi-polar tensioning of experience, exposed to the high sun of his meetings with Heidegger, should not be seen simply in the pathological terms of his being "ill—incurably," for in a sense it is a rational response. (That it is Heidegger who provides this diagnosis raises again the question of where reason and madness lie.) We are caught between horror and happiness, horror and hope, our lives suspended over an abyss, whatever strategies we may devise for failing to face up to this. We (so it must seem) wisely find ways to live with this, without succumbing to the madness that eventually consumed Celan. Few have his cause. But we live unwisely if we live in denial.

How do these thoughts, and *The Meridian*'s manifestation of something both thematically and stylistically aligned with them, compare with Cavell's extraordinary discussion of *The Rime of the Ancient Mariner*, the disturbing, supernatural poem by Samuel Taylor Coleridge?[20] The poem's narrative involves following the line of the mariner's voyage due south toward the pole (down a longitudinal, meridian line), and then his return, but in a changed state. The world to which the mariner returns—call this his home, call this the world—has been, by steps, deadened and then reanimated. He is by turns stricken by guilt, touched by redemption. The settlement achieved at the end is one of a return to the ordinary as to an ordinary that has been jeopardized—threatened, to put this philosophically, by skepticism. Cavell takes Coleridge to be taking on Immanuel Kant no less—that is, as depicting the natural human frustration at inability to grasp things-in-themselves, the natural human reaction of rejection (skepticism), and the eventual recognition of the need for a different kind of response. To pull these thoughts together would be to recognize the tensioned, troubled nature of our condition. This is a condition that we evade, to be sure, by multiple strategies of bad faith.

Bad faith takes surreptitious forms. Positive psychology and the idealization of well-being are contemporary expressions of this, but then so is that orientation to life that imagines it to be amenable in principle to rational planning and control without remainder. That these are prominent in public policy and practice today scarcely needs demonstration. Even if they provide a space in which virtues of a kind would seem to be exercised, in the end they are bourgeois and nihilistic. But it is the more specifically philosophical bad faith that predictably provokes Cavell. It is easy to see the pertinence of Coleridge's depiction of the ghost-ship and the personification of Life-in-Death as suggestive of Cavell's preoccupation with examples of false animation. In fact, the idea of a false animation is there in his diagnosis of philosophy's construction of and response to skepticism. Recalling the Ghost in the Machine, Cavell sees Coleridge's "picture of animated bodies . . . as a parody of what a certain kind of philosopher, a person in a certain grip of thought, takes the human being, hence human society, to be."[21] Further, *The Ancient Mariner*'s figuring of the killing of the albatross evokes the related thought of a world that has been deadened at our hands, where claims to knowledge have been, let us say, subjected to exorbitant demands.

Yet, once the connection between this narrative and *The Meridian* is raised, questions present themselves of a different order, extending this allegory of thought. The Mariner's ship strays from the temperate zone toward a frozen landscape in which the ship is locked in ice. Becoming free from this is the result, so it seems, of an act of violence or sacrifice, the killing of the albatross. Yet the return voyage passes through a region where, with no wind or current, the ship is unable to move and where, once again, thought is stymied. The vertical trajectory might be read as extending toward poles of subjectivity and objectivity. Its Antarctica might suggest the fixity of the thing-in-itself. It might suggest the fixity (and fixations generated by) the unconscious. Cavell reads the parable as taking on Kant, no less, but also as presaging the thought of Freud. He announces at the start of the essay that he reads

> the line in question to be (among other things, no doubt) the line implied in [Kant's *Critique of Pure Reason*] "below" which or "beyond" which knowledge cannot penetrate. On Kant's view, the effort to breach it creates, for example, skepticism and fanaticism, efforts to experience what cannot humanly be experienced. Coleridge's poem demonstrates that Kant's lined-off region can be experienced and that the region below the line has a definite, call it a frozen, structure. This way of interpretation (say as a romantic craving for experience, as if doubting whether one now has an experience to call one's own) is not incompatible with interpretations of the poem as of the Fall; indeed it provides an interpretation of that interpretation. [22]

In fact, the journey down across a line is suggestive in multiple ways. Transgressing the line or limit of propriety, crossing a boundary between sanity and madness, the allusions here extend to the question of the limits of what can be said or, that is, put into lines. These are lines that, of necessity, Celan crossed in his work as a translator, and that, with insistent, tenacious precision, he exploited in his writings, his poetry most obviously. The task of the translator, its necessary crossing of lines, opens onto the exercise of judgment; and is it not especially in the crossing of a line that one is exposed *to* being judged? Celan's insistence on the meridian, his exposure to the madness of a midday sun, keeps faith, so it seems, with Emmanuel Levinas's call for insomnia: The evil of the world calls upon us not to go to sleep. This deprives him of the axis of latitude that provides the diurnal passage of night and day.

In closing, however, let me find a more temperate tone in order to recall what I called the internal relation between the concepts of event, narrative, address, and reception. Such connections are apparent in Celan's encounter with Heidegger, to be sure, but also in the circumstances attending the death of Yochanan Budick. These events help to reveal possibilities and impossibilities of language that are in danger of being denied, in public policy and practice, throughout our social world, and to the detriment of our moral lives. These are possibilities writ large in the experience of translation. If there is a "trauma" to the "birth of culture within oneself," there is little in contemporary education that acknowledges this. Cavell's concept of voice and Derrida's account of the poetic alike require finding something new in our expression, and this relates to giving an account of ourselves in what we say—not as our personal story, but as our response to the world. This is simultaneously a response to the other human being. If we are serious about imparting hope, if we are serious about the possibilities of forgiveness, possibilities so painfully tested in *Todtnauberg*, we must recognize that these things will not be achieved without openness in our engagement in language, without preparedness to be addressed, without a readiness to respond. These aneconomies of language condition the possibility of forgiveness and hope. And we can educate and live in a way that honor these matters. This is part of our responsibility to the world.

NOTES

1. But is there not something to note within English itself, with its divided roots? Consider, for a start, "translate" (v.) itself, which originates in the early fourteenth century and means "to remove from one place to another" or "to turn from one language to another." This in turn derives from the Old French *translater* and directly from the Latin *translatus* ("carried over"), which serves as a past participle of *transferre* ("to bring over, carry over") and obviously connects with "transfer" and comprises the roots *trans-* and *latus* ("borne," "carried"). A similar notion is behind the Old English word it replaced, *awendan*, from *wendan*, which means "to turn, direct" and connects, again obviously, with the contemporary "wend."

2. Stanley Cavell, *A Pitch of Philosophy: Autobiographical Exercises* (Cambridge, MA: Harvard University Press, 1996), vii.

3. Emily Budick, "Sense and Sensibility: Stanley Cavell's Philosophy of Moral Manners," in *Walden in Tokyo: Stanley Cavell and the Thought of Other Cultures*, edited by Naoko Saito and Paul Standish (manuscript under review).

4. Cavell, *A Pitch*, 50.

5. Ibid., vii.

6. Ibid., vii.

7. Ibid., 14.

8. "The Argument of the Ordinary: Scenes of Instruction in Wittgenstein and Kripke" appears in *Conditions Handsome and Unhandsome*, 64–100. Cavell sees the passage concerning the turning of the spade as epitomizing Wittgenstein's idea of teaching and learning, and he provides a fascinating equivocation about where the exhaustion of justifications leaves the teacher, one possibility of which is that he might wait and lean on his spade. See the title essay in Stanley Cavell, *Philosophy the Day after Tomorrow* (Cambridge, MA: The Belknap Press of Harvard University Press, 2005).

9. Ibid., 14–15.

10. Ensuing references to Celan's poems are to the *Selected Poems and Prose of Paul Celan*, translated by John Felstiner (New York: W. W. Norton and Co., 2001).

11. Pierre Joris, "Celan/Heidegger: Translation at the Mountain of Death," paper presented at the "Poetic Thought & Translation" Conference, Wake Forest University, October 1988.

12. George Steiner, *Heidegger* (Chicago: University of Chicago Press, 1991), p. xxxii.

13. The name "Todtnauberg," already resonant with the sound of death (German, *Tod*), also resounds with Organisation Todt, a Nazi construction company, named after Fritz Todt, that built autobahns and, later, major fortifications and concentration camps.
14. Reported by Clemens Podewils in "Namen," 70. Cited in James Lyon, *Paul Celan and Martin Heidegger: An Unresolved Conversation, 1951–1970* (Baltimore: Johns Hopkins University Press, 2006), 270.
15. This is taken from what appears to have been the draft of a letter to Heidegger. See Lyon, *Paul Celan*, 207 and 235, n. 23.
16. Lyon, *Paul Celan*, 210–11.
17. Paul Celan, *The Meridian*, trans. Jerry Glenn, in Jacques Derrida, *Sovereignties in Question: The Poetics of Paul Celan*, ed. Thomas Dutoit and Outi Pasanen (New York: Fordham University Press, 2005), 175–85, esp. 181.
18. Celan, *The Meridian*, 185.
19. Derrida, *Sovereignties*, 159.
20. Coleridge's poem was first published in 1798 but later reworked at different stages, with a marginal gloss added.
21. Cavell, *In Quest of the Ordinary: Lines of Skepticism and Romanticism* (Chicago: University of Chicago Press, 1988), 54.
22. Ibid., 50.

BIBLIOGRAPHY

Emily Budick. "Sense and Sensibility: Stanley Cavell's Philosophy of Moral Manners." In *Walden in Tokyo: Stanley Cavell and the Thought of Other Cultures*, edited by Naoko Saito and Paul Standish (manuscript under review).

Stanley Cavell. *In Quest of the Ordinary: Lines of Skepticism and Romanticism*. Chicago: University of Chicago Press, 1988.

———. *Conditions Handsome and Unhandsome: The Constitution of Emersonian Perfectionism*. Chicago: University of Chicago Press, 1990.

———. *A Pitch of Philosophy: Autobiographical Exercises*. Cambridge, MA: Harvard University Press, 1996.

———. *Philosophy the Day after Tomorrow*. Cambridge, MA: The Belknap Press of Harvard University Press, 2005.

Paul Celan. *The Meridian*, trans. Jerry Glenn. In Jacques Derrida, *Sovereignties in Question: The Poetics of Paul Celan*, edited by Thomas Dutoit and Outi Pasanen. New York: Fordham, 2005.

———. *Selected Poems and Prose of Paul Celan*, trans. John Felztiner. New York: W. W. Norton and Co., 2001.

Jacques Derrida. *Sovereignties in Question: The Poetics of Paul Celan*, edited by Thomas Dutoit and Outi Pasanen. New York: Fordham, 2005.

Pierre Joris. "Celan/Heidegger: Translation at the Mountain of Death." Paper presented at the Poetic Thought & Translation Conference at Wake Forest University, October 1988.

James Lyon, Paul Celan, and Martin Heidegger. *An Unresolved Conversation, 1951–1970*. Baltimore: Johns Hopkins University Press, 2006.

Clemens Podewils, "Namen/Ein Vermächtnis Paul Celans." In *Ensemble. Lyrik, Prosa, Essay* 2, 1971.

George Steiner. *Heidegger*. Chicago: University of Chicago Press, 1991.

Ludwig Wittgenstein. *Philosophical Investigations*, edited by G. E. M. Anscombe and R. Rhees. Oxford: Blackwell, 1953.

Chapter Five

From Radical Translation to Radical Translatability

Education in an Age of Internationalization

Joris Vlieghe

Witnessing today an increasing internationalization of higher education, we are also up to new challenges. One of these is that, more and more, students and teachers no longer speak one and the same language. This implies, in many cases, that they have to rely on a language over which they don't have full command. More often than not this language is English, or more accurately put, a more or less distorted version of it—sometimes referred to as "Global Englishes" or "Globish." Giving a twist here to a term coined by Willard Van Orman Quine, I would refer to these circumstances as conditions of "radical translation."[1] In this chapter I deal with the challenges and opportunities that come along with radical translation, from a perspective that is both philosophical and educational. To be clear, my intent is not to stress the problematic character of this situation (viz., that it deprives students form learning opportunities, that it is a symptom of the marketization of higher education gone mad, etc.), nor am I looking for concrete and workable solutions. Rather, I want to flesh out *what it means* to educate and to be educated under these modified circumstances. Moreover, I argue that radical translation could also be taken in a positive and even in an inherently *educational* sense. Therefore, my aim in this contribution is to rethink the very meaning of education in view of particular conditions we experience today.

The view I develop here departs from a more common definition of education that refers to processes with fixed outcomes such as the transfer of tradition and knowledge, socialization, qualification, and so forth. In this

73

chapter, on the other hand, I take education as referring to an event, namely, to the possibility of a destabilization of fixed meanings, of self-transformation and of a new beginning, individually and collectively. I elaborate my ideas by drawing from the philosophies of two thinkers whose life work is concerned with the role that language plays in the formation of subjectivity and community: Stanley Cavell and Giorgio Agamben. The combination of these two at first sight unrelated philosophical perspectives is not meant as a mere theoretical exercise of comparing different intellectual traditions and pointing out (anticipated) differences and (unexpected) similarities.[2] On the contrary, I want to show that both thinkers address most timely, existential, and societal issues, and that a combined reading of Cavell and Agamben offers a vocabulary for thinking in new ways about education, language, and internationalization.

One and the other have analyzed the human condition as a situation in which translation cannot be avoided. Although I focus in this chapter on radical translation, that is, on circumstances in which we are forced to speak a foreign language, and moreover one over which we have no full command, much of what Cavell and Agamben talk about applies to the relationship one has with one's native language, too. They defend the idea that one *always* remains a stranger to language, and so translation isn't necessarily an intercultural or interlinguistic matter. The reason why I go deeper into the issue of learning and teaching in a multilingual context is that it offers a most tangible example of the educational possibilities radical translation might bring about. With Cavell and Agamben I show that lack of control over one's own words shouldn't only be regarded as a failure or as a difficulty to be overcome, but also as a condition for profound change, that is, a condition for education to take place.

LOST IN TRANSLATION AND THE CHALLENGE OF COMING TO LIVE A COMMON WORLD

Rather than starting with general and abstract considerations, I first discuss a concrete case, taken from my own experiences as a university teacher. In the past years, I have been teaching philosophy of education at a postgraduate level in international program, in Belgium, Germany, and the United Kingdom. This involves teaching in English to groups of highly diverse students who, the majority of them, are NNS—non-native speakers. Moreover, being a native Dutch speaker myself this has given cause to an at first sight highly artificial situation in which nobody speaks his or her "own" language. Furthermore, having a background in continental philosophy, I demand my students to engage with a lot of German literature (in English translation), and with ideas and concepts that cannot easily be translated (*Bildung, Bildsamkeit, Erziehung, Übung*, and many more such terms).

I must admit that at times students and I run into serious communication problems, and that there are many occasions at which students, but also I myself, don't manage to come up with the appropriate words and expressions. It is a matter of course that how hard we try and do our best, the flow of our words is frequently interrupted by stammering. This, of course, might feel quite embarrassing. In my own case, this often happens at the moment I realize that I have just translated a Dutch expression word for word into a nonexisting English formulation. On a more positive note, we also avoid difficulties that arise when listening to native English speakers, as they have a penchant for using many colloquial expressions. I cannot speak for my students, but I have to concede the fact that sometimes I just decide not to say something or that I express something utterly different from what I intended to (often stock phrases) just because I cannot find the right words. And this doesn't apply to spoken words only. When I mark assignment papers, it is not an exception for me to find that students have completely erroneous conceptions of what certain terms mean or what a particular philosopher has said.

At first sight, all this might seem most undesirable, as high quality teaching and learning are under jeopardy (a most delicate situation in view of the tuition fees foreign students have to pay). At a more philosophical level, it is easy to draw from this illustration the conclusion that, as a result of linguistic barriers, a true and profound communal understanding is out of reach. Moreover, it could be argued that an element of alienation and even of violence is involved because students (and teachers) are deprived of the possibility to express themselves in their mother tongue, and because they have to give in to speaking a foreign language. Therefore, conditions of radical translation actually support the linguistic imperialism of the English language, as there is no choice but turning to what happens to be today's academic lingua franca.

It is not my intention to question the severity of the many problems that come along with lacking linguistic competence and having to face situations of radical translation. Nonetheless, I would like to open another perspective on this issue that highlights a more positive side. Rather than denying or downplaying the many misunderstandings, barriers, frustrations, and feelings of (sometimes extreme) unease and powerlessness, I defend the idea that the circumstances of lacking full and final command over language may lead to a strong educational experience. In order to substantiate and clarify the claim that this experience of impotence shouldn't necessarily be regarded as problematic, I first turn to a distinction John Dewey makes in his pragmatist philosophy of communication.[3]

In his work Dewey criticizes a naïve, though frequently shared assumption behind what we actually do when we speak with one another. According to this prevailing belief, communication is all about guaranteeing a perfect understanding between speaker and interlocutor. Communication is successful if the identity between what is expressed and what is understood is ensured. This view implies that we first need a shared background in order to reach a common understanding: We must agree on basic beliefs about what the world is like, on the definition of the words we use, on ideas regarding what constitutes a valid argument, and so forth (even if the majority of these assumptions remain implicit). Therefore there is *the need to live in a common world* before we really can begin talking. Without such a background our talk is mere gibberish.

Over and against this view, Dewey proposes to look at communication from another angle, namely, as a common endeavor *to make* sense to one another: Commonality shouldn't be regarded as a starting point or as a necessary condition, but rather as a result. When successful, *we first come to live a common world*—a world that isn't given beforehand but is the fruit of our efforts. This world is only temporary and it has to be built time and again. Thus, what is really at stake when we speak with one another is that we make something *happen*, that we create something *new*—something that is new with each effort to come to mutual understanding. More importantly, what Dewey suggests is that an obsession with identity as a precondition for "true" understanding might actually prevent us from coming to live a common world. Whereas the first view deems any situation in which full transparency is unattainable as problematic at the outset, the second view implies that it is precisely this ideal of transparency itself that poses a problem that needs to be overcome, or at least, that it is a false ideal that should be abandoned. When we desire such an unreachable goal, we wind up with a form of relativism, which gives us the perfect excuse for not having to address and be addressed by people who are different from us, and for not having to work out things together. After all, if we can't truly understand one another, we are prisoners of the languages we speak, and we all remain entrapped in our own worlds.

According to this view, if we have no common language there is no common world. In a way, this is true, but Dewey would add that a common world is precisely something we still need to make, again and again. This is also to say that a lack of control over the situation doesn't inevitably pose a threat to commonality. On the contrary, it is this lack that prompts us to establish commonality: There is no "we" before we engage in understanding one another. A "we" is only constituted in every endeavor we undertake. In a sense this is a fairly accurate description of what happens in my classroom. Neither the absence of a shared linguistic and cultural background nor the lack of control over the lingua franca prevent students and teacher from trying to come to a communal understanding. If things work out, which is—to be honest—far from evident and certainly not the rule, something *new* is established that is not dependent upon something that existed beforehand.

However, I don't believe Dewey's analysis covers everything there is to say about this situation. This is because, in view of his pragmatist background, Dewey focuses on arriving at a successful answer to communication troubles that may cross our paths. Even if he admits that whatever it is we make in common is only a temporary, changeable, and precarious result, it is still a *result* that brings a *solution* to a problem. As such, a Deweyan account might ignore or miss out on the importance of things than cannot and should not be resolved. In this text I defend the view that under these particular conditions there is indeed the possibility of an experience of *newness*, but this draws from a sense of *impotence* rather than from coming up with a solution. Referring to the work of Cavell, who is particularly critical of Dewey on this point, this might be called a sense of *dissolution.*[4] In the next sections I argue, with Cavell, that we should take more seriously the experience of lacking control and being lost in (radical) translation. Rather than eventually overcoming this loss, it can be argued that this absence of control is vital to what it means to be a human being. And, moreover, that experiencing true community is dependent upon experiencing dissolution.

LANGUAGE AND SELF-LOSS: DEFINING AND DEFYING WHO WE ARE

At first sight Cavell's ideas seem to echo Dewey's point of view. Cavell, as an admirer of Emerson, defends an uncompromising *antifoundationalism*, which he describes as "transforming or replacing founding with finding."[5] This is to say that there is no need for having firm and fixed grounds that guarantee and justify that our common understanding is *truly* a common understanding—that is, foundations that could convince the skeptic (à la Quine perhaps) that we *really* grasp what others say. What matters is that we actually come to such an understanding, in the double sense of comprehending one another and agreeing with one another. We have to look for it and *find* it. If so, this event forms, and therefore *founds* a "we," a community. Cavell refers to this as "finding as founding."[6] In fact, Cavell develops here Ludwig Wittgenstein's observation that we shouldn't come to an understanding (i.e., a shared opinion) *about* language, but to an understanding (i.e., a real agreement) *in* language.[7] We don't need to look for something *external to* our own linguistic practice in order to explain that it is possible (or for that matter, as the skeptic believes, impossible) to do what we already do. Instead, we need to strive at what in Wittgenstein reads as *Übereinstimmung* (which literally means a correspondence of *Stimme*, that is, of voices), while remaining fully *within* our linguistic nature—language being our "form of life."[8]

This is, I would argue, on a par with Dewey's stress on making common understanding happening. Moreover, Dewey's ideas are in line with Cavell's *quest for the ordinary*. This pursuit—which is actually more a recovery of something that was already visibly there, but most difficult to actually experience because it is so plainly obvious—testifies to a radical *antimetaphysical* stance. Following Nietzsche here, a metaphysical viewpoint could be said to resonate with the all-too-human desire of having faith in constructs that transcend the concrete, material, cluttered, and imperfect world we live in, and of aspiring for an ideal and perfect reality (which, for instance, happens when we cherish the idea, criticized by Dewey, that we should only be happy with those forms of understanding that are based on a pure and flawless identity between the speaker's mind and the interlocutor's mind). As such, Cavell's philosophy appeals to *relying* on what we actually can experience, over and against the futile but enchanting project of substituting the world as represented in otherworldly categories for the world as it is given. This is the way in which Cavell interprets *self-reliance* in Emerson's work.[9] Although this expression might suggest otherwise, self-reliance regards not so much the actualization of a pre-given, authentic self, as it concerns an attitude toward one's own life that allows experience to take place, and to be affected by and changed by it. However, experience is not something we easily like to undergo. This explains why we have the tendency to mistrust our senses and to seek refuge in a metaphysical heaven. Self-reliance should thus be the object of cultivation and education.

Again, this seems to converge with Dewey's own defense of trusting whatever it is we come up with in our mutual efforts of reaching understanding, as messy, imperfect, and unstable as the outcome might be. Yet, there is, as I indicated, a crucial difference between Cavell's and Dewey's views. The latter doesn't fully leave behind foundationalist and metaphysical yearnings, because he is only concerned, in the end, with coming up with solutions, and thus with regaining control over situations in which we find ourselves "lost in translation."[10] In my understanding, the whole of Cavell's philosophy aims at showing that this lack of command is not a problem to be solved. Rather, dissolution forms a condition we should accept. Moreover, it regards a condition that *defines* us and *defies* us: Being lost in translation is not only vital to what it means to be a human being (and partake in human community), but it also prevents us from ever being able to decide what humanity and community finally mean.

To Cavell, *every* instance of speaking involves self-loss, even if things might appear to be the opposite at first. When we reflect upon the use of our own native language, most of the time we experience it as an instrument we fully possess and control. And yet, as Cavell underscores in *The Senses of*

Walden, "Words come to us from a distance; they were there before we were: we are born into them. Meaning them is accepting that fact of their condition."[11] In speaking there is always something that precedes us: Language has a *fierce public character.* We have no choice but to use words spoken by others, which means that we have to appropriate something with a potency and efficacy of its own. In fact, this is an idea expressed by Heidegger when he claims that *language (itself) speaks* ("die Rede redet"), which can be easily illustrated by having a look at ways in which language actually *affects* us. For example, the nominalization of verbs, as in "No smoking!" has an effect on us that is much more powerful than an expression like "it would be nice if you would do without smoking" ever could. It is as if the first expression is a command that comes from nowhere—as if it is a timeless and universal expression the contrary of which is utterly unthinkable.[12] As such, language has its own objective force.

Another, perhaps even more important, dimension of language that points to the fact that it precedes its users and escapes their control is the *"fierce ambiguous character"* of the words we use.[13] In his "Excursus on Wittgenstein's Vision of Language" Cavell asks, "Why haven't we arranged to *limit* words to *certain* contexts, and then coin new ones for new eventualities? . . . We learn the use of 'feed the kitty,' 'feed the lion,' 'feed the swans,' and one day one of us says 'feed the meter,' or 'feed in the film,' or 'feed the machine,' or 'feed his pride,' or 'feed wire,' and we understand, we are not troubled. Of course we could, in most of these cases, use a different word. . . . But what should be gained if we did? And what would be lost?"[14] There is a good reason, Cavell suggests, why we don't. In some way this ambiguity defines and defies who we are. As creatures of language we must decide whether or not we can use a given word for a new situation we are confronted with. We have no choice but to discuss and to come to an agreement about the appropriateness of saying that two people of the same sex can be "married," that genetically improved species should be called "crops," that someone we only know through social media counts as a "friend," that online payment units are genuine bit "coins," and so on. Of course we could invent new words each time we meet with a new situation, and the many technological revolutions we witness today give us more than enough occasion to do so. But, as these examples make clear, we then escape our responsibility to seek for an agreement on the meaning of the world we must *commonly* inhabit. The quality of our living-together is dependent upon it.[15]

So, as we are speaking beings, we are continuously obliged to negotiate about the criteria for applying the terms we use. At the same time, it is precisely by doing so that a "we" is created. What is at stake in these discussions is indeed whether or not a person who uses "friend" to refer to a Facebook contact is still, as Cavell says in the above quote, "one of us." But "us" in this expression isn't something with a clear meaning or something that is given from and for all eternity. On the contrary, the very fact that we *must* engage in a discussion is a precondition for change. An existing way of ordering communal life is being *defied*. The point to take here is that the dissolution that follows from the ambiguity of language isn't a deplorable flaw we should try to overcome. Of course, from a practical angle it could be seen as a nuisance, but on a second view this lack of control over our language is an important part of what it means to be part of a human community.

REMAINING CHILDREN THROUGHOUT OUR LIVES

Now, in the passage I just quoted at length, Cavell not only refers to the unavoidable negotiations that inevitably come with language being our form of life; he also refers to the learning of common uses of language, that is, to the initiation into this form of life. At this level, too, it is clear for Cavell that language precedes us. Cavell gives the example of his daughter learning the meaning of the word "kitty" and, having "correctly" used it a number of times, one day suddenly used the same word when stroking a piece of fur.[16] Cavell comments on this, using a most perceptive metaphor: "If she had never made such *leaps* she would never have walked into speech."[17] Becoming a competent language-user isn't merely a matter of, smoothly and step-by-step getting the hang of using the right expressions in the appropriate situations. Rather than taking *steps*, it involves *leaping*. This includes a letting go of one's foothold: One has to leave behind firm ground and take a risk—not being certain that one will land without hurting oneself or that one will land at all. Therefore, the child's attempts to become a speaking human being do not necessarily imply their own guarantee of success: Whether or not something will come about, whether or not what one says makes sense, remains utterly unsure.

This analysis of what is involved in acquiring a language has implications that exceed the stage of childhood in a developmental sense. The struggle with words, as exemplified in the above example, shouldn't be taken as a mere illustration, but as a paradigmatic account of what it means to be a creature of speech. We *always* have to make leaps when using language, and so *we remain children throughout our lives*. This might explain why Cavell defines philosophy as "education of grownups."[18] As a rule, adults tend to define childhood as a negative and exceptional state, that is, childhood as a condition of *not yet* being an adult, which justifies the need for education—a view that implies that one cannot meaningfully educate grownups. However, Cavell seems to suggest looking at things the other way around: We are all children (even at an adult age) in that education can happen anytime, especially when we are confronted (once more) with the necessity of leaping into language.

However, this is not something we easily admit to, as grownups that is, because of the fluent command we happen to have over our *mother* tongue. Therefore, Cavell is particularly interested in Henry David Thoreau's experiments in conducting a new life near Walden Pond, the reporting on which is noted down for his readers in what he calls *father* tongue mode. [19] Leaving aside here obvious gender-related biases that could be advanced against such a division, it makes sense to oppose two different ways of relating to one's "own" language. More precisely, Cavell comments that for Thoreau, when writing *Walden*, language no longer appears "as an extension but as an *experience* of speech." [20] On the one hand, there is language as we normally use it for expressing thoughts and feelings. On the other hand, there is language insofar as it becomes itself an object of experience. As speakers of our mother tongue we are in full command over the meaning of what we intend to say. However, there are moments in which we come to realize that "our" language isn't really *ours*. Then mother tongue is no longer "our own" tongue. We speak father tongue.

Now, Cavell's ideas are particularly helpful in describing what happens in the multilingual classroom example I started from. Having to speak a non-native language, everyone (and in this case, the teacher included) is constantly *leaping* into language. Therefore an intense *father tongue experience* may come about. There is a strong awareness that we are *children* in a Cavellian sense: that we are not in (full) possession of our language. Two remarks should be made at this point. First, I might be suggesting here that the distinction between mother and father tongue only applies to situations where native and foreign tongues coexist. However, this is not the case. What is at stake is that one can relate in two divergent ways to language *as such*—that is, in a normal and fluent mode, as opposed to a mode that makes us experience something about the human condition. It makes thus perfect sense to say that one also can (and must) relate to one's own native tongue (e.g., as a monolingual speaker) under the mode of father tongue. Even when proficient in a given language, there are moments of acute consciousness that the language one takes for granted isn't a possession, but rather a reality that is not of one's own making. The above-discussed examples of the fact that we are, as language speakers, necessarily heirs to an existing language, and of the fierce ambiguity of ordinary language, form cases in point. The basic idea is thus that insofar as we are *linguistic* beings and insofar as language is our form of life, we may find ourselves utterly dispossessed. We experience that we are children—that we remain to be strangers to "our" language. We *always* stutter and make leaps.

Second, the father tongue experience has been defined, so far, in a negative way. However it can also be formulated more affirmatively. More precisely, what is at stake when we find ourselves in a state of dissolution could be rephrased as a strong and direct experience of the possibility of *a new beginning*. In this context Cavell also uses the Thoreauvian expression *re-birth*.[21] In order to flesh out this positive side, I turn in the next part to the work of Giorgio Agamben. Whereas the figure of the child in Cavell is only dealt with in an unsystematic manner, Agamben has built the whole of his thought around the idea of a constitutive childhood, which he calls *infantia*—referring to the Latin root *fari*, "to speak." Infants are literally lacking the ability of speech. Reflecting on this it will become clear that experiencing dissolution might have a positive and, more precisely, *educational* dimension, too.

IMPOSSIBILITY EQUALS POSSIBILITY

In one of his earliest books, Agamben turns upside-down an old Aristotelian belief that has informed much of the history of philosophy in the West, namely, that human beings, although they have a lot in common with animals, are also clearly distinct from them. This is because the essential features that define "us" as humans is that we can think and speak. Whereas animals can at most express actual states of pain, pleasure, and desire, it is only humans that possess a symbolic system allowing them to transcend the present, to represent what is absent, and to have abstract and complex thoughts. Over and against this, Agamben argues that both humans and animals are fully linguistic creatures. The critical difference, however, is that whereas animals are already within language, humans are *always in the process* of entering the sphere of language—and they never fully succeed. Animals are thus in full possession of their language. They *have* language, whereas humans don't. Therefore all humans are *infants*, creatures that are "deprived of language."[22] With every act of speech we can only try to appropriate a language that remains external to us and over which we finally lack control.

At first this might just seem an inversion of an existing metaphysical scheme, and therefore Agamben's ideas might still testify to the belief that humans have essential traits that determine them. And yet, what is at stake in this reversal is precisely a way to state that we have no essence. What turns us into *human* beings is that we have to face certain conditions without having right answers as to how we should respond to these conditions—there are only an infinite number of possible responses.[23] As Agamben says, "The fact that must constitute the point of departure for any discourse on ethics is that there is no essence, no historical or spiritual vocation, no biological destiny that humans must enact or realize. This is the only reason why something like an ethics can exist, because it is clear that if humans were or had to be this or that substance, this or that destiny, no ethical *experience* would be possible—there would be only be tasks to be done."[24]

Here Agamben makes clear that the experience of lacking an essence turns us into beings that have to take up the responsibility for leading a good life, individually and collectively. I would add that this is the reason why something like *education* can exist, too. The whole idea of education only makes sense if we are creatures of possibility rather than of necessity. Only beings that can begin anew at any time and that can be transformed profoundly without being fully determined by a fixed destiny are *educable* beings. Furthermore, I would like to draw attention to the use of the word *experience* in the above quote, to which Agamben also refers as *experimentum linguae*.[25] First, what is implied here is that *infantia* is not a matter of some theoretical insight about the human condition, but an existential category. It regards something we have to live through as people (rather than only having to think or talk about). Second, the Latin verb *experiri*, from which the word "experiment" is derived, refers to taking a risk, seeking out danger, putting oneself at stake. And so, this experience is not so much an enriching experience (in the sense that we learn from experience and become stronger persons), as it is one of *self-loss*—not unlike dissolution in the philosophy of Cavell.

Experimentum linguae typically takes place at moments during which we are faced with what Agamben calls "the materiality of language."[26] We get an intense awareness of the words we utter insofar as they are physical realities (written or spoken), and so we start to stutter, experience writing block, and the like. We can't go on. No longer being able to express ourselves, we (temporarily) lose control, and therefore we go through a situation of *impossibility*. However, Agamben shows that exactly here something unique can be experienced that remains absent under normal conditions, that is, when we are in full command over the meaning of our words. More precisely, we have a strong experience of language *itself*. This regards something that is presupposed in any act of meaningful language but that normally remains implicit and that can only be indicated by using expressions such as "that there is language" and "that we can speak."[27]

What Agamben means to say here is actually not expressible *in* language. As language-users we haven't much alternative but to say things like "we can do *this*, we cannot can do *that*." So, it doesn't make sense just to say, "I can." Nonetheless that is exactly what is at stake in *experimentum linguae*: the experience that we are creatures of possibility, rather than of necessity. Again, this is not something to fathom at a theoretical level, but an experience one should live through. And this experience is something we can only have under conditions of lack of possibility. It is only in moments of impotence that we can realize what it actually means "to be able." For this Agamben coins the term *potentiality*—to distinguish it from *mere* situations of possibility in which potentiality (the experience of possibility *as such*) is already actualized in one fixed direction or another. Another way of making his point clear is to say that our actual capacity to do *this* and to do *that* turns us blind to the very fact that we actually *can* do this and that.

The paradoxical conclusion to draw from all this is that *impossibility equals possibility*.[28] In *not* being able to find the appropriate words, we might experience something that normally goes unnoticed because of the fluency of our speech, but that is of the utmost importance nonetheless, namely, that we *can* speak. In the end, *experimentum linguae* is also an unconditionally positive and affirmative experience. To give a more concrete illustration, Agamben refers to the story of Damascius, the last leader of the Athenian Academy, closed down in 529 CE by the Christian emperor Justinian the Great. As an exile living in Persia, Damascius had been completely paralyzed intellectually, because he didn't succeed in "thinking the unthinkable" (i.e., articulating in speech or thought the final ground that renders speech and thought possible). After a year of torment, however, Damascius suddenly realized that the very writing tablet on which he tried to express and structure his ideas was the solution to his problems: "What he has until then been taking as the One, as *the absolutely Other of thought*, was instead *only the material*, only the *potentiality* of thought."[29]

This anecdote nicely underlines Agamben's idea that experiencing potentiality requires a confrontation with impotence that, at the same time, is also on occasion to grasp—not theoretically but existentially—what "being able" means in the first place. On the one hand, there is a confrontation with the materiality of language, and this is a disempowering event—as it prevents Damascius from expressing what he needs to express. On the other hand, it is only by taking this materiality fully seriously that Damascius experiences what he, as a linguistic creature, is capable of. Only then things change profoundly: "Now [Damascius] could break the tablet, stop writing. Or rather, now he could truly begin. . . . That which can never be first let him glimpse, in its fading, the glimmer of a beginning."[30]

Moreover, this story also shows that looking for some principle that transcends our own human practices in order to explain or to justify what we already can do is completely wrong-headed. When turning back to the tablet in its full materiality, Damascius realizes that there is nothing outside or beyond the *ordinary*. As he says, "There is no absolutely Other of thought."[31] At this point Agamben's radical immanent philosophy seems on a par with Cavell's antimetaphysical and antifoundationalist stance. This is also to say that when Agamben refers to experiencing potentiality by using the term *infantia*, he is not talking about childhood as a phase, say, as a prelinguistic and presymbolic stage of sheer innocence and happiness to which we might return during *experimentum linguae*. On the contrary, *infantia* refers to an experience we have insofar as we are linguistic beings. As such this experience can happen any time we speak. It regards a *possible experience* that isn't a return to something lost, nor is it the fulfilment of a destiny in a time still to come. Rather, it is an *experience of pure possibility* that follows from a complete affirmation of life such as it is.

DISSOLUTION, FREEDOM, AND RADICAL TRANSLATABILITY

Coming back to the multilingual classroom situation I began with, it is most important to note here that, as a moment of disempowerment and dissolution, it might also be an occasion for experiencing *infancy*. So, in my reading, the crucial thing here is, *pace* Dewey, not only that students (and teachers) make something happen in common, but first and foremost that an experience of *a new beginning* might be furthered. We affirm that we can speak. In confrontation with unfamiliar words, or with words we cannot fully master, we might also give new life to these words, and start all over again with these words. What is at stake here could be called a *sense of freedom*. To clarify this, I return a last time to Cavell's oeuvre. In his analysis of the child that comes into language, Cavell says that the child's leaping takes place on the "meadows of communication."[32] On the meadows, one can leap everywhere—with feelings of joy, rapture, and freshness. As such, leaping involves a confirmation of freedom, not in the sense of an absence of restraints that hinder the full actualization of ourselves, but, on the contrary, in the sense that there are no clear direction and destination, and that the future is entirely undetermined. As such we may also get "dissolved" from our existing selves. Or in Thoreau's words: we might experience *rebirth*.

In conclusion, drawing from Cavell's and Agamben's ideas on a constitutive childhood, it can be argued that on experiencing not to be in possession of "our" language—something that most typically happens under conditions of radical translation—the opportunity may be granted to live through a truly important *educational* moment. The openness and freedom that come about undercut established orderings of our individual and collective existences and involve a profound self-transformation at both these levels. This possibility of a revival of ourselves and of a renewal of our common world is dependent upon a strong experience of "being able." Therefore, I suggest that we regard the conditions of radical translation we might meet in today's globalized world of higher education as offering the possibility of *radical translatability*. The potentiality at stake here involves more than just an issue of translation (i.e., coming to a communal understanding). It also regards an *experience of* translat*ing* (i.e., an experience of what it means that we *can* come to such an understanding, and therefore that our selves and our world *can* be rejuvenated). Moreover, this translatability implies the possibility of suspending any fixed ordering or destination. What may happen here is indeed thoroughgoing or *radical*. And, in a most profound sense such occurrence should be called *educational*. Because, everything literally can begin *anew*.

NOTES

1. This term refers to a thought experiment laid out in *Word and Object* (Cambridge, MA: MIT Press, 1960). Here, Quine describes a similar situation (composing a translation manual for a language that is completely unrelated to one's own) in order to make a case for the ultimate indeterminacy of translation. Succinctly put, Quine argues that even if we believe we have sufficient reasons for assuming that we fully understand speakers of another language, it is always thinkable on logical grounds that we are mistaken.

2. Usually, Agamben and Cavell are regarded as philosophers that belong to completely divergent linguistic and intellectual traditions. Nonetheless, during a study period in the United States, Agamben at one point was a student of Cavell and participated in the seminars Cavell held on Hollywood film at Harvard University. See David Kishik, *The Power of Life: Agamben and the Coming Politics* (Stanford, CA: Stanford University Press, 2012), 1.

3. John Dewey, *Experience and Nature* (New York: Dover, 1958). Cf. Gert Biesta, "No Education Without Hesitation: Exploring the Limits of Educational Relations," *Philosophy of Education Yearbook* 2012: 1–13.

4. Cf. Naoko Saito and Paul Standish, "What's the Problem with Problem-Solving? Language, Skepticism, and Pragmatism," *Contemporary Pragmatism* 6, no. 1 (2009): 153–67.

5. Stanley Cavell, *This New Yet Unapproachable America* (Albuquerque: Living Batch Press, 1989), 109.

6. Ibid., 77.

7. Ludwig Wittgenstein, *Philosophische Untersuchungen*, trans. Mary Anscombe (Oxford: Blackwell, 2011), §241. Cf. Sandra Laugier, "Transcendentalism and the Ordinary," *European Journal of Pragmatism and American Philosophy* 1, no. 1 (2009): 12.

8. Cf. Sandra Laugier, *Recommencer la philosophie* (Paris: Vrin, 2014), 77–86.

9. Cf. Laugier, "Transcendentalism and the Ordinary," 15.

10. Cf. Naoko Saito, *"Lost in Translation* and Education for Understanding Other Cultures," Round Table at the 14th Biennial Meeting of the International Network of Philosophers, University of Calabria, Cosenza, Italy, August 20–23, 2014.

11. Stanley Cavell, *The Senses of Walden*, second ed. (San Francisco: North Point Press, 1981), 64.

12. This example is discussed in greater detail in Gunther Kress, *Literacy in the New Media Age* (London: Routledge, 2003), 75–78.

13. Cavell, Stanley, *The Claim of Reason: Wittgenstein, Skepticism, Morality, and Tragedy* (New York: Oxford University Press, 1979), 180. My emphasis.

14. Ibid., 180–81; italics in original text. Cavell's remark could also be read against the background of another, "standard" criticism of the desire to do away with the ambiguities of language, the type we find in Orwell's Newspeak. Whereas Orwell most rightfully warns against a reduction of the number of words we use, which might actually reprogram our whole conceptual apparatus and turn us into people who no longer can imagine an alternative to the existing course of things (good, ungood, and dubblegood instead of good, bad, and excellent), Cavell seems to suggest that a limitation isn't always to be dreaded.

15. Cf. Stefan Ramaekers and Joris Vlieghe, "Infants, Childhood and Language in Agamben and Cavell: Education as Transformation," *Ethics and Education* 9, no. 3 (2014): 292–304.

16. Cavell, *Claim of Reason,* 172.

17. Ibid. My emphasis.

18. Ibid., 125.

19. In Thoreau the experience of father tongue refers to his own historical conditions, as he was disaffected by the rhetoric of a new American nation that spoke to many of his peers, but that no longer spoke to him and that forced him to go and live a new, experimental life.

20. Stanley Cavell, *A Pitch of Philosophy* (Cambridge, MA: Harvard University Press, 1996), 41. My emphasis.

21. Cf. ibid.

22. Giorgio Agamben, *Infancy and History*, trans. Liz Heron (London: Verso, 1993), 65.

23. This is an idea that parallels Heidegger's analysis of *Dasein*: We have no choice but to respond to the fact that we are born, that our existence is finite, that we have to live with others even if they are completely different from us, etc.

24. Giorgio Agamben, *The Coming Community*, trans. Michael Hardt (Minneapolis: University of Minnesota Press, 1993), 43. My emphasis.

25. Agamben, *Infancy and History*.

26. Ibid., 3.

27. Giorgio Agamben, *Potentialities: Collected Essays in Philosophy*, trans. Daniel Heller-Roazen (Stanford, CA: Stanford University Press, 1999), 39–47.

28. In stating this, Agamben again clearly echoes some basic Heideggerian ideas. According to Heidegger, the consciousness of death and profound boredom, that is, experiences that pose a limit to the project of self-realization, are a call to take seriously our own potentiality-for-being [*Seinkönnen*] (Cf. Giorgio Agamben, *The Open: Man and Animal*, trans. K. Attell [Stanford, CA: Stanford University Press, 2002], 49–70).

29. Giorgio Agamben, *Idea of Prose*, trans. Michael Sullivan and Sam Whitsitt (Albany: State University of New York Press, 1995), 34. My emphasis.

30. Ibid.

31. Ibid.

32. Cavell, *Claim of Reason*, 172.

BIBLIOGRAPHY

Agamben, Giorgio. *The Coming Community*. Translated by Michael Hardt. Minneapolis: University of Minnesota Press, 1993.

———. *Infancy and History*. Translated by Liz Heron. London: Verso, 1993.

———. *Idea of Prose*. Translated by Michael Sullivan and Sam Whitsitt. Albany: State University of New York Press, 1995.

———. *Potentialities: Collected Essays in Philosophy*. Translated by Daniel Heller-Roazen. Stanford, CA: Stanford University Press, 1999.

———. *The Open: Man and Animal*. Translated by K. Attell. Stanford, CA: Stanford University Press, 2002.

Biesta, Gert. "No Education Without Hesitation: Exploring the Limits of Educational Relations." *Philosophy of Education Yearbook* 2012: 1–13.

Cavell, Stanley. *The Claim of Reason: Wittgenstein, Skepticism, Morality, and Tragedy*. New York: Oxford University Press, 1979.

———. *The Senses of Walden*. Second edition. San Francisco: North Point Press, 1981.

———. *This New Yet Unapproachable America*. Albuquerque: Living Batch Press, 1989.

———. *A Pitch of Philosophy*. Cambridge, MA: Harvard University Press, 1996.

Dewey, John. *Experience and Nature*. New York: Dover, 1958.

Kishik, David. *The Power of Life: Agamben and the Coming Politics*. Stanford, CA: Stanford University Press, 2012.

Kress, Gunther. *Literacy in the New Media Age*. London: Routledge, 2003.

Laugier, Sandra. "Transcendentalism and the Ordinary." *European Journal of Pragmatism and American Philosophy* 1, no. 1 (2009): 1–17.

———. *Recommencer la philosophie*. Paris: Vrin, 2014.

Quine, Willard Van Orman, *Word and Object*. Cambridge, MA: MIT Press, 1960.

Ramaekers, Stefan, and Joris Vlieghe. "Infants, Childhood and Language in Agamben and Cavell: Education as Transformation." *Ethics and Education* 9, no. 3 (2014): 292–304.

Saito, Naoko. "*Lost in Translation* and Education for Understanding Other Cultures." Round Table at the 14th Biennial Meeting of the International Network of Philosophers, University of Calabria, Cosenza, Italy, August 20–23, 2014.

Saito, Naoko, and Paul Standish. "What's the Problem with Problem-Solving? Language, Skepticism, and Pragmatism." *Contemporary Pragmatism* 6, no. 1 (2009): 153–67.

Wittgenstein, Ludwig. *Philosophische Untersuchungen.* Translated by Mary Anscombe. Oxford: Blackwell, 2011.

Chapter Six

Problems in Translation

Ian Munday

In this chapter I draw on the work of Stanley Cavell and Gilles Deleuze to attempt a critique of the current tendency within schooling[1] to view education in problem-solving terms. I try to show that, in quite different ways, Cavell and Deleuze expose problem "solving" as a repressive way of going on, or at least show how problem-solving may prevent us from going "on." Whereas Cavell is concerned with the ways in which problems dissolve only to start up again, Deleuze distinguishes between "real" and "false" problems. Different understandings of "translation" are central to the arguments presented here. In the last part of the chapter I draw on Gordon Bearn's critique of Cavell to bring these approaches into conversation.

CAVELL AND TRANSLATION

The first part of the chapter draws on Cavell and the particular understanding of translation that he employs. It will be helpful to say something about that before introducing these ideas to issues surrounding problem-solving in education. Cavell's treatment of the term "translation" owes much to his readings of Ralph Waldo Emerson and Ludwig Wittgenstein. This is discussed in some detail in Naoko Saito and Paul Standish's article "What's the Problem with Problem-Solving? Language, Skepticism, and Pragmatism," and I shall stick quite closely to their letter while summarizing it. Saito and Standish argue that Cavell's understanding of translation is not about translating one language into another in which a foreign language can be "juxtaposed against the original."[2] Rather, translation is "something already woven into the process of the acquisition of the original language,"[3] which is always evolving—words are translated from English into English.[4] This takes us away from a metaphysical understanding of the world that pictures language as a representational symbolic system. Instead, we should think of language (and therefore the world) as constantly evolving. Just as language (and world) is in translation, so are we: "Language is already in translation, in movement in the self, and we in turn, are always already in translation."[5] Consequently, this understanding of translation involves a kind of transfiguration of selves and forms of life:

> Cavell refers to the notion of translation sporadically, but it is a thought that permeates his writings. For example, "*Walden,*" he writes, "can be taken as a whole to be precisely about the problems of translation, call it transfiguration from one form of life into another" (Cavell 2006, 17). The accent here is at once religious and Wittgensteinian. A form of life cannot be realised through the specifics of particular language-games, and these, being *language*-games, are always themselves in transition or on the way. Nor can such a life be realized in one language-game alone: one must move between language-games that, by their very nature, will be more or less incommensurable.[6]

The "translation" or "transfiguration" described here is not a synonym for any sort of transformation whatsoever. Rather it points to something ordinary that is internal to the operation of language whereby the movement within the language we encounter is simultaneously a movement in the self. To be moved in this way is not something we have "full" control over.

Whether we like it or not we will move between language games, whether that involves an experience of going to university and encountering the ways in which a discipline such as philosophy is worded or through being inducted into the language games of the jobs or professions we join. Until about ten years ago I was a high school teacher in England. I still recall the shock of the linguistic induction into this profession. There was a "strategy" for pretty much everything, and a lot of "terms" cropped up that seemed to be drawn from psychology. Stimulate the reptilian brain. Accommodate kinesthetic learners. There would also be plenty of slogans. Are the children "learning to learn"? How can we get them to "maximize their potential"? "Our school is about 'inclusion.' We are an 'including school.'" In short, the language of teaching is rich (is this really the right word?) in acronyms, slogans, and technical terminology. It takes a while to adjust to this language. At first it induces fear and insecurity—and the feeling that everybody seems to understand what is going on except me. With "experience" the language becomes second nature and provides the linguistic competence and horizon for professional life. It binds you to the fellow members of the professional community. Induction into the profession works only too well. If you have any "common sense," you play by the rules and learn to speak the language fluently. After a while you will be in jargon stepped in so far that, should you wade no more, returning were as tedious as go o'er.[7]

However, some may try to step back, or refuse the pull that would drive them forward. They (or should I say "we"?) perhaps lack common sense. Perhaps we are "lunatics." When summarizing the section of *The Claim of Reason* that features "lunatics,"[8] Stephen Mulhall writes:

> We learn the criteria-governed use of words in certain contexts, and are then expected to project them into further contexts, but nothing *insures* that this will happen (not books of rules, and not universals); the fact that it does happen is a matter of sharing our routes of interest and feeling, a sense of similarity and disparity, seeing the pattern or point in going on with words in a certain way— all the whirl of organism that Wittgenstein calls "forms of life." For Cavell, human speech and activity, sanity and community, rest on nothing less than this attunement in our natural reactions or responses to reality.[9]

On this view, those who reject the language of the teaching profession described above are not lunatics. Rather, they fail to share the same routes of interest and feeling that run through that language. It is worth stressing that people who are "attuned" are not lunatics either. They may, however, exhibit symptoms of repression. Think again of what Saito and Standish say about translation: a life cannot "be realized in one language-game alone: one must move between language-games that, by their very nature, will be more or less incommensurable."[10] Allowing ourselves to move or be moved between language games may have a therapeutic dimension that militates against such repression. The discussion of problem-solving and education below attempts to take this dimension on board.

Before launching into that discussion, however, it should be quite apparent that there is a certain dissonance between the various registers that are sounded in the course of this chapter, especially between the language of complex philosophy and the language of schooling with its mixture of technical terminology and "ordinary" language. Shakespeare has also been briefly butchered. The reader will have experienced a jarring of discursive registers that may seem strange and perhaps "inappropriate"; academic decorum usually requires consistency in this regard. I want, for the sake of scholarly seriousness, to thematize this "inappropriateness" and see it as a critical dimension of a chapter in which movement between language games is not simply discussed but is also enacted.

PROBLEMS

Let us begin our discussion of problem-solving, education, and translation by considering an "educational" scene. This scene is real (though you may doubt my sincerity here). It was featured in a training event on poetry given to English teachers from a high school in England.

Scene 1

> A man came from the local authority to provide training to members of staff to English teachers at a secondary school. One part of the training day was devoted to providing ideas for teaching "disaffected" students. As is quite typical on these occasions the advisor began by reminding the teachers of the importance of catering for different learning styles—kinesthetic, auditory, and visual. He then demonstrated how one might accommodate the needs of different learners when studying the poem "Vultures." One of the figures presented in the poem is the Commandant at Belsen. The Commandant is presented as a loving family man and the poem clearly tries to address the moral complexity of his situation. In the first task (designed to accommodate kinesthetic learners) the teachers were asked to leave their seats and imagine a line between two poles (chairs) representing absolute good and absolute evil. The line incorporated a numerical system in which 1 represented absolute good and 10 absolute evil. The teachers were then asked to grade the commandant to determine his position on the scale.

One of the things that I enjoy most about this scene is that when I recount it to people, it can elicit such different reactions. Colleagues in the English and philosophy departments and peers from philosophy of education have tended to laugh or look at me in disbelief or ask if I'm making it up or get a bit angry that this is what schooling has come to. In contrast, teachers present at the event and some colleagues in education have tended to think that this scene demonstrates an extremely creative approach to teaching and learning. When I have introduced the scene to education students by asking them to participate in the activities, the response has been largely positive. However, one or two students have, on each occasion, refused to take part.

Why should the scene elicit such different reactions? Having been both a schoolteacher and an academic who spends part of his time teaching teachers, I believe I am qualified to speculate, or perhaps "translate" English into English.

When I asked those few students why they refused to participate in the activity they tended to think that it was weirdly contrived. Teaching children that there are such things as absolute good and evil (and that there is a ten-point dividing line between these two realms) sounded like a ridiculously oversimplistic, if not dangerous, depiction of the moral life. Their objection was to the content of the task and the way it is set up. Peers and colleagues in philosophy and philosophy of education have never felt the need to explain their amusement at or distaste for this scene as though it were so obviously stupid that they'd be wasting their breath. So why is this scene heard so differently by teachers/student teachers?

I believe that it is difficult to understand the enthusiasm among teachers for the scene without having been a member, however peripheral, of the tribe. On my first day of teacher training some fourteen years ago we were told in our very first session that teaching English was no longer about teaching English and that these days we "teach students not subjects." This sounds like (and possibly is) nonsense. To try to account for what it might mean I want to consider the notion that teaching itself has been translated into and naturalized as a problem-solving process. In the United Kingdom a problem-solving approach to education has become ubiquitous. Teachers tend to see themselves as problem-solvers: "How do I get Alice to focus on her work and learn? Which strategies will help me overcome her apparent indifference? Alice's failure is a problem I must help her to overcome—she will then be a successful learner." Teachers engaged in what is variously called action research, practitioner research, and teacher research are inquiring into their own practice so as to solve problems in the classroom:

> Let us assume that you have identified some aspect of your professional practice in your classroom that is puzzling you. You may have noticed that one particular technique you use to encourage effective learning does not appear to be working as well as it used to, or that another is working very effectively. You may have seen something in the news or read something in the educational press that reminded you of your classroom or at least caused you to wonder how it might apply to your own professional situation. At this point you have taken the first step as a researcher in that you have identified an educational issue that might need resolving. We could generalise by saying that much educational research focuses on interesting puzzles that have been identified by practitioners.[11]

Much of the research conducted by academics in education departments is dedicated to solving problems—what better way is there to demonstrate impact? In the most extreme cases researchers are trying to solve problems regarding teacher research conducted by teachers who are adopting a problem-solving research strategy to demonstrate the impact of problem-solving approaches in the classroom that involve trying to teach students how to problem-solve. With regard to skills-based curricula, problem-solving is perhaps the "thinking skill" par excellence.

Let us return to Scene 1 and read it against this context. Teachers start with a problem—an assumed ignorance and disaffection on the part of students with regard to the subject matter. Indeed, the subject matter itself becomes something to be overcome and solved. It is not that there is a right place to stand on the line between absolute good and evil exactly (though justifications for standing in a particular place may lead to some sort of consensus). Rather, it is the framework itself that supposedly provides a platform for saying anything at all. In this sense an obstacle (the poem's difficulty/obscurity) has been overcome and students are given a "voice." This is seen as progressive: Before they couldn't speak about the poem— now they can. For anybody who has tried to teach a group of disaffected teenagers, the appeal of the approach advocated by our expert may well seem strong. I couldn't get anywhere with this lot and now I can. Moreover, the approach appears to be politically inclusive, "nice" even.

TRANSLATING THE SCENE

Up to this point, the way in which I've been using the word "translation" is meant to marry with Cavell's treatment of that term. The very existence of the educational scene described above, along with its differing reception, seems to provide some evidence of a relative incommensurability between language games and a situation in which people "barely" seem to share the same language. More significantly, the appeal of the scene may signal a repression of alternative language games.[12]

To further explore what such repression involves and relate it to the problem-solving approach within teaching, let us consider a short section from Cavell's essay "Philosophy the Day after Tomorrow"[13] (taken from his book with the same title) and a fragment from *Philosophical Investigations* that he takes to epitomize Wittgenstein's approach to teaching and learning: "If I have exhausted the justifications [for following the rules of mathematics or of ordinary language as I do], I have reached bedrock and my spade is turned. Then I am inclined to say, 'This is simply what I do.'"[14] Cavell maintains that the reading of this scene has achieved consensus in the United States where the teacher's gesture is taken to be a display of power. Reaching bedrock is a political gesture, a "speaking for the community and its settlements, demanding agreement, threatening exclusion."[15] In direct contrast, Cavell views this scene as a display of weakness that may serve to enlighten the teacher. In other words, Cavell focuses on the affective, perhaps literary, aspects of this scene (which he calls a "phantasm"). He focuses on the fact that Wittgenstein rather than "saying," "This is simply what I do" is "inclined" to say it, and this means that the words are never actually said. Instead we have a period of silence.[16] Problems are not solved but temporarily "dissolved."[17] The smoothness of the educational experience is interrupted. Either teacher or student will break the silence when something new can be said that will transfigure what has been said so far. Such an experience may well be traumatic.

For Cavell, good philosophers (and good teachers) know when to be silent and when to break that silence. Philosophy (and teaching and learning) should therefore be about knowing when something is worth saying and when it is not. But how should what is worth saying be decided? Surely the point is that it is decided in a kind of confrontation (which may or may not be fractious) between teacher and student. This way, philosophy (and the same can be said for teaching) will not speak into the void with an "impersonal metaphysical voice."[18] Rather philosophy/teaching will be oriented toward the other and what "interests" her or him. However, the notion of what "interests" us has quite an unusual inflection in Cavell's outlook. "Interest" here is bound up with things mattering in ways that cannot be reduced to instrumental or abstract/metaphysical factors. So things do not "matter" in Cavell's sense "just" because they are useful or true. Rather, they matter because we care about them. I find the echo of this in Gordon Bearn's claim that "nobody cares about truth, just truth"[19] and take the emphasis here to be on the words "cares" and "just." It is not as though truth was something we would want to dismiss, but rather that something being true should connect to our ordinary concerns. Those concerns cannot be with truth alone if it is abstracted from our immediate "concerns" and desires. Consequently, "if it is part of teaching to undertake to validate these measures of interest, then it would be quite as if teaching must, as it were, undertake to show a reason for speaking at all."[20] In this sense, good teaching has a therapeutic aspect in that it shows itself as "a struggle against melancholy, against being overtaken by pointlessness."[21]

With all this in mind, let us return to teaching conceived of as problem-solving and to Scene 1. The problem-solving approach presented here represents an attempt to supersede the kind of deadlock that Cavell and Wittgenstein see as so important to a good education. The rather bizarre platform (that takes the form of zones good and evil and the ten-point scale) marks a repression of the call to silence leading to the kind of pointless "chatter" that Cavell is so opposed to, or perhaps disgusted by. Cavell and Wittgenstein's teacher is constantly open to problems dissolving before reappearing transfigured after periods of silence. Here, objectives cannot be ticked off, and just as things seem to move forward, we are pulled back again as things are transformed. Receptiveness to this allows for creative translations. As Saito and Standish note, our confrontations with literature provide exemplary instances of cases where this kind of translation or transfiguration may take place. Here, we may move from the voice of the mother tongue to speak with the "father tongue."[22] The presentation of the commandant seems to be an exemplary instance for the possibility of doing just this. "Voice" here is not just about saying anything. An impasse is what allows for the emergence of a "voice." In Scene 1 that voice is repressed by the way in which things are set up; the teacher feels she "knows" her students—they are "disaffected." Along with all this there is an assumed metaphysics regarding what a poem is—that poems have some sort of Platonic identity that can be worded in lots of different ways. This identity supposedly remains the same whatever pedagogical strategy you employ—all roads lead to Rome and are seen as equally valid. Intrinsic to this rather metaphysical understanding of meaning is the attempt to achieve some kind of metalevel or point from which to understand and master poems—a platform from which to speak. Resisting the urge to supply such a platform may lead to frustration and confusion but, for Wittgenstein and Cavell, such things are integral to a good education.

DELEUZE AND PROBLEM-SOLVING

Having considered a Cavellian approach to translation and problem-solving in schooling (where problems are dissolved rather than solved), I want to move on to a consideration of a rather different approach to these issues by looking at the work of the French philosopher Gilles Deleuze. Though Deleuze provides a rich discussion of problems he does not, to my knowledge, speak of translation. Therefore, discussing his philosophical approach in terms of translation is my own doing and I can therefore take the blame or praise regarding its appropriateness.

Deleuze's and Cavell's philosophies differ at an ontological level. Like Jacques Derrida and Martin Heidegger, Cavell's philosophy is antifoundationalist in the sense that there is no metaphysical meaningfulness to a universe that exists behind our words. Our words "word" the world. Cavell is therefore interested in translations within a language and the transfiguration of selves that accompany such translations. Deleuze is equally critical of the metaphysics of presence. However, his philosophy is, in some respects, foundational in a nonmetaphysical sense. To get a sense of what this means, let us begin with the distinction that he makes between what is "actual" and "virtual." On the face of it, one would perhaps imagine that this would be a distinction between what is "real" and "simulated" (or something along these lines). However, what Deleuze means is quite different. The "actual" and "virtual" represent two interlinked realms. To think in terms of the "actual" is to approach things from "this" side of representation as concretized entities. To consider their virtual aspect we need to travel to the "other side of representation."[23] Here is Deleuze:

> Let us assume a concept with indefinite comprehension (virtually infinite). However far one pursues that comprehension, one can always think that it subsumes perfectly identical objects. By contrast with the actual infinite, where the concept is sufficient by right to distinguish its object from *every* other object, in this case the concept can pursue its comprehension indefinitely, always assuming a plurality of objects which is itself indefinite. Here again, the concept is the Same—indefinitely the same—for objects which are distinct. We must therefore recognise the existence of non-conceptual differences between these objects.[24]

What are "non-conceptual differences"? What might this have to do with what is beyond representation? What could this say to a discussion of translation? I believe that what Deleuze is trying to say here is that the way in which the world is divided up comes about as a kind of translation of "sensuous" singularities into things that are made to appear the same through their "actualization." This introduces a different understanding of difference. An example might be going for a drive. Looking at going for a drive in "actual" terms, we can identify me, my car, the road, and everything around about—the scenery, weather, whatever. Now one can look at things from this side of representation (what is enshrined in our language) and note that the same drive is not the same drive. Though I might be following the same road, I can never exactly cover the same bits of it. The weather or the light will never quite be the same. I won't have the same things on my mind. This is all true enough when looked at in "that" way. But what if we take something like the weather? This is commonly thought to be something that happens out there—the light is different because the weather is different. To look at this in another way, to talk of the weather at all is to abstract away from our singular experience in (rather than of) a moment in the world where pointing to the weather is just one way we have of abstracting and generalizing from that singularity. This abstraction derives not from the identity of a weather that is already there as "weather" but from the virtual intensities (or non-conceptual differences) that are connected and fused to generate the concept of weather, an abstraction that is repeated and memorized.

What can be said of the weather can be said of all abstractions/actualizations and this must include "me." There must be a "virtual" me who precedes the abstraction into the conscious rational agent I might think myself to be. Deleuze's understanding of the "virtual" captures a powerful metonymic force that precedes identity and emphasizes connection—the sort of thing that might touch me when it matters that my family might be me. What an "individual" is must clearly be something more than the rational agent of the Enlightenment or its more ordinary cousin, the free thinking/choosing individual—the sort of person that most of us probably think we are. Instead the individual might be thought of as a site where "thought takes place,"[25] though not the kind of thought "possessed" by a rational being. This is not to say that we are not rational agents, but that this only accounts for what we are from this side of representation. Moreover, rational thought must still retain the model of a coherent self that thinks, while the approach advocated here dissimulates the self through "intense, beauteous particles."[26] Of course we can repress or fight off the expression of these variations or we can try to reintensify patterns that give consistency to our lives and try to bring significance to them. It is important to try to forget our attachment to actual things.[27] This involves the recognition that, at some level, all representations and concepts of identities are illusions that can stall our becomings. In this sense, clinging too hard to actualizations is a form of repression. We must allow ourselves to be untranslated and retranslated if we are to live well.

REAL AND FALSE PROBLEMS

One way of beginning to approach Deleuze's understanding of problems is to consider it in relation to the kind of problem-solving approach found in self-help manuals. This is because the "self" that needs help is perceived in "actual" terms and treated as a bounded entity. Moreover, the self, or at least one aspect of the self, is treated as a problem to be overcome. Conventional approaches to problem-solving must be "problematic" for Deleuze because they tend to understand things in terms of fixed identities (the problem-solver, the problem). Moreover, such approaches work with finalities rather than becomings—once you've solved the problem, then that's it. Given what has just been said, it may seem odd that Deleuze should speak about "problems" at all; yet he does. Deleuze maintains that "as opposed to solutions, problems must be thought of as true or false."[28] Here again is Deleuze:

> There are no ultimate or original responses or solutions, there are only problem-questions, in the guise of a mask behind every mask and a displacement behind every place. It would be naïve to think that the problems of life and death, love and the difference between the sexes are amenable to their scientific solutions and positings, even though such positings and solutions necessarily arise without warning, even though they must necessarily emerge at a certain moment in the unfolding process of the development of these problems. The problems concern the eternal disguise.[29]

Given the first part of this quotation we can see that the sort of thing philosophers often treat as problems must be something rather different from what Deleuze is talking about. If a true problem requires a "guise of a mask behind every mask," then a false problem can be false because it is "overdetermined—that is, it allows its solutions to be judged in terms of truth and falsity (*Is the cat on the mat?*)."[30] So, if the sort of things that some philosophers (and just philosophers) bother themselves with are false problems, what would a "real" problem that has no final solution look like? When approaching such problems we have to do something seemingly contradictory. In his reading of Deleuze, James Williams[31] notes that what we should do is allow our actions to connect with everything that has brought them about while simultaneously forgetting everything. I take this to mean that good thinking (which is also a kind of "feeling") involves a kind of repression as we make a case for something but with "real problems" this will be overcome as we veer off in new directions and "connect" in other ways. The ways of connecting and forgetting that "false" problems present are already laid out for us by either a single answer or a series of possible answers depending on the rules we must accept as being legitimate. It is possible that the question "Is the cat on the mat?" might start to look like "real" problems if it continues to be productive. Barring an existential crisis, where I'm not sure if

I'm imagining cats on mats, then it will not. In the next section I will consider what this might mean for schooling.

PROBLEMS AND SCHOOLING

Think of a science class in which the teacher wants to get a class of very young children to understand how to classify various objects into their ascribed scientific categories. This is not just about getting them to know which things are plants and which things are rocks. They need to be able to develop the knowledge and skills to come across new things and make these classifications. This involves the "problem" of looking at things and being able to work out what they are. Deleuze may have seen this as a false problem. Williams can, I think, throw some light on why this might be so:

> In order to allow children (and adults) to learn about the different consistencies of the plant world, botanical gardens allow them to touch hard, sticky, prickly, spongy plants through holes in an opaque screen. The children's ideas and sensations of these properties are heightened when they cannot see the plant and where there are elements of discovery in emerging sensual contrasts. Deleuze wants us to connect to the pure variations that ideas and sensations may connect to: becoming harder, softer, pricklier, spongier. This does not necessarily imply connecting more comprehensively to more actual cactuses and coconuts. For Deleuze, the things that operate in the processes that bring us about and make us into individuals are not actual objects and the knowledge we may gain from them but the sensual variations and the variations in ideas that take place in order for actual things to gain a living significance for us. [32]

The kind of experience that the children are exposed to here is something that the above-mentioned problem-solving approach to science brackets off or deems irrelevant. Ideas can so easily be abstracted away from "emerging sensual contrasts." This kind of abstraction may become a blockage to the kind of living significance actual things may have for us. I am not arguing that children should not be taught to classify objects in accordance with scientific categories, but rather that the problem-solving approach that accompanies this is incredibly limited and should be regarded as only one part of our experience of things in the world. In this sense, "How do I relate to the things in my environment?" is a real problem whereas "How do I scientifically classify these objects?" is not. Indeed, the latter question is not a "real" problem because the virtual dimension of existence is ignored. Ignoring that dimension turns problems into things that can be solved. The point is that problems are "real" problems because they persist as problems—they cannot be nullified by solutions or exist as islands. They generate intensities "because" they cannot be negated by solutions. If we return to Scene 1, the question of how to read the commandant's behavior would be a real problem but the apparatus used by the teacher to elicit an answer represses the various possibilities for connecting and forgetting. "Where should I stand on the line?" is not a real problem. Moreover, the treatment of literature presented in Scene 1 has no time for poetry as a kind of sensual experience.

COMPARE AND CONTRAST

I believe that both Deleuzian and Cavellian approaches to translation and problem-solving provide rich opportunities for offering a critique of the contemporary culture of schooling. Indeed, both writers have interesting and important things to say about the repressive aspects of a problem-solving approach. It is perhaps the way in which repression is handled that most separates them. In "Sensual Schooling: On the Aesthetic Education of Grownups"[33] Bearn argues that Cavell's (and Wittgenstein's) philosophy is itself repressed because it does not acknowledge singularities. Bearn mentions philosophy's much loved "goldfinch." We can decide that what has fallen from the tree is a goldfinch in terms of Austinian criteria, where we keep asking questions about how I know that it is a goldfinch until we reach an agreement that it is or isn't such a thing. Or we could do the same thing with Wittgensteinian grammar and establish its identity based on the difference between goldfinches and eagles, doves, and bullfinches. Or we can realize the limitations of this way of going on by opening ourselves to this goldfinch now as it meets and merges with the currents of the wind, as it seems to leave a trail of red in the sky behind it, as it's call merges and blends with the rush of the water beneath it.[34]

With J. L. Austin, in addition to Wittgenstein and Cavell, goldfinches are problems that are quickly solved before we move on to more grown-up matters. For Deleuze and Bearn, goldfinches would be part of the problem, "How do I relate to the things in my environment?" Bearn writes: "Cavell's education is to bring us up, a second time to adulthood."[35] In this scenario, the first time we are brought up to adulthood is through acclimatization to the criteria of actualizations—the sort of thing described earlier in the science lesson. Philosophy as the "education of grownups" reflects our growing dissatisfaction with those criteria. In contrast, for Bearn, a better philosophy "is not what we normally think of as philosophy at all. It is not about growing up; it is about becoming children. Growing green." We might also wonder if the significance of silence and pause in Cavell and Wittgenstein's writings may signal a kind of repression. Are we not continuing to connect and forget (though we will not be conscious of this) through the "apparent" silence?

I have a fair bit of time for Bearn's critique of Cavell. The kind of translation that Cavell deals with is a very "human" matter whereas Deleuze and Bearn dissimulate the human through intense particles. However, though the silence (construed as absence) may be illusory, it is certainly not experienced as such. Indeed, our experience of education, of writing say, can often be fairly traumatic and our experience of translation may not always be one that we find "affirmative." Moreover, "growing green" might be less pleasurable than it sounds. There are, I think, some points of convergence between Cavell and Deleuze. Near the beginning of this chapter I mentioned that Scene 1 was greeted with laughter or horror by some. Cavell often talks about language as an appeal to the "ear." This would seem to capture the more sensual dimension to the way language can appeal to or disgust us and how this is woven through both our ordinary exchanges and experiences of education.

NOTES

1. The context I have in mind is British, but it is likely that readers from outside the United Kingdom may well find that what is described here resonates with their own experiences of schooling.

2. Naoko Saito and Paul Standish, "What's the Problem with Problem-Solving? Language, Skepticism and Pragmatism," *Contemporary Pragmatism* 6, no. 1 (2009): 160.

3. Ibid.

4. Ibid.

5. Ibid.

6. Ibid., 160–61.

7. Macbeth to Lady Macbeth: "I am in blood / Stepped in so far that, should I wade no more, / Returning were as tedious as go o'er," act 3, scene 4, lines 142–44.

8. Stanley Cavell, *The Claim of Reason: Wittgenstein, Skepticism, Morality, and Tragedy* (New York: Oxford University Press, 1979), 111–25.

9. Stephen Mulhall, ed., *The Cavell Reader* (Oxford: Blackwell, 1996), 31.

10. Saito and Standish, "What's the Problem with Problem-Solving?" 160–61.

11. Anne Campbell, Olwyn McNamara, and Peter Gilroy, *Practitioner Research and Professional Development in Education* (New Delhi: Paul Chapman Publishing, 2004), 1.

12. It is worth mentioning that Saito and Standish's discussion of translation features in an article dedicated to a critique of the problem-solving dimension of Dewey's pragmatism. Following Cavell, they argue that Dewey's pragmatism reflects a kind of repression with regard to translation and transfiguration within language ("What's the Problem with Problem-Solving?" 161). Sadly, there is no space to discuss the significant differences between Dewey's account of problem-solving and the one presented above. However, it is worth mentioning that Dewey is regularly cited in the educational literature on problem-solving as though he were its hero and figurehead. The translations and forms of repression that brought about this state of affairs are deserving of a full paper.

13. Stanley Cavell, *Philosophy the Day after Tomorrow* (Cambridge, MA: The Belknap Press of Harvard University Press, 2005), xl–l.

14. Ibid., 112.

15. Ibid., 113.

16. Ibid., 112.

17. Saito and Standish, "What's the Problem with Problem-Solving?" 161–64.

18. Paul Standish, "In Her Own Voice: Convention, Conversion, Criteria," *Educational Philosophy and Theory* 36 no. 1 (2004): 94.

19. Gordon Bearn, "Pointlessness and the University of Beauty" in *Just Education*, ed. Pradeep Dhillon and Paul Standish (London: Routledge, 2000), 245.

20. Cavell, *Philosophy the Day after Tomorrow*, 115.

21. Ibid., 116.
22. Saito and Standish, "What's the Problem with Problem-Solving?" 162.
23. Bearn, "Pointlessness and the University of Beauty," 248.
24. Gilles Deleuze, *Difference and Repetition* (London: Continuum, 2004), 15.
25. James Williams, *Gilles Deleuze's* Difference and Repetition*: A Critical Introduction and Guide* (Edinburgh: Edinburgh University Press, 2003), 6.
26. Bearn, "Pointlessness and the University of Beauty," 248.
27. Williams, *Gilles Deleuze's* Difference and Repetition, 10.
28. Ibid., 130.
29. Deleuze, *Difference and Repetition*, 132.
30. Williams, *Gilles Deleuze's* Difference and Repetition, 130–31.
31. Ibid., 5.
32. Ibid., 7.
33. Gordon Bearn, "Sensual Schooling: On the Aesthetic Education of Grownups," in *Stanley Cavell and the Education of Grownups*, ed. Naoko Saito and Paul Standish (New York: Fordham University Press, 2012), 88–118.
34. Ibid., for a deeper discussion of these differences.
35. Ibid., 94.

BIBLIOGRAPHY

Bearn, Gordon. "Pointlessness and the University of Beauty." In *Just Education*, edited by Pradeep Dhillon and Paul Standish, 230–58. London: Routledge, 2000.
———. "Sensual Schooling: On the Aesthetic Education of Grownups." In *Stanley Cavell and the Education of Grownups*, edited by Naoko Saito and Paul Standish, 88–118. New York: Fordham University Press, 2012.
Campbell, Anne, Olwyn McNamara, and Peter Gilroy. *Practitioner Research and Professional Development in Education*. New Delhi: Paul Chapman Publishing, 2004.
Cavell, Stanley. *The Claim of Reason: Wittgenstein, Skepticism, Morality, and Tragedy*. New York: Oxford University Press, 1979.
———. *Philosophy the Day after Tomorrow*. Cambridge, MA: The Belknap Press of Harvard University Press, 2005.
Deleuze, Gilles. *Difference and Repetition*. London: Continuum, 2004.
Mulhall, Stephen, ed. *The Cavell Reader*. Oxford: Blackwell, 1996.
Saito, Naoko, and Paul Standish. "What's the Problem with Problem-Solving? Language, Skepticism and Pragmatism." *Contemporary Pragmatism* 6, no. 1 (2009): 153–67.
Standish, Paul. "In Her Own Voice: Convention, Conversion, Criteria." *Educational Philosophy and Theory* 36, no. 1 (2004): 91–106.
Williams, James. *Gilles Deleuze's* Difference and Repetition*: A Critical Introduction and Guide*. Edinburgh: Edinburgh University Press, 2003.

Chapter Seven

Pragmatism and the Language of Suffering

From James to Rorty (and Orwell) and Back Again

Sami Pihlström

INTRODUCTION

William James's "pragmatic method," as articulated in his key philosophical work, *Pragmatism* (1907), is reinterpretable as a philosophical method seeking to ground metaphysical inquiry in ethical reflection and evaluation. James introduces the pragmatic method—originally formulated by Charles S. Peirce in the 1870s—in Lecture II by suggesting that when seeking to determine the meaning of our "ideas" (e.g., concepts, conceptions, beliefs, theories, and worldviews), we should look into the possible (conceivable) practical effects they and/or their objects might have in human experience and habits of action.[1] Thus formulated, this is a method of "translation": Ideas need to be translated into (possible, conceivable) action in order for us to be able to determine their meaning. In Lectures III and IV, James illustrates this method by applying it to some metaphysical problems, including theism vs. materialism (atheism), the concept of substance, freedom, as well as monism versus pluralism. On my reading (which I won't be able to substantiate here), in all these cases, the pragmatic method is a method of assessing the rival views ("ideas") from an ethical perspective.

But what does it mean, for James, to evaluate our ideas from an ethical perspective, or to translate metaphysics into ethics? The pragmatic method remains hopelessly vague if it simply encourages us to look for the practical meaning of metaphysical (and religious/theological) views in their ethical impact, unless we have some idea about how to go on investigating that impact.[2] Here, I believe, we should take the further step of interpreting the pragmatic method as a method of taking seriously the "cries of the wounded"[3] in relation to the various metaphysical views or theories that could be proposed regarding these matters at issue. It is a method that looks into the possible *futures* of the world in which we live, focusing on what the different metaphysical views "promise" and on whether they can function as philosophies of hope, especially from the point of view of the "wounded," the sufferers or the victims of evil. This is a profoundly ethical undertaking. Far from maintaining that our metaphysical problems ought to be solved first—or that we could simply get rid of them—in order to turn to ethical problems later, James is suggesting that we should begin our metaphysical inquiries from the ethical examination of the practical relevance of the rival metaphysical ideas that have been or can be proposed, and that this ethical examination can only take place if we focus on how "the wounded" would respond to this or that world-picture being true.

This discussion of what I call the ethical grounds of metaphysics (and, more generally, the metaphysics-ethics entanglement) in *Pragmatism*, and pragmatism, ought to be placed in a context of a more generally ethically oriented reflection on issues of fundamental human importance, especially evil and suffering. As both the opening and the closing of *Pragmatism* indicate, James is deeply conscious of the significance of the problem of evil, and he is strongly opposed to any philosophical and theological attempts (e.g., theodicies) to explain evil away or to justify its existence. This is another example of Jamesian pragmatist metaphysics ultimately grounded in ethics. The metaphysical controversy between monism and pluralism, in particular, invokes the problem of evil. James offers an ethical argument against monism and in favor of pluralism by pointing out that the former, unlike the latter, leads to an irresolvable theodicy problem.

The problem of evil is not merely an example by means of which we may illustrate the Jamesian pragmatic method. Much more importantly, it offers a *frame* for James's pragmatism more generally. The problem of evil provides an ethical motivation for exploring, pragmatically, metaphysical issues that ultimately need to be linked with ethics. This exploration takes place in a world in which theodicies are no longer possible (if they ever were). No theodicist consolation is an option, James argues, for an ethically serious thinker. What we may call Jamesian *antitheodicism* is therefore a crucial element of his pragmatic method framed by the problem of evil.

TRANSLATION AND ACKNOWLEDGMENT

The basic view defended in this chapter should be understood as an attempt—albeit a largely implicit one—to contribute to the discussion of pragmatism and *the understanding of other cultures and traditions in the context of "the philosophy of translation."* Pragmatism is sometimes regarded as a philosophy committed to, or at least in the danger of sliding into, something like *cultural relativism*. This is a picture of pragmatism often associated with Richard Rorty's and some of his followers' "postmodernist" neopragmatism (though Rorty himself always resisted being classified as a relativist, insisting on being an "ethnocentrist," "ironist," and "antirepresentationalist" instead). Relativism, quite independently of how Rorty's pragmatism in particular ought to be interpreted, becomes highly problematic as soon as we truly want to make sense of intercultural communication and translation. Radical relativism, in particular, in a sense views cultures and languages as mutually non-intertranslatable, hermetically sealed. Accordingly, translation—or philosophy as translation—is something through which we may respond to the threat of relativism.

The essential point here is that *a* (though not necessarily the) key to cultural universality beyond mere relativity can be found in the kind of real evil and suffering that James takes fundamentally seriously and urges us to take seriously whenever applying the pragmatic method to our beliefs and ideas. Suffering unites human beings across cultures, or *ought to* do so, at least, and any culturally sensitive moral philosophy seeking to avoid (radical) relativism must therefore adopt a "realistic spirit" about evil.[4] Avoiding relativism by emphasizing the universal, transcultural significance of evil and suffering does *not* entail any implausible theory of absolute ethical standards, however, nor any assumption of the intertranslatability of all culturally variable views on good and evil. Any reasonable discussion of evil and suffering takes place in a cultural context. The cultural universality of evil and suffering must not be confused with the implausible idea that forms of (culturally universal) evil and suffering would not be (necessarily) culturally localized and interpreted.

The problem of evil, I argue, emerges as a "transcendental" frame, a transcultural (albeit not therefore culturally neutral or noncultural but, rather, always inevitably culturally [re-]interpreted) condition making ethical seriousness possible. By framing our pragmatist approach to metaphysics and religion, and its ethical grounding, in terms of the problem of evil, we may also advance a form of pragmatism (indebted to James) that may significantly serve philosophies of intercultural dialogue and mutual understanding, even though our possible success in this task will not be examined in any detail in this chapter. This transcendental and transcultural character of the topic of evil and suffering indicates why we may see pragmatism as enabling us to "translate" experiences of evil and suffering across cultural boundaries. Such translations are always needed—in a broad sense of translation irreducible to mere transmission of linguistic meanings from one language to another—precisely because of the culturally particular, unique ways in which those experiences emerge. This is the sense in which "philosophy as translation" is implicitly present throughout my discussion.

The phrase "philosophy as translation," primarily drawn from R. W. Emerson and Stanley Cavell, figures heavily through this entire volume. It would be extremely interesting—in a more comprehensive undertaking than the scope of this chapter allows me—to more explicitly connect the pragmatist view developed and defended here with the kind of Cavell-inspired views on truth as translated that many other contributions to this volume focus on.[5] It might also be possible to view the antitheodicism I am defending as a response to the kind of *skeptical* predicament that Cavell, drawing from Ludwig Wittgenstein, emphasizes—that is, as an attempt to live with the existential anxiety of the skeptical predicament. Moreover, the broad notion of translation we may draw from Cavell would enable us to view the challenge of translating expressions of evil and suffering as something inherent in human culture, in our life with language, itself.[6]

There are also other Cavellian or quasi-Cavellian themes that will come up in my Jamesian and Rortyan pragmatist context. One of them is *ordinariness* ("the ordinary"), to be explored briefly below in the context of the criticism of Rorty put forth by James Conant (another Cavell-inspired thinker). Another Cavellian theme relevant here is *acknowledgment*: We may say that, according to James, theodicies strikingly fail to acknowledge the suffering individual, or the victim of evil. Utilizing the distinction between acknowledgment and knowing—fundamental in Cavell's analysis of our relation to skepticism and otherness[7]—we may see theodicies as hopeless attempts to *know* the reasons of suffering (to know God's harmonious cosmic plan, if one is a theist, or possibly the teleological structure of history, if one works in terms of a secular theodicy), whereas the ethically appropriate attitude to the suffering other, and to the other's suffering, is *acknowledgment* rather than knowledge.[8]

However, my approach is also slightly (again implicitly) critical of Cavell in the sense that I am rather strongly recommending pragmatism—Jamesian rather than Rortyan—as an approach to the kind of existential issues of evil and suffering I am exploring, in contrast to Cavell's tendency to somewhat downgrade the importance of pragmatism, especially in relation to thinkers like Emerson and Thoreau.[9] Even so, I am willing to acknowledge a significant common ground between Jamesian pragmatism, on the one hand, and Cavellian (and/or his Emersonian and Wittgensteinian) ideas, on the other. James might even be seen as a bridge between pragmatism on the one side and Cavell (even with his reservations regarding pragmatism), on the other. More detailed issues concerning the relation between James and Cavell would certainly deserve further scrutiny.

Even though I started my reflections from James's pragmatism, my main focus in the following will be on Rorty's neopragmatism—and, more specifically, his reading of George Orwell's *Nineteen Eighty-Four*. I will try to show how Jamesian antitheodicism is actually challenged, rather than being further developed, by the Rortyan approach to evil, suffering, and pragmatism. Conant's insightful critique of Rorty's reading of Orwell will be utilized in this context. The crucial challenge for the pragmatist, I will suggest, is to find a place to stop on the way down the slippery slope from James to Rorty (or Rorty's Orwell—or, *horribile dictu*, O'Brien).

It is through James's pragmatic method that we will actually be led to Rorty. James famously argued that in *every* genuine metaphysical dispute, some practical issue is, however remotely, involved. If there is no such issue involved, then the dispute is empty. Jamesian pragmatism is thus both influenced by and in contrast with the Kantian (somewhat proto-pragmatist) idea of the "primacy of practical reason" in relation to theoretical reason. For Immanuel Kant, the metaphysical ideas of God, freedom, and immortality are only vindicated by the practical, instead of theoretical, use of reason. The Jamesian pragmatist, however, goes beyond Kant in emphasizing not simply the "primacy" of ethics to metaphysics but their *inseparability* and *entanglement*. Pragmatist inquiries into metaphysical topics, such as James's, lead to the radical claim that metaphysics might not, in the last analysis, even be *possible* without a relation to (or a translation into) ethics: Pragmatically analyzed, we cannot arrive at *any* understanding of reality as we humans, being ourselves part of that reality, experience it, without paying due attention to the way in which moral valuations and ethical commitments are constitutive of that reality by being ineliminably involved in any engagement with reality possible for us.[10] Ethics, then, plays a "transcendental" role constitutive of any metaphysical inquiry we may engage in. Ethics is thus the realm of the practical (in a Kantian sense) to which the metaphysical needs to be "translated" in order for metaphysical issues to be truly humanly meaningful. In this sense, pragmatism is deeply about a kind of ethical translation of the metaphysical.

We still need to determine in more detail *how* exactly the ethical becomes involved in, or even a criterion for, the metaphysical. This does *not* happen with reference to any specific moral theory, that is, not by requiring metaphysics to serve some specific ethical good, as defined in some such theory, whether utilitarian, deontological, or virtue ethical. On the contrary, James's pragmatic pluralism must be extended to cover the plurality of humanly possible approaches to ethical reflection. There is no single correct moral theory but a plurality of "voices" we need to carefully listen to whenever we seek to reflect on what we ought to do and how we ought to think. This pluralism is closely related to James's resolute *antireductionism*—his emphasis on the irreducible significance of individual perspectives, whether religious, metaphysical, political, or moral.

In addition to the pragmatic method, we might say that in a sense the Jamesian approach to the metaphysics of substance, or of theism, is an application of the pragmatist conception of truth. Our ideas expressed or expressible by means of such concepts—our metaphysical views and commitments—are pragmatically "true" or "false" insofar as they put us in touch with ethically significant experiences. The truth of a metaphysical view can be assessed by means of the pragmatic criterion of its ability to open us to the cries of the wounded. It is right here, in a pragmatist ethically colored and structured metaphysics, that truth, in James's memorable phrase, "happens to an idea." And it is right here that Rortyan neopragmatism comes to the picture as a development of Jamesian ideas.

NINETEEN EIGHTY-FOUR AND THE PROBLEM OF TRUTH

I have elsewhere[11] at considerable length defended a resolutely antitheodicist reading of James and an antitheodicist way of developing pragmatism generally—as a philosophical contribution to the discourse on evil, but also more comprehensively as a contribution to the examination of the relations between ethics and metaphysics. The basic idea of this reading was sketched in the introductory section above. What we should now consider is the way in which this antitheodicism is, first, rooted in *Kantian* antitheodicism, and secondly, threatened by a certain kind of problematization of the notions of *truth* and *reality* that James's own pragmatism takes some crucial steps toward. In this context, we will have to expand our horizon from James's *Pragmatism* to Rorty's neopragmatism and especially to Rorty's treatment of Orwell. Why they are relevant to our concerns here needs some explanation.

According to Rorty, famously, *cruelty* is the worst thing we do. This is, one might suggest, another pragmatist version of the above-discussed Jamesian principle according to which we should always listen to the cries of the wounded. There is a kind of *holism* involved in Rorty's position, just like in James's: "Don't be cruel" could be regarded as a meta-principle governing all other moral principles (and, to put it in a Kantian way, governing the choice of all moral principles), yet itself (like all more specific principles, and unlike the Kantian meta-principle, the categorical imperative) fallible and revisable, even though it may be difficult or even impossible to imagine how exactly it could fail—just like it is impossible to imagine, in the context of Quinean holism, what it would really be like to falsify a logical or mathematical principle.[12] There are, *pace* Kant, no *unconditional* ideals or principles, either for James or for Rorty, while both pragmatist philosophers do operate with broader and more inclusive (as well as narrower and less inclusive) moral views and principles. Whereas for James the broadest imaginable principle seems to be the requirement to realize the largest possible universe of good while carefully listening to the cries of the wounded, for Rorty an analogous role is played by the liberal principle of avoiding cruelty and realizing individual freedom as fully as possible. All ethical requirements, including these, are contingent and in principle fallible, as everything is contained in a holistic, revisable totality of our ongoing ethical thought and conversation. (Analogously, we may say, the transcendental is contained in the empirical, and vice versa.)

In his essay on Orwell, Rorty rejects the realistic reading of *Nineteen Eighty-Four*, according to which the book defends an objective notion of truth in the context of a penetrating moral critique of the horrible and humiliating way in which Winston is made to believe that two plus two equals five.[13] Consistently with his well-known position (if it can be regarded as a "position" at all), Rorty denies that "there are any plain moral facts out there in the world, . . . any truths independent of language, [or] any neutral ground on which to stand and argue that either torture or kindness are preferable to the other."[14] Orwell's significance lies in a novel redescription of what is possible: He convinced us that "nothing in the nature of truth, or man, or history" will block the conceivable scenario that "the same developments which had made human equality technically possible might make endless slavery possible."[15] Hence, O'Brien, the torturer and "Party intellectual," is Orwell's key invention; Orwell, crucially, offers *no answer* to O'Brien's position: "He does not view O'Brien as crazy, misguided, seduced by a mistaken theory, or blind to the moral facts. He simply views him as *dangerous* and as *possible*."[16]

The key idea here, according to Rorty, is that truth as such does not matter: "What matters is your ability to talk to other people about what seems to you true, not what is in fact true."[17] Famously, in *Nineteen Eighty-Four*, Winston's self is destroyed as he is made to believe that two plus two equals five and to utter, "Do it to Julia!" when faced with his worst fear: the rats. Rorty points out that this is something he "could not utter sincerely and still be able to put himself back together."[18]

The notion of *sincerity* is central here, as it leads us to the way in which Immanuel Kant discusses theodicies in his 1791 essay, "Über das Misslingen aller philosophischen Versuche in der Theodicee" ("On the Miscarriage of All Philosophical Trials in Theodicy"), a largely neglected short piece that usually does not get the kind of attention that Kant's more famous doctrine of "radical evil" does (not to speak of the main works of his critical philosophy).[19] I believe we should follow Kant in rejecting theodicies not only for intellectual but also for ethical (and, therefore, religious) reasons; indeed, James (as I have interpreted him above) is, in this sense, a Kantian. As Richard Bernstein points out in his introduction to what is one of the most important contributions to the problem of evil in the twenty-first century, Kant's rejection of theodicies is a crucial part of his critical philosophy:

Insofar as theodicies aim at theoretical knowledge about God, they are not merely contingent failures but, much more strongly, impossible and *must* fail, given the limitations of human reason; on the other hand, it is precisely by limiting the sphere of knowledge that Kant, famously, makes room for faith.[20] Kant, therefore, is "the modern philosopher who initiates the inquiry into evil without explicit recourse to philosophical theodicy" and hence also leads the way in our attempt to rethink the meaning of evil and responsibility "after Auschwitz."[21] Kant writes about evil in a conceptual world entirely different from the one occupied by his most important predecessors, such as Gottfried Leibniz. This Kantian conceptual world is, if my argument in the earlier sections of this chapter is on the right track, shared by James (and other pragmatists), even though pragmatism more generally is also critical of Kant's aprioristic approach to philosophy in general. We might say that Kant's antitheodicism was "translated" into a pragmatist antitheodicism by James.

The details of Kant's analysis of the failures of theodicies need not concern us here. I just want to emphasize the way in which Kant invokes the Book of Job as an example of the only "honest" way of formulating an "authentic" theodicy—which, for him, actually seems to be an antitheodicy. Job's key virtue, according to Kant, is his *sincerity* (*Aufrichtigkeit*), which establishes "the preeminence of the honest man over the religious flatterer in the divine verdict":[22]

> Job speaks as he thinks, and with the courage with which he, as well as every human being in his position, can well afford; his friends, on the contrary, speak as if they were being secretly listened to by the mighty one, over whose cause they are passing judgment, and as if gaining his favor through their judgment were closer to their heart than the truth. Their malice in pretending to assert things into which they yet must admit they have no insight, and in simulating a conviction which they in fact do not have, contrasts with Job's frankness.[23]

For Kant, the leading feature in Job's virtuous character was not, then, his patience in suffering (as many traditional, particularly Christian, interpreters of the Book of Job might suggest), but his inner sincerity, integrity, and honesty. Indeed, Job protests against his suffering in the poetic dialogues of the book; he does not simply endure his fate or quietly suffer, but complains and insists on the injustice of his adversities.[24] Thus, Job's honesty of heart, rather than his alleged patience, is his greatest virtue.

Toward the end of the essay, Kant discusses the moral evil of insincerity—of our tendency "to distort even inner declarations before [our] own conscience"—as "*in itself evil* even if it harms no one."[25] Thus, he seems to be saying in so many words that speculative, rationalizing theodicies—the kind of theodicies manifested by Job's friends—are themselves exemplifications of evil. They are also evil in a very specific sense: They do not acknowledge the Kantian—and more generally Enlightenment—ideal of free, autonomous, and responsible thinking based on the idea of inner truthfulness. They are therefore revolts (not primarily against God but) against humanity itself, conceived in a Kantian way. We might even say that the insincerity of theodicist thinking does not recognize the essential human capacity for freedom and responsibility, for the kind of autonomous thinking that is the very foundation of morality. It is not implausible, it seems to me, to suggest that James could have sympathized with, or indeed implicitly shared, this Kantian line of thought in his criticism of theodicies. For James, too, there is something ethically fundamentally insincere in theodicies.

A fundamental distinction between truth and falsity is, however, necessary for the concepts of sincerity and truthfulness, and given the role these concepts play in Kantian antitheodicism, such a distinction is necessary for the antitheodicist project generally as well, also in its Jamesian reincarnation. Now, insofar as Rorty's pragmatism carries Jamesian pragmatism into a certain extreme, one is left wondering whether there is any way to stop on the slippery slope arguably leading from James to Rorty (and eventually bringing in, with horror, Orwell's O'Brien). Reality, shocking as it often is, must still be contrasted with something like unreality, while truth and truthfulness must be contrasted not only with falsity but also with lying and self-deception, and possibly other kinds of loss of sincerity and truthfulness that may follow from the collapse of the truth-versus-falsity distinction itself. What we find here is, as we may say, the problem of realism in its existential dimensions. This is, arguably, the core pragmatic meaning of the problem of realism—or even an approach to the problem of realism framed by the problem of evil in a Jamesian manner.

Insofar as the distinction between truth and falsity collapses, as (in a sense) it does in *Nineteen Eighty-Four*, the very project of antitheodicy, which (I believe we may argue) is based on and depends on the Kantian notion of *Aufrichtigkeit* (sincerity),[26] becomes threatened. Truthfulness itself collapses here. Hence, this is another very special message and problem of Orwell, an implicit warning of his great novel: there is no theodicy available even in this negative sense, no happy end or moral harmony available, *even by going through antitheodicism*. Taking evil seriously entails acknowledging that we constantly run the risk of losing whatever truthfulness we might be capable of possessing, and of thereby losing the sincere attitude to evil and suffering that antitheodicists like Kant and James have found crucially important for an adequately (or even minimally) ethical attitude to suffering. Thus, the Orwellian challenge (or warning) lies right here: Is there, or can there be, or can we at least imagine, *such evil that makes antitheodicy itself impossible* by destroying the very possibility of Kantian *Aufrichtigkeit* (by destroying the truth vs. falsity distinction that is necessary for truthfulness or sincerity)? This *fragility of antitheodicy*, the fragility of sincerity necessary for antitheodicy, is a crucial dimension of the more general fragility of the moral point of view; we can consider it a *meta-antitheodicy*. By destroying Winston's capacity for sincerely uttering something and still being able to "put himself back together," O'Brien not only engages in evil that lies (almost) beyond description and imagination but also leads us to imagine the possibility of evil that renders (Kantian) antitheodicy itself impossible. This will then collapse the Jamesian antitheodicist approach as well, given that it starts from a kind of pragmatic softening of the notion of objective truth culminating in the "truth happens to an idea" view that we found characteristic of James's ethically grounded metaphysics.[27]

METAPHYSICS AND THE ORDINARY

While James (on my reading) only resisted certain metaphysically realistic forms of metaphysics, especially Hegelian monistic absolute idealism (and corresponding metaphysical realisms), without thereby abandoning metaphysics altogether, Rorty's reading of Orwell is based on his rejection of *all* forms of metaphysics. In his view, Orwell tells us that "whether our future rulers are more like O'Brien or more like J. S. Mill does not depend . . . on deep facts about human nature" or on any "large necessary truths about human nature and its relation to truth and justice" but on "a lot of small contingent facts."[28] Now, this is hard to deny, at least in a sense; various minor contingent facts have enormous influence on how our world and societies develop. This is also a very important message of Rortyan *ironism* in general: Our firmest moral commitments, our "final vocabularies," are all historically contingent. But the worry is that if we entirely give up (even pragmatically rearticulated) objective truth, we will end up giving up the very possibility of sincerity, too, and that is something we need for resisting the future of all possible O'Briens' (paradoxically) theodicist newspeak seeking to justify evil, suffering, and torture. It is one thing to accept, reasonably, historical contingency and to reject overblown metaphysics of "deep facts about human nature"; it is quite another matter to give up even a minimal pragmatic sense of objective truth required not only for sincerity but for the very possibility of sincerity (and, hence, for the possibility of insincerity as well, because insincerity is possible only insofar as sincerity is possible, and vice versa).

I am not saying that Rorty (or James) is wrong, or has a mistaken conception of truth (or facts or history or anything). What I am saying is that *if* Rorty is right (whatever it means to say this, given the disappearance, in Rorty's neopragmatism, of the distinction between being right and being regarded as being right by one's cultural peers), then we are in bigger trouble than we may have believed. Jamesian pragmatism seems to take the correct, indeed vital, antitheodicist step in refusing to philosophically justify evil and suffering. This step was initially made possible by Kant's antitheodicism, which is rooted in the Book of Job, as we briefly saw. However, insofar as Jamesian pragmatism develops into—or is, in the course of the pragmatist tradition, transformed or translated into—something like Rorty's neopragmatism, which lets the notion of truth drop out as unimportant, the end result is not only an insightful emphasis on historical contingency (and on the role of literature in showing us fascinating—and dangerous—contingent possibilities) but also the possible fragmentation of sincerity itself, which seems to depend on a relatively robust distinction between truth and falsity. Antitheodicy thus becomes fragmented through that fragmentation. What this shows is, I suppose, a quasi-Rortyan point: Orwell is more important, and O'Brien more dangerous, than we might have thought. But it also shows that Rorty in effect deprives us of certain linguistic, literary, and philosophical resources that we might have seen Orwell equipping us with.

This criticism of Rorty (which is also, implicitly, a qualified criticism of Jamesian pragmatism, though *not* a proposal to give up that pragmatism but, rather, to carefully rethink its current value, being aware of its potential problems) comes close to James Conant's highly detailed—and devastating—attack on Rorty's reading of Orwell.[29] According to Conant, Rorty is committed to (indeed, obsessed by) the same philosophical prejudices as his metaphysically realist opponents are in claiming that notions such as objective truth, facts, or historical truth are not in the focus of Orwell's worries. Thus, Conant argues that Rorty fails to see that there is an "ordinary" way of using these and related concepts that need not be construed either metaphysically realistically or antirealistically (or in a Rortyan deflated manner); hence, "when our intellectual options are confined to a forced choice between Realist and Rortian theses . . . we are unable to recover the thoughts Orwell sought to express."[30] Conant obviously does not dispute Rorty's (or Orwell's) emphasis on historical contingency, but he argues that in a perfectly ordinary sense, "the demise of 'the possibility of truth'" could still be very scary.[31] In Conant's view, Orwell's novel is primarily "about the possibility of a state of affairs in which the concept of objective truth has faded as far out of someone's world as it conceivably can,"[32] and therefore it is directly relevant to our antitheodicist concerns here.

Conant contests in a thoroughgoing manner Rorty's deflated reading of O'Brien's character as someone who *simply* enjoys torturing Winston and seeks to "break him" for no particular reason.[33] Truth and truthfulness occupy a central place in Orwell's analysis of what is really frightening in totalitarianism; in this way, the debate between Rorty and Conant on these notions in the context of *Nineteen Eighty-Four* directly continues—without their drawing any attention to it—the antitheodicist argumentation we find in Kant's theodicy essay, referring to the Book of Job.[34] O'Brien's "unqualified denial of the idea that (what Orwell calls) 'the concept of objective truth' has application to the past"[35] can be directly applied to Job's sincerity about *his* past: Job knows he did not sin, and therefore his suffering cannot be a punishment for sin, yet he does suffer; the availability of objective truth (about the past, in particular) is needed to make sense of the very possibility of Job's firm rejection of his so-called friends' allegedly consoling, albeit theodicist, speeches. Such (inner) freedom and the availability of the concept of objective truth are inseparable:

> What [Orwell's] novel aims to make manifest is that if reality control and doublethink were ever to be practiced on a systematic scale, the possibility of an individual speaking the truth and the possibility of an individual controlling her own mind would begin simultaneously to fade out of the world. The preservation of freedom and the preservation of truth represent a single indivisible task for Orwell—a task common to literature and politics.[36]

No matter how exactly we should read Orwell and Rorty, this is a fundamental link between freedom and truth, a link also needed to make sense of the very idea of antitheodicy in its Kantian and Jamesian meaning. In particular, the preservation of freedom and truth—the task Conant argues is shared by literature and politics—is inseparably intertwined with the need to fight against "the corruption of language," which corrupts our concepts and, thus, thought itself.[37] Insofar as theodicism itself is a corruption of thought—as, according to James, it seems to be—and insofar as theodicist writing will inevitably end up corrupting the language we use for talking about evil and suffering, a genuinely antitheodicist philosophical project will have to take very seriously this literary-cum-political challenge (which, a pragmatist philosopher should add, always has an ethical core). While Conant in my view surprisingly finds no reason to refer to Hannah Arendt's analyses of either totalitarianism or evil, the kind of corruption of language he does speak about would, in my view, be readily comparable to the well-known concept of the banality of evil, which is also based on a kind of newspeak and loss of autonomous thought—along with, horribly, a loss of the very possibility of an antitheodicist rejection of the moral inappropriateness of theodicies.[38]

These reflections should make us appreciate the fact that the ways we speak about evil and suffering are constitutive of the ethical and political world we live in—and thus more generally constitutive of the human world, like language in general is constitutive of any reality humans are able to inhabit and thus also of any arena of potential meaningfulness (or loss of meaning) where translation as a "movement of meaning" takes place. Insofar as this is correct about language, meaning, and translation in general, theodicies may be seen as "mistranslations" of human meanings—as mistaken and misleading ways of attaching meaning to meaningless suffering. The corruption of language inherent in theodicism corrupts our way of being human.

This, at the most radical level, is what theodicies can do to us. And this is why the Orwellian way of drawing attention to the ways we speak is vitally important for us.

Finally, just as our language addressing evil, suffering, and morality may become corrupt, the very discourse of sincerity (Kantian *Aufrichtigkeit*) can become corrupt, and one form of such corruption is shown by Orwell himself, for instance in the passage in which O'Brien tells Winston that his (Winston's) surrender to the Party must be out of his own free will: "We do not destroy the heretic. . . . We convert him, we capture his inner mind, we reshape him. We burn all evil and illusion out of him; we bring him to our side, not in appearance, but genuinely, heart and soul."[39] From this horror, I think, only literature—not philosophy, I'm afraid, or at least not philosophy alone—can save us. The kind of theodicist language James (like Kant) attacks is itself a corrupted language, manifesting a fundamentally insincere attitude to the reality of evil—as insincere as a straightforwardly antirealist denial of the reality of evil would be. A corrupted and insincere language is also impossible to *translate* across cultural boundaries into ethically adequate expressions of human suffering.

CONCLUSION: THE SICK SOUL AND CORRUPTION

The Orwellian warning manifested by O'Brien's troubling character is something that, I submit, only Jamesian-like sick souls can truly appreciate. In *The Varieties of Religious Experience*, James tells us that the sick souls are those who, in contrast to the "healthy-minded," maintain that "the evil aspects of our life are of its very essence, and that the world's meaning most comes home to us when we lay them most to heart."[40] The sick souls, then, are those "who cannot so swiftly throw off the burden of the consciousness of evil, but are congenitally fated to suffer from its presence."[41] Reflecting on the reality of evil and suffering, acknowledging human helplessness and sadness even when life seems happy and easy, we may be led to maintain (with James) that "[t]he completest religions would . . . seem to be those in which the pessimistic elements are best developed"—that is, "religions of deliverance," according to which one has to "die to an unreal life" in order to be "born into the real life."[42]

The concept of the sick soul is, for James, a concept to be employed in the psychological and philosophical description and explanation of certain kinds of religious attitudes and ways of living and thinking. However, given the close relation between religion and ethics in James, this concept can, I believe, be used in ethical contexts bracketing the actual religious aspects of, say, conversion. We may say that the sick soul takes seriously—ethically seriously—the evil and suffering around her or him in the world even if she or he never experiences this as a *religious* problem (or perhaps, as we also might say, never translates an originally religious problem into a fundamentally ethical one). The sick soul, then, acknowledges, to move back to Orwell (and Conant's debate with Rorty) again, that it is imaginable that we might be led into a situation in which humanity itself would fade out from the world along with truth and the possibility of free thought: Winston is, according to O'Brien, "the last man."[43]

Does one actually have to *be* a sick soul in the Jamesian sense in order to be able to be ethical at all? Well, I think the answer is no, in a sense roughly comparable to the sense in which you do not have to be a transcendental idealist (in a Kantian context) in order to have objective experiences, even if you do have to be a transcendental idealist (according to Kant) in order to be able to philosophically account for the possibility of objective experience. Thus, we may reconstruct the Jamesian argument as maintaining that you must be a sick soul in order to be able to account for the possibility of ethics. The problem we have been dealing with throughout this chapter is (in non-Jamesian terms) transcendental rather than empirical. The concept of the sick soul, like antitheodicism, is *constitutive of the possibility of the ethical*, not for anyone's actually being, or failing to be, ethical (like the concept of truth is constitutive of sincerity). Only the sick soul (transcendentally speaking) is ethically uncorrupted. Being a sick soul in this sense is an infinite challenge.

Insofar as we detach the notion of the sick soul from its immediate context in the psychology of religion, we may say that James writes in the same intellectual and spiritual setting in which Richard Bernstein, Susan Neiman, and some other contemporary philosophical and political theorists of evil operate, a context in which evil is a challenge to our attempt to find life meaningful at all—a context *very* different from the theoretical context typical of mainstream evidentalist and theodicist philosophers of religion.[44] Acknowledging evil and the potential disharmony and even absurdity of life (individual and social), as well as the limits of philosophical theorization and reflection on these matters, while affirming an active, melioristic attitude (against an unavoidably tragic background), can be seen as a key Jamesian contribution to the problem of evil and to the challenge to reflect on the relations between religion, metaphysics, and morality arising from this problem. According to James, as I read him, we should never philosophically theorize in a theodicist manner about the potential "harmonious" justification, accommodation, or meaningfulness of evil and suffering. We should, rather, acknowledge evil and its victims by not attempting to explain it, or their sufferings, away; and we should simply fight against evil instead of accepting it by justifying it. Moreover, we should fight against the corruption of acceptance. All of this is an attempt to articulate, in a noncorrupted language, what it means to try to listen to the "cries of the wounded."

When we pragmatically evaluate the success of pragmatism in responding to evil and suffering antitheodicistically, thus offering an ethical argument for pragmatism, *this* line of argument itself needs to take seriously the anti-theodicist requirement that (I have argued) James finds necessary for the pragmatic method. Whether it can do so in the end (all the way down) depends on finding a solution to the threatening loss of truth—loss of sincerity—that pragmatism would slide into, if the deflated Rortyan reaction to Orwell were (though I hope, and have tried to argue, that it isn't, at least not necessarily) the inevitable outcome of James's approach. Only if we can resolve this Rortyan-Orwellian issue can we even attempt to offer any illuminating response to the nagging (quasi-Cavellian) question of what's the use of translating our concern with acknowledging the suffering other into a vocabulary of Jamesian pragmatism.

NOTES

Early versions of this study were presented in conferences on "philosophy as translation" based on the SPIRITS project led by Naoko Saito (Kyoto University) at the Helsinki Collegium for Advanced Studies (November 2014) and, more substantially, at the University College London Institute of Education (February 2015). Some related material was also presented as parts of my joint papers with Sari Kivistö at the subsequent SPIRITS conferences at the University of Helsinki (December 2015) and Kyoto University (March 2016). For helpful comments and criticism, I should like to thank Russell B. Goodman, Vincent Colapietro, Henrik Rydenfelt, Naoko Saito, Paul Standish, Sandra Laugier, Heikki J. Koskinen, and Sigridur Thorgeirsdottir, in particular. My greatest debt is to Sari Kivistö, to whom I owe some of the fundamental points about Kant and *Aufrichtigkeit*, as well as Orwell.

1. My references to James's *Pragmatism: A New Name for Some Old Ways of Thinking* (1907) are to the critical edition in *The Works of William James*, ed. Frederick H. Burkhardt, Fredson Bowers, and Ignas K. Skrupskelis (Cambridge, MA and London: Harvard University Press, 1975). For the original formulation of the pragmatic method, see, in particular, Charles S. Peirce, "How to Make Our Ideas Clear" (1878), in *The Essential Peirce* (2 vols.), vol. 1, ed. Nathan Houser (Bloomington: Indiana University Press, 1992).

2. I think much of my own work on this—cf., for example, Sami Pihlström, *Pragmatist Metaphysics: An Essay on the Ethical Grounds of Ontology* (London: Continuum, 2009)—doesn't go deep enough in this respect. However, see also Sari Kivistö and Sami Pihlström, *Kantian Antitheodicy: Philosophical and Literary Varieties* (Basingstoke: Palgrave Macmillan, 2016), chapter 4, which offers a considerably more comprehensive treatment of the topics of the present essay.

3. This phrase comes from William James, "The Moral Philosopher and the Moral Life" (1891), in *The Will to Believe and Other Essays in Popular Philosophy* (1897), in *The Works of William James* (1979).

4. I am borrowing the notion of a realistic spirit (though no specific views) from Cora Diamond, *The Realistic Spirit* (Cambridge, MA and London: The MIT Press, 1991), which focuses on Wittgenstein and Gottlob Frege rather than James.

5. The various conferences and other activities of the Kyoto-based SPIRITS project led by Naoko Saito have also employed the vocabulary of "philosophy of translation" and "truth as translated."

6. On the "truth in skepticism," see Stanley Cavell, *The Claim of Reason: Wittgenstein, Skepticism, Morality, and Tragedy* (New York and Oxford: Oxford University Press, 1979), especially 45, 115, 241; see also Stanley Cavell, *The Senses of Walden: An Expanded Edition* (Chicago: University of Chicago Press, 1992; first published 1981), especially 106–7, 133.

Given the topic of evil and suffering, particularly relevant here would be Cavell's essay, "Hope against Hope" (1985), in Stanley Cavell, *Emerson's Transcendental Etudes* (Stanford, CA: Stanford University Press, 2003), 171–82, which explicitly links Emerson with Kant (specifically Kant's essay, "The End of All Things"). Regarding our ethically appropriate reactions to evil and suffering in this context, invoking the Emersonian concept of hope in particular, see chapter 4, "Rebuking Hopelessness," by Paul Standish, in this volume.

7. See again Cavell, *The Claim of Reason*. The notion of acknowledgment is, of course, fundamental to the existential project of living with our skeptical (Wittgensteinian) predicament.

8. See also the analysis of theodicism as a failure of acknowledgment in Kivistö and Pihlström, *Kantian Antitheodicy* (cited above). On Cavell's significance for the philosophy of religion, see Espen Dahl, *Stanley Cavell, Religion, and Continental Philosophy* (Bloomington: Indiana University Press, 2014); on acknowledgment in this context, see Dahl's chapter 3. Dahl does not discuss Cavell's relation to pragmatist philosophy of religion, but the topics he examines (including acknowledgment, guilt, and forgiveness) have interesting analogies in the pragmatist context, too.

9. Cf. Stanley Cavell, "What's the Use of Calling Emerson a Pragmatist?" in Morris Dickstein, ed., *The Revival of Pragmatism: New Essays on Social Thought, Law, and Culture* (Durham, NC: Duke University Press, 1998), 72–80.

10. It may be worth noting that the radical "humanist" pragmatist F. C. S. Schiller, who was influenced by James (and whose influence on James is acknowledged by the latter in many places), even published an article with the title, "The Ethical Basis of Metaphysics" (*International Journal of Ethics* 13, 1903); the essay is reprinted in Schiller's *Humanism: Philosophical Essays* (London: Macmillan, 1903).

11. Cf. Sami Pihlström, *Taking Evil Seriously* (Basingstoke: Palgrave Macmillan, 2014), as well as Kivistö and Pihlström, *Kantian Antitheodicy*, chapter 4.

12. According to Quine's famous holism, logical and mathematical beliefs (or sentences) are in principle on a par with empirical scientific beliefs (or sentences). See W. V. Quine, "Two Dogmas of Empiricism" (1951), in Quine, *From a Logical Point of View* (Cambridge, MA: Harvard University Press, 1953; rev. ed. 1980), chapter 2. Cf. Morton White's extended pragmatic holism also covering (unlike Quine's) ethics and normativity: White, *A Philosophy of Culture: The Scope of Holistic Pragmatism* (Princeton, NJ: Princeton University Press, 2002).

13. For the realistic reading, also directed against Rorty's own pragmatism, see, for example, Peter van Inwagen, *Metaphysics* (Boulder, CO: Westview Press, 1993), 69; and H.O. Mounce, *The Two Pragmatisms* (London: Routledge, 1997), 211–18.

14. Richard Rorty, "The Last Intellectual in Europe: Orwell on Cruelty," in Rorty, *Contingency, Irony, and Solidarity* (Cambridge: Cambridge University Press, 1989), 173.

15. Ibid., 175.

16. Ibid., 176.

17. Ibid. This is followed by the well-known Rortyan one-liner, "If we take care of freedom, truth can take care of itself" (Ibid.).

18. Ibid., 179.

19. The essay was first published in *Berlinische Monatsschrift*, September 1791, 194–225; it is available, for example, in Wilhelm Weischedel, ed., *Immanuel Kant: Werke in zehn Bänden* (Darmstadt: Wissenschaftliche Buchgesellschaft, 1983), vol. 9. For an English translation, see Immanuel Kant, *Religion and Rational Theology*, trans. and ed. Allen W. Wood and George Di Giovanni (Cambridge: Cambridge University Press, 1996), 20–37 (with the translator's introduction, 21–23). In referencing, even though I am citing the English translation, the standard *Akademie-Ausgabe* numbering will be used. For Kant's theory of radical evil, see Book I of his *Religionsschrift* (*Religion innerhalb der blossen Vernunft* [1794], in *Werke in zehn Bänden*, vol. 9). I cannot examine the much-discussed theory of radical evil in this chapter. For secondary literature focusing on the theodicy essay, see, for example, Johannes Brachtendorff, "Kants Theodizee-Aufsatz—Die Bedingungen des Gelingens philosophischen Theodizee," *Kant-Studien* 93 (2002), 57–83; and Elizabeth C. Galbraith, "Kant and 'A Theodicy of Protest,'" in Chris L. Firestone and Stephen R. Palmquist, eds., *Kant and the New Philosophy of Religion* (Bloomington and Indianapolis: Indiana University Press, 2006), 179–89. As Gal-

braith notes (182), it was presumably David Hume who "awoke Kant from his dogmatic slumbers" regarding theodicy—as well as, more famously, the capacities of human reason more generally. The theodicy essay is of course a very late work of Kant's; in his precritical writings, he seems to have favored a basically Leibnizian theodicy. My Kantian-inspired discussion in the rest of this section is indebted to, and partly borrowed from, a more comprehensive inquiry into this topic that I have undertaken with Sari Kivistö: cf. Kivistö and Pihlström, "Kantian Anti-Theodicy and Job's Sincerity," forthcoming in *Philosophy and Literature* 40, no. 2 (2016); see also Kivistö and Pihlström, *Kantian Antitheodicy*, chapter 1.

20. Richard Bernstein, *Radical Evil: A Philosophical Interrogation* (Cambridge: Polity Press, 2002), 3–4.

21. Ibid., 4. For Bernstein's insightful reading of Kant's theory of radical evil, see ibid., chapter 1.

22. Kant, *Theodicee*, AA 8:267.

23. Ibid., AA 8:265–66.

24. See also John T. Wilcox, *The Bitterness of Job: A Philosophical Reading* (Ann Arbor: University of Michigan Press, 1989), for a reading of Job according to which Job's protest goes as far as to be blasphemous. Wilcox emphasizes God's *amoral* creation and world order in contrast to Job's demands for moral justice. Thus, according to Wilcox (see chapter 10, in particular), Job moves from an initial "moral bitterness" to an appreciation of amoral nature created by God, and the Book of Job argues that a "high religion" rejects the "orthodox" idea that God guarantees a moral world order. (One might say that Wilcox's Job is proto-Nietzschean rather than proto-Kantian.) C. Fred Alford doesn't quite agree with the view that Job engages in blasphemy but does maintain that when Job's patience "is at an end," his "rage borders on heresy." See Alford, *After the Holocaust: The Book of Job, Primo Levi, and the Path to Affliction* (Cambridge: Cambridge University Press, 2009), 16.

25. Kant, *Theodicee*, AA 8:270.

26. This is argued in some detail in Kivistö and Pihlström, "Kantian Anti-Theodicy and Job's Sincerity."

27. Note that I am not claiming that James would be committed to any explicitly Kantian antitheodicy. His antitheodicism, in my view, is Kantian in the broader sense of arguing that it is a necessary condition for the possibility of a moral point of view that evil and suffering are not explained away or justified. He rejects precisely the kind of rationalizing justification that Job's "friends" paradigmatically offer. My worry is whether this Kantian approach works in the overall context of Jamesian pragmatism, with its softened notion of truth.

28. Rorty, "The Last Intellectual," 187–88.

29. James Conant, "Freedom, Cruelty, and Truth: Rorty versus Orwell," in Robert B. Brandom, *Rorty and His Critics* (Oxford, MA and Cambridge: Blackwell, 2000), 268–342. See also Richard Rorty, "Response to James Conant," ibid., 342–50. Conant's essay is, in my view, one of the best critical discussions of Rorty's project in general, by no means restricted to the interpretation of *Nineteen Eighty-Four*—yet, as it focuses on that book and Rorty's reading of it, it does show us something about the fundamental philosophical relevance of Orwell's novel.

30. Ibid., 279–80. I take it as obvious that Conant's views on the ordinary are to a considerable extent indebted to his long engagement with Cavell's thought.

31. Ibid., 285–86.

32. Ibid., 297. He also says the novel "is perhaps as close as we can come to contemplating in imagination the implications of the adoption of a resolutely Rortian conception of objectivity (that is, a conception in which the concept of objectivity is exhausted by that of solidarity)" (ibid., 307). This formulation is better than the one quoted in the main text above because it avoids involving the notion of a state of affairs that might itself be regarded as a remnant of old "Realist" metaphysics.

33. See ibid., especially 290.

34. Note how different Orwell's views on totalitarianism, at least on Conant's reading, are from Hannah Arendt's well-known ideas, in which the concentration camp is the epitomization of totalitarianism. See Arendt, *The Origins of Totalitarianism* (New York: Schocken Books, 2004; first published 1951). For Orwell, such atrocities are peripheral; hostility to truthfulness is the "really frightening" thing. (Conant, "Freedom, Cruelty, and Truth," 295). Note, however,

also that Rorty charges Conant of confusing truth with truthfulness ("Response to James Conant," 347). When Conant says that the "capacity of individuals to assess the truth of claims on their own" threatens "the absolute hegemony of the Party over their minds" (ibid., 299), a natural reference would be the Kantian account of the Book of Job as committed to the idea of Job's truthfulness—even in relation to divine hegemony. Of course, Job finally puts a word on his mouth and speaks no more, but even then he does not give up his sincerity and inner truthfulness; rather, he just gives up the possibility of speech itself.

35. Ibid., 308.

36. Ibid., 310.

37. Ibid., 313.

38. On the banality of evil, see Hannah Arendt, *Eichmann in Jerusalem: A Report on the Banality of Evil* (London: Penguin, 1994; first published 1963). Conant's lack of interest in Arendt is not my only complaint against his views, although here I have mostly just relied on his argument against Rorty. I am also quite unhappy with his hostility (shared by Rorty, of course) toward metaphysics in general (he does not seem to appreciate the possibility of the kind of ethically oriented pragmatist metaphysics outlined here) and with his "new Wittgensteinian" rather unarticulated employment of the concept of the "ordinary," which Rorty himself also finds problematic (see "Response to James Conant," 345, 349). I certainly agree with Conant that the kind of objective truth whose availability (in principle) is presupposed by the antitheodicist project is not necessarily equivalent to metaphysically realistic correspondence truth; yet, I am not quite sure if the mere appeal to the "ordinary" is philosophically helpful here (and to this extent I agree with Rorty rather than Conant—or, indeed, Cavell). This essay, however, is not the proper place to settle such issues.

39. This horrible description of an ironic corruption of sincerity is quoted by Conant ("Freedom, Cruelty, and Truth," 340 n.197).

40. William James, *The Varieties of Religious Experience: A Study in Human Nature* (New York: New American Library, 1958; first published 1902), 114.

41. Ibid., 116.

42. Ibid., 139.

43. Conant, "Freedom, Cruelty, and Truth," 312–13. Perhaps the "last man" is a sick soul. Perhaps only a sick soul will remain uncorrupted.

44. See, for example, Bernstein, *Radical Evil*; Susan Neiman, *Evil in Modern Thought: An Alternative History of Philosophy* (Princeton, NJ: Princeton University Press, 2004); for a mainstream attempt at a theodicist argument in philosophy of religion, see Peter van Inwagen, *The Problem of Evil* (Oxford: Clarendon Press, 2006). I criticize van Inwagen from a perspective largely indebted to (though not identical with) Bernstein and Neiman's in Pihlström, *Taking Evil Seriously* (for a discussion of James and the sick soul in that book, see chapter 2).

Chapter Eight

Communication as Translation

Reading Dewey after Cavell

Megan J. Laverty

> Knowing how to continue . . . isolates or dramatizes the inevitable moment of
> teaching and learning, and hence of communication, in which my power
> comes to an end in the face of the other's separateness from me.
> —Stanley Cavell[1]

Both Stanley Cavell and John Dewey, two of America's most important
philosophers, affirm philosophy's practical orientation and insist that its central project is our primary existential concern, namely, the question of how to
live. In their view, philosophy should have an impact on our lives. Despite
this shared vision, however, Cavell conspicuously distances his ordinary language philosophy from Dewey's pragmatism.[2] I will argue, in agreement
with Hilary Putnam, that Cavell is "too harsh on Dewey and inclined thus to
overplay the differences."[3] To this end, I will rehearse Cavell's reservations
about pragmatism and then offer a rereading of Dewey that highlights the
role of translation inherent in his philosophy of communication, showing him
to be just as committed to the dynamism in the relationship between the
fixation of our thought in words and the elusiveness of meaning.

CAVELL'S RESERVATIONS ABOUT DEWEY'S PRAGMATISM

Natural language figures prominently in the philosophies of Cavell and
Dewey. Both envision it as inherently practical and participatory. They see
mutual intelligibility as neither given nor guaranteed, but as something to be
achieved as individuals bring community into being. This "projective vision
of language" entails that linguistic criteria and shared norms are constituted

as words are used.[4] According to Cavell and Dewey, this is no easy task. Conscientious effort, communicative labor, psychological discipline, and experimental open-mindedness must be exercised if, to quote Stephen Mulhall, "human beings [are] to see and hear themselves in the words and deeds of other human beings."[5] Moreover, our use of language necessarily involves individual responsibility *and* community: If words are used without thought, their meaning becomes merely conventional; if words are used too idiosyncratically, they become unintelligible to others.

Despite believing that we have been cast adrift in a groundless sea of words, Cavell, following Ludwig Wittgenstein, illuminates "the astonishing extent" of our attunement to linguistic criteria and shared norms.[6] This attunement is blind in the sense that we use language unaware that we are uniquely responsible for the criteria governing its successful use; we do not see the precariousness of our own condition. Although "nothing insures that we will make, and understand, the same projections," the fact that this happens, and happens repeatedly, is determined by what is shared: "Routes of interest and feeling, modes of response, senses of humor and of significance and fulfillment, of what is outrageous, of what is similar to what else, what a rebuke, what forgiveness, of when an utterance is an assertion, when an appeal, when an explanation—all the whirl of organism Wittgenstein calls 'forms of life.'"[7] The reason our attunement, though blind, so effectively facilitates communicative success is that it tethers our shared language to our shared experience.

As Naoko Saito points out, however, Cavell recognized that our natural willingness to attune with linguistic criteria and shared norms risks "conformity of the self to language, and of the self to itself."[8] Words become mere words and fail to place the individual in the world. When language and self are lost to each other, ordinary lives become characterized by "quiet desperation" or "silent melancholy."[9] Thus, Cavell argues that the autonomy of language and the self must constantly be reestablished. Traversing the abyss from a state of loss to rebirth is arduous: We must labor to express ourselves and to be found reasonable by others. This labor is not just technical, but ethical.

Like Cavell, Dewey views ethics as a dimension of language-use, but he is less captivated by the astonishing extent of our attunement. He locates the ethical dimension of language-use in delicately balanced forms of associated living and emphasizes the utter fragility of our values: creative self-expression, human companionship, fulfilling endeavors, and a meaningful life. Although our concepts are integrated into the traditions that we inherit, their continued existence relies on our renewed and ongoing engagement with them. The danger, in Dewey's mind, is not conformity, but complacency: a failure on the part of individuals to search for new and deeper meanings by seeking out greater possibilities for community—and vice-versa. Instead of settling for the narrow horizons of our practical lives, we should seek to expand those horizons by engaging in conversations that compel us to speak in surprising ways. According to Dewey, it is just as important *not* to mean what we say, because the experience of stretching our conceptual limits serves to instill a practice of reflection; what we mean is to be discovered through human interaction.

For Dewey, the groundlessness of human language and community is a source of strength, rather than weakness. Assuming full responsibility for our language and community allows us to trust and improve human experience. Philosophical superstitions, such as the assignation of moral value to only a handful of characteristics identified as virtues, thwart meaningful inquiry into the nature and significance of human speech and activity. [10] The traits that we recognize as emphatically moral, such as courage, honesty, and patience, are, in Dewey's view, intimately connected "with thousands of other attitudes which we do not explicitly recognize—which perhaps we have not even names for."[11] Naming and recognizing these "thousands of other attitudes" requires creating new forms of human association and becoming. Ultimately, Dewey proposes that even the question of our humanity—whether we are fatally flawed or fallen—be subject to inquiry.

Cavell takes Dewey to be "handing over" the question of our humanity not to philosophy but to the social sciences, and it is a source of his misgivings about Dewey's pragmatism. He considers Dewey's focus on the business of what works as a "betrayal of what philosophy has centrally been and still centrally can be."[12] According to Cavell, Dewey misses the question of philosophy, and whether it is even necessary or possible, because he naively endorses science and scientific knowledge. He focuses on the initiation, development, and fulfillment of inquiry, holding that initiation occurs by means of disruption to our routine ways of understanding, development is propelled by the scientific method, and fulfillment results from activity. Thought moves from problematic situations to their actual solutions. If there are limits to thought, then they are historically contingent and can, in principle, be overcome.

Cavell suspects Dewey's willingness to relinquish philosophical questions to the social sciences betrays a uniquely American assumption that enlightened self-interest begets social cohesiveness, and vice-versa; his reconstruction of philosophy accords with a mythical understanding of America and what it means to be an American. But it is not Dewey's invocation of a familiar cultural myth with which Cavell takes issue. In fact, in his own work Cavell seeks to retrieve the voices of Ralph Waldo Emerson and Henry David Thoreau as both distinctively American and essentially philosophical. [13] It is rather Dewey's having failed "to create a distance within familiarity" by interrogating what is repressed or lost that Cavell laments. [14] Cavell depicts Dewey's endorsement of scientific knowledge as failing to acknowledge the absolute limits of thought and thereby repressing essential elements of our humanity.[15]

Cavell is more suspicious than Dewey of the standardization of meaning that secures communication and community. He thinks that culture inhibits the human voice just as much as it enables it and is resistant to the ordinary transmission of settled messages because he worries that it deadens certain sensitivities and propensities, represses distinctive voices, and thwarts self-expression. His concern is that our thinking be made our own and that others come to endorse it as reasonable. Thus, he emphasizes the inner agenda of *freedom*, understood as "mastery of what one does and says."[16] For Cavell, language is to be used expressively as opposed to instrumentally if humans are to find and become themselves. Such use constitutes a release from "self-imprisonment toward the light of the instinct of freedom."[17] Richard Eldridge explains that this "conversion of, and from within, experience" involves encounters with strangeness, trials, and perils.[18] In Saito's words, we find ourselves through "the moment of leaving the familiar, of acquiring the sense of strangeness within the ordinary, or say, of radical departure from within home."[19] This moment of departure creates the distance necessary for reconfiguring our relationship to the world.

If the education of grownups begins with estrangement from ourselves and our lives, then self-transformation is "from the inmost to the outmost." According to Cavell, Dewey misses this "internal perspective."[20] As a reader of Emerson and Thoreau, Cavell never could find his way back to Dewey's writings and a world vastly different from his own; a world that is without "the heights of modernism in the arts, the depths of psychoanalytic discovery, the ravages of the century's politics, the wild intelligence of American popular culture."[21] Although Cavell may have a point about the deficits of Dewey's world, he fails to grasp the role of communication in Dewey's thought. If Cavell is gripped by "the romance of expressive freedom," Dewey is gripped by the romance of inclusive communion. He thinks that there is nothing more human than our desire to achieve understanding through rare moments of human connection—the making of something common—which, like the escape from our common finitude, is ultimately impossible. Misapprehension and misunderstanding are foundational to human language and community: it is only through the labor of working through misunderstanding that we establish common meaning. For this reason, conventional language-use and its standardized meanings should not be taken for granted, for not only is it necessary for communication, it is also a testament to the success of our conjoint undertakings.

Dewey defines conjoint undertakings as "cooperative, in that response to another's act involves contemporaneous response to a thing as entering into the other's behavior, and this upon both sides."[22] Cooperative activity occurs when an individual responds to the meaning of another individual's speech and behavior. He or she perceives the "thing" as it figures in the other's experience; in other words, he or she incorporates that individual's perspective. A "cross-reference," or translation, between the two perspectives occurs. In the next section, I explain why such intralingual translation is commonly undertaken without our being aware of it. I do so with reference to Louise Glück's poem "Averno," which describes being ignored and misconstrued on the grounds of age. The experience represents a breach in communication because the speaker and the spoken-to fail to exist for one another as "guardians of meaning."[23]

A CALL FOR INTRALINGUAL TRANSLATION

The English word "translation" derives from the Latin *translatio* ("transporting"), which comes from the verb *transferre* ("to carry over"). At its most basic, interlingual translation is the attempt to render in one language an utterance or text that has already been articulated in another; the translation aims to produce something comparable to the original utterance or text. Ultimately, the aim of interlingual translation is cross-cultural understanding. It is thus no surprise that globalization has increased the necessity and prominence of interlingual translation, as evidenced by the proliferation of translator-training programs and the emergence of the new interdisciplinary academic field of Translation Studies.[24] This field has enjoyed rapid growth, and various forms of translation research have made methodological, theoretical, and pedagogical advances. This highlights the critical role of interlingual translation in the history of letters, colonization, and economic expansion.

Contemporary scholars agree that interlingual translation theory rests "on particular assumptions about language use, even if they are no more than fragmentary hypotheses that remain implicit or unacknowledged."[25] Generally, such assumptions are either instrumental or hermeneutical. The *instrumental* theorist identifies a word's meaning with its referent. The word is thought to correspond or "point to" the relevant item in the world. The meaning relationship is ostensive, as exemplified in Wittgenstein's early picture theory of language. The *hermeneutical* theorist assumes that the meaning of a word is provided by the social conventions that govern the intentions and expectations of its use. Both assume that native speakers convey meanings so directly to one another that no effort of translation is needed.

The instrumentalist view, that utterances have ostensive meaning, has been famously challenged by such philosophers as Wittgenstein, Cavell, and Iris Murdoch.[26] Murdoch, for example, argues that "[L]anguage is far more idiosyncratic than has been admitted. . . . Words are the most subtle symbols we possess and our human fabric depends on them. The living and radical

nature of language is something which we forget at our peril."[27] She thinks
that we succumb to this peril—we forget the "living and radical nature of
language"—because the apparent constancy of our word use *conceals* conceptual change. For Murdoch, "knowing what a word means" has two senses:
although words can be understood in a conventional sense—for example, the
meanings of terms like "table," "chair," and "coat" are readily appre-
hended—most are understood in depth, that is, "an altering and complicating
process, takes place" when we use or hear them.[28] For the purpose of this
discussion it will be useful to consider an example.

The dying, elderly narrator of Louise Glück's poem "Averno" reflects: "It
is terrible to be alone. / I don't mean to live alone— / To *be* alone, where no
one hears you."[29] The narrator lives in the care and companionship of his
grown-up children; this includes visits, conversations, meals, admonitions,
bickering, advice, and assistance. They perceive him to be losing his facul-
ties, talking about things "no one can see" to disguise the fact that he "can't
remember anymore the word for chair."[30] He resents that their view of him
has become overdetermined by age: He is now just like other old people. His
utterances no longer have a bearing on what his children think, except to
signify his advancing senility. They are indistinguishable from other evidence that demonstrates the inevitable erasure of human capacities by time;
they are simply phenomena of gerontology. His children view their father's
loss of independence and agency as a loss of authority. Neither does he
participate in the guardianship of meaning, nor does he offer a perspective on
what it means to live well.

While the ailing father knows that he is "preparing to be a ghost," he
believes that his impending death has deepened his understanding of *life*'s
"impermanency" and lack of "solidity."[31] Too frail to fully articulate his
view, this deepened understanding takes effect in the narrator's memory and
fantasy. His attention is captivated by the cyclical nature of the seasons,
arrivals and departures of trains and travelers, farming, fire, accidents, in-
clement weather, and inhospitable places. Death, he discovers, is not the only
occasion on which individuals disappear from this world.

He longs to share this insight with his children but, given their apparent
disregard for what he says, he settles for dreaming of companions similarly
claimed by such questions as, "*Is there any benefit in forcing upon oneself
the realization that one must die?*" and "*Is it possible to miss the opportunity
of one's life?*"[32] The father's commitment to these questions, as questions for
us, reveals an appreciation for how they animate thinking about the everyday: tea, chairs, illness, labor, travel, trains, fire, mist, and snow.

The father wants his children to recognize that he shares in what Cora
Diamond calls "a life with concepts."[33] He seeks their acknowledgment that
his conceptual inhabitance of life stands in a normative relationship to their
own (as theirs do to his). In other words, he wants them to realize that his

utterances and understanding serve as a potential corrective to theirs, and vice-versa. This realization requires an exercise of translation on their part. For example, they might need to recall occasions on which they lacked independence and agency (like their father) and yet meant what they said (like their father). Or they might need to call to mind more familiar things and then trace out connections between those things and what their father says about spirit. The father, too, would have to give up some of his certainty in an effort to inhabit the world that his children inhabit.

Even with translation, however, the father's yearning for complete mutual understanding is unrealizable due to the improvisational nature of grammatical and existential normativity. There is no linguistic or existential authority that can mediate between him and his children. This is true not only in instances of a radical conceptual rift, like the one between the father and his children, but also in acts of seemingly commonplace and straightforward communication. Since any way of going on is effectively as meaningful as any other, individuals must respect "the other's equal claim to authority."[34] They must seek to share in the thoughts of others as they accept the contingency of their own thinking, and they must strive "to assimilate, imaginatively, something of another's experience" in the articulation of their own thought.[35] Thus we must continue to strive toward mutual understanding, even though it cannot be completely achieved.

DEWEY'S PHILOSOPHY OF COMMUNICATION

Dewey enjoyed extended visits to China, Japan, Turkey, South Africa, and Mexico, among other places, at a time when such travel was uncommon and arduous by today's standards. He used these opportunities to lecture, teach, and explore varieties of education scarcely known in the United States at the time. As he expended a great deal of energy and resources on these trips, it is safe to assume that he implicitly upheld a philosophy of interlingual translation, although to my knowledge he did not articulate it in his published corpus.[36] It is also safe to assume that Dewey did not articulate such a philosophy because, like Cavell and other post-Wittgensteinian philosophers, he conceived of *intralingual* translation as always already at work in natural language, and so would likely have conceived of *interlingual* translation as an extension of the same phenomenon. He argued that the meanings of utterances within a single language are neither fixed nor static, but rather constantly altered through use. He acknowledges translation's imperfectability and defends its necessity in his philosophy of communication.

At the beginning of chapter 5 of *Experience and Nature,* Dewey introduces the sacrament of transubstantiation as a benchmark for our thinking about communication, writing: "Of all affairs, communication is the most wonderful. That things should be able to pass from the plane of external pushing and pulling to that of revealing themselves to man, and thereby to themselves; and that the fruit of communication should be participation, sharing, is a wonder by the side of which transubstantiation pales."[37] In other words, for Dewey, communication is analogous to and yet even more miraculous than transubstantiation; it is, he explains, "ultimately worthy of awe, admiration and loyal appreciation."[38]

Transubstantiation and communication both involve conversion. Transubstantiation converts the wine and bread into the blood and body of Christ and language converts existence into experience. The "signs and symbols" that are the means of communication—"gestures, pictures, monuments, visual images, finger movements"—do not simply represent the elements of experience; rather, they *create* experience by converting the senseless push and pull of qualitative immediacies into meanings or objects of thought.[39] The conversion of existence into experience is a form of communion because meanings or objects of thought can be shared. According to Dewey, "events cannot be passed from one to another, but meanings may be shared by means of signs."[40]

The view that meanings, and not events, are shared might appear counterintuitive in the face of our commonsense belief that language describes, and therefore comes *after*, shared human events. Indeed, it can sometimes seem that language actually impedes individuals' ability to share an event. According to Dewey, however, these events cannot be shared because they cannot be thought; they exist on "the plane of external pushing and pulling."[41] Although sensory immediacies can be qualitatively differentiated, they remain "dumbly rapturous,"[42] and to be without language is to be submerged in a "rapid and roaring stream of events."[43] Only language transforms this senseless flow into experiences, parsing its contents into objects of thought or, alternatively, things with meaning. As the objects of thought, these contents "become capable of survey, contemplation, and ideal or logical elaboration."[44] Thus, contrary to the aforementioned commonsense belief, it is not that our "conceptual capacities are exercised on non-conceptual deliverances of sensibility," but rather, as John McDowell argues, that "conceptual capacities are already operative in the deliverances of sensibility themselves."[45]

Just as language is instrumental for the organization and actualization of human experience, communication is instrumental for all forms of human engagement, ranging from the mundane to the accomplished. But communication is also, to use Dewey's term, "final," that is to say, it is "a sharing whereby meanings are enhanced, deepened, and solidified in the sense of communion."[46] This sense of communion holds an "intrinsic delight" or "inhering fascination" for us.[47] We feel momentarily "detached from immediate instrumental consequences of assistance and cooperative action."[48] As something that we undergo, this "conjoint communicated experience" feels like an act of grace, inspiring incomprehension and gratitude.[49] Unlike transubstantiation, the sacrament of communication is not the exclusive preserve of ordained priests. It is a gift that excludes no one. Dewey's deep democratic impulse is reflected in his identification that something as universal *and* as commonplace as communication redeems us through communion.

Dewey cautions, however, against "separating [the] instrumental and final functions" of communication.[50] Communication can and should, he argues, be used instrumentally to establish common purposes and cooperative activities,[51] but there is a danger of focusing exclusively on the instrumental function of communication, namely that it reinforces the erroneous view that the grammar that governs what we mean is fixed and transparent. As individuals are far too limited with respect to the scope and variety of their cooperative activities, they must rely on the final function of communication to expand and enhance their shared meanings.[52] Focusing exclusively on the final function of communication, however, is "luxurious and corrupting for some; [and] brutal, trivial, harsh for others."[53] The aim, then, is to achieve a rhythmic balance between the two functions.

Dewey defines rhythm as the "ordered variation of changes," or "rationality among qualities."[54] He conceives of it as the "universal scheme of existence, underlying all realization of order in change," apparent in the changing seasons, the diurnal transition from day to night and then day, the alternation between undergoing and acting, and the life cycle from birth to death.[55] Rhythm divides existence into measures that allow for variation in intensity: "Certain forms grow strong against the weaker forms."[56] For this reason, he sees modulation—that is, knowing where to put the emphasis and for how long—as the chief problem of life. If there is "order, rhythm and balance," then it "means that energies significant for experience are acting at their best."[57]

Dewey's account of rhythm highlights that human interactions do not always move from disequilibrium toward equilibrium, and communication need not always resolve misunderstanding and achieve consensus. While most of the time we assume a common background—"it is silently sup-plied and im-plied as the taken-for granted medium" of exchange—were we to inspect it we would find impasses and ruptures.[58] We derive meanings from experience. Given that "experience is not a rigid and closed thing; it is vital and hence growing,"[59] it is impossible to predict the "increment of meaning" that will be left as its intellectual deposit.[60]

Dewey considers the child's acquisition of language to be illustrative of the inevitability and uncertainty of the meaning-making process. He cites an example of the child who begins with whatever significance he can get out of his interactions with the family dog. This shapes his expectations and behavior, as he eagerly tries to apply the concept with each new experience. The concept (in this case, "dog") becomes, according to Dewey, "a working tool of further apprehensions, an instrument of understanding other things."[61] Dewey's boy anticipates that the next "dog"—which turns out to be a horse—will be furry, friendly, four-legged, and brown. He is capable of revising his understanding in light of this new experience because he is acutely aware that his concepts are nothing more than hypotheses. For this reason, they are "always open to development through use."[62] Dewey concludes that "[in] learning to understand and make words, children learn more than the words themselves: they gain a habit that opens a new world to them."[63] It is a habit of conceptual malleability in which the indefiniteness of meaning is enacted with every new experience.

As individuals age and their lives become more settled, however, their eagerness to be estranged from their own worlds with a view to discovering new ones diminishes. This state of affairs is unsurprising, given that adults are subject to the tyranny of habit. This leads to another reason for the inevitably jagged character of the common background. For although adults may live as if their meanings were stable and satisfactorily given, experience teaches otherwise. There is simply no limit to the "emancipation and enlargement of experience."[64] As Dewey explains, "experience may welcome and assimilate all that the most exact penetrating thought discovers."[65] Even the most mundane objects, activities, and relationships can be seen in a fresh light, opening "new vistas of experience."[66] Abstract thought is our ability to imaginatively move the mind from the familiar toward the unfamiliar, and through this process of defamiliarization it brings the background into view. In this sense, the unfamiliar, which is the source of our misunderstandings, is as foundational to thought and communication as the familiar: it not only illuminates each individual's conceptual background but also alters its topography. Thus while a certain standardization and stability of meaning is necessary, deep differences in experience and understanding remain.

Thus, Dewey argues, individuals must not allow their utterances to proceed "on a superficial and trivial plane" by assuming that all meanings are *concrete* or, alternatively, wholly and satisfactorily given.[67] Such an assumption reveals an orientation unreflectively "dominated by the past, by custom and routine."[68] Dewey acknowledges that meanings are inevitably fixed "*by the demands of practical life,*" compelling individuals to behave in an environment as if it were comprised of such fixed entities as clothes, houses, yards, meals, schools, and trains.[69] It is for practical reasons that individuals grasp the popular meanings of words. Much of the time, our thinking and conversations go "within the limits of what is implied or understood"[70] and the demands of practical life make it imbecilic to "dig up" and formulate the common background that we take for granted in our communications.

Yet, the vagaries of language make us vulnerable "to mis-apprehension, mis-understanding, and mis-taking," and result in occasions on which individuals are called upon to inspect and examine that taken-for-granted common background.[71] In an effort to discover the root of the misunderstanding, individuals must expose "what was unconsciously assumed" to the light of day.[72] Glück's poem "Averno" illustrates this kind of misunderstanding. The dying narrator's children have forgotten that communication is participatory, that is, it requires individuals to continually reestablish what is "made common in at least two different centers of behavior."[73] Meaning is never wholly in the mind, but unfolds *in* and *with* the world. The children think "they know the outcome" of aging and death.[74] Yet, they fail to realize that the aspects of aging and death that they take as given—senility, filial responsibility, healthcare, insurance, and funeral services—reveal the concretization of meanings that have had the "strange and troublesome corners . . . rubbed off."[75] The father attempts to reintroduce those "strange and troublesome corners" by engaging his children in conversation.

Speaking a language is an endlessly creative task; there is no limit to the meanings that humans can make and share.[76] As Murdoch points out, it is "something progressive, something infinitely perfectible."[77] Here, in different terminology, Murdoch echoes Dewey's view that meanings are "purely relative to the intellectual progress of an individual; what is abstract at one period of growth is concrete at another; or even the contrary, as one finds that things supposed to be thoroughly familiar involve strange factors and unsolved problems."[78] There are no rules, however, for balancing the concrete and the abstract, the instrumental and the final. There are no guidelines for when to familiarize the strange or to destabilize the familiar. It ultimately comes down to the "disposition and tact of the individual in the particular case."[79] The finer the balance between these elements, the deeper our mutual understanding, and the fuller our participation in life. Dewey writes that "[v]arious phases of participation by one in another's joys, sorrows, sentiments and purposes, are distinguished by the scope and depth of the objects that are held in common, from a momentary caress to continued insight and loyalty."[80] Thus, he concludes that it is by means of understanding the common things—"a flower, a gleam of moonlight, the song of a bird"—that our "lives reach a deeper level."[81]

Full and complete meaning eludes us, just as full and complete mutual understanding eludes us. As humans, we do not know all there is to know about being human. Rather than "move beyond" our ordinarily practical lives, Dewey directs us to something we already know: By engaging more fully in life we widen our acquaintance with persons, practices, and things.[82] Such a broadening of our acquaintance uniquely enables us to discover new and unforeseen possibilities, deepen our conceptual understandings, and increase the reach of our responsibility. The more deeply an individual understands a concept, the greater his or her capacity to appreciate its significance in others' lives. To recognize the truth of this we only need to recall Glück's poem. Had the grown-up children Glück describes been willing to suspend their concrete meanings long enough to complicate and deepen them by means of a conversation with their father, they might have been able to understand him. This would have raised profound and difficult questions about how they should live. Transcendence and mystery are not absent from Dewey's philosophy. Quite the opposite: these ideas are ubiquitous in his thought and ultimately bound up with what he takes to be the most fundamental aspects of language and communication.

CONCLUSION: CONDITIONS OF IMPOSSIBILITY IN DEWEY'S THOUGHT

Many read Dewey as prioritizing conjoint human activity and valuing communication as simply an important means by which to achieve that end. I have argued that he inverts this means-end relationship, suggesting that Dewey sees *communion* as humanity's ultimate priority, and considers conjoint human activity, and the communication it involves, as an invaluable way to initiate, problematize, and effect such communion. The view that communion and communication are more fundamental than activity and ends-fulfillment originates in Dewey's anthropological outlook. He writes: "We are made for conversation with our kind. When we are not urged into talk by the necessities of mutual dependence and assistance, we are brought to it by an inner push: communicate and share in the communications of others we must."[83] Dewey thinks individuals have no choice but to communicate, and consequently he is concerned that so many of us "do so much and say so little."[84] More to the point, he worries that we conceive of conversation as yet one more activity.

There is a qualitative difference between activity and communication, however, that Dewey highlights in the following passage:

> Thinking about events and celebrating them in tone and color and form might become more important than being an event. It is even possible that temporary abstinence from the course of events for the sake of conversing about them might moderate their violence, and by tempering power render it more stable. And then when the great change in the event does come, you and your children will be infinitely more prepared for it. For you will have developed a frame of mind which gives meaning to things that happen; and to find a meaning, to understand along with others, is always a contentment, an enjoyment. Events that have no attributed meanings are accidents and if they are big enough are catastrophes. By sufficient preliminary conversation you can avert a catastrophe. For nothing is a catastrophe which belongs in a composed tale of meanings.[85]

This passage could be read as endorsing overtly pragmatist themes: Dewey argues that our reason for thinking, and for engaging in conversation, is to achieve greater control over life's events. He claims that we avert catastrophes by being able to account for them. In other words, we minimize the occurrence of accidents by attributing meaning to the things that happen. Such a reading fails, however, to grasp the import of Dewey's philosophy of communication, an import that is made plainer when his philosophy is read in light of what I have argued, and different dimensions come into view.

In the passage above, Dewey refrains from making categorical assertions. He simply observes that thinking about events "might become more important" than participating in them or, to use his words, "being an event." He characterizes thinking as "celebrating [events] in tone and color and form." Here, he conceives of thinking as poetic rather than strategic: The aim is to describe the event in terms of its felt impact. The stress is on the aesthetic dimension of the experience. Dewey believes that such thinking occurs in conversation. Undoubtedly, an effect of such conversations is to render our world more stable and predictable, such that potential catastrophes become mere accidents. This allows us to minimize life's disruptive forces. Dewey also emphasizes that these conversations develop "a frame of mind which gives meaning to things that happen." Developing such a frame of mind is no small achievement because to "find a meaning" is to "understand along with others." It entails consonance, conjointness, and cooperation.

To converse, according to Dewey, is to speak and listen, to gesture and respond to gestures, as well as to read and write. Dewey does not privilege writing as Cavell does, but this is not because he considers it an indulgence—we only need to consider the thirty-seven volumes of Dewey's collected works.[86] Dewey does not distinguish reading and writing from speaking and listening; they are all valuable means of thought and communication. They contribute to "a frame of mind which gives meaning to things that happen" by simultaneously renewing our linguistic conventions and expanding upon them. Dewey read widely, traveled abroad, and wrote extensively in an effort to be in perpetual conversation with diverse others. While he knew that this conversation could be demanding—requiring interlingual and intralingual translation—he relished the profound feelings of contentment and joy that accompanied the fellow feeling associated with finding meanings and understanding others.

Dewey accounts for the feelings of contentment and joy with reference to our deep need to "communicate and share in the communications of others." Thinking, which involves conversation, is deeply fulfilling for human beings. To quote Phillip W. Jackson, Dewey considers it "the consummate act of human freedom."[87] To live *is* to live in community with others; to live in community with others *is* to inhabit "a composed tale of meanings." Dewey's point is not that individuals inevitably cast identity in some narrative form; rather, the tale we tell is composed of meanings. Meanings are shared. An expansion of meanings entails an expanded and reorganized composition of the tale. Here, Dewey focuses on the fact that our understanding of the human condition—the tale that we tell about ourselves—alters according to whom we admit as being one of us and under what terms we admit them.

In this context, a tale is composed in two senses. It gets created through the combination of meanings. It also facilitates composure: Feelings are less brute, overwhelming, and erratic. A person need not repress potentially dangerous or disruptive feelings in order to appear poised. Even dangerous feelings can be engaged intelligently if their source, nature, and significance are properly understood. Dewey suggests that we think about events in an effort to avoid violent upheaval, tragic misfortune, debilitating catastrophe, and traumatic disaster. This extends far beyond the solving of immediate problems; it is thinking about events so that life might be made more humane for all living creatures. Dewey is calling for justice on a global scale—it is a call that has gone largely unheeded.

This lengthy passage sits somewhat at odds with Dewey's proclivity for pragmatist-inspired problem-solving. Although it is "buried deep within his lengthy corpus of writings,"[88] David Hansen gives it significance. He reads it "as a call to accept fully the possibilities of communication, and thus of meaning, and thus of *coming into life* rather than settling for mere existence."[89] I build upon this and read Dewey as negating the "primacy of practice," which raises a question about his pragmatism.[90] Cavell argues that Emerson's negation of the primacy of practice is what distinguishes him from Dewey.[91] Recasting Emerson as a perfectionist in this way, Cavell squarely situates Dewey on the other side of the practical divide: as a pragmatist. Unlike Cavell, I am not willing to situate Dewey so squarely and definitively on either side of this proposed philosophical divide, though I am undecided over whether Dewey is less a pragmatist or whether "the limits of pragmatism are not nearly as narrow as critics and even defenders suppose," as Vincent Colapietro asserts.[92] While I agree with Colapietro that "[to] read Dewey reductively as a pragmatist or instrumentalist is to miss more than half of his meaning," and that "to read him in this manner means failing to hear *his* distinctive voice," I am concerned about the consequence of dividing philosophy into schools of thought.[93]

Dewey worried about this also. He knew that the meanings of texts are not transparent. Their lack of transparency compels individuals to impute meaning to them by calling to mind more familiar words and ideas and then tracing out connections to the text. As readers, we cannot avoid drawing upon received understanding, such as our knowledge of established philosophical schools of thought, in order to make sense of the text. All reading and speaking requires an effort at intralingual translation. For this reason, we can never be sure we have heard the philosopher's distinctive voice.

While I read Dewey against a post-Wittgensteinian background—having encountered pragmatism relatively recently, following my immigration to the

United States in 2000—there are historical precedents for such an ordinary language approach in the writings of such American philosophers as Richard Rorty and Richard J. Bernstein.[94] Although I am not in a position to resolve this debate regarding the character of pragmatism, my reading of Dewey's writings on communication goes some way to proving Dewey's point. If language is participatory in the sense that meaning must be made common in at least two individuals, then the substance of Dewey's philosophy is rediscovered each time someone tries to make sense of it anew. The meaning of Dewey's philosophy is not merely the sum of all past imputed meanings, because it is internal to the nature of human experience that there are meanings yet to be found. Indeed, each reading of his work, he would argue, is an act of intralingual translation, and as such it involves the recognition, internal to the nature of meaning, that we always enlist concepts that transcend our current and future understanding of them. For Dewey, and for me, this situation is an occasion neither for despair nor for despondency, but for hope.

NOTES

I would like to thank my research assistant Tomas Rocha for all of his time and effort, the contributors to this volume for their sympathetic criticism, and Diana Barnes, Rachel Longa, Naoko Saito, and Paul Standish for their comments on an earlier draft.

1. Stanley Cavell, *The Claim of Reason: Wittgenstein, Skepticism, Morality and Tragedy* (New York and Oxford: Oxford University Press, 1979), 122.

2. See Naoko Saito, "Philosophy as Education and Education as Philosophy: Democracy and Education from Dewey to Cavell," *Journal of Philosophy of Education* 40, no. 3 (2006): 347–48; Paul Standish and Naoko Saito, "Introduction," in *Stanley Cavell and the Education of Grownups*, ed. Naoko Saito and Paul Standish (New York: Fordham University Press, 2012), 1–18; Richard Shusterman, "Putnam and Cavell on the Ethics of Democracy," *Political Theory* 25 no. 2 (1997), 193–214.

3. Standish and Saito, "Introduction," in *Stanley Cavell and the Education of Grownups*, 6.

4. Hilary Putnam, "Philosophy as the Education of Grownups—Stanley Cavell and Skepticism," in *Reading Cavell*, ed. Alice Crary and Sanford Shieh (London and New York: Routledge, 2006), 119–30.

5. Stephen Mulhall, *Stanley Cavell: Philosophy's Recounting of the Ordinary* (Oxford: Clarendon Press, 1994), 68. Cited in Richard Eldridge, ed., *Stanley Cavell* (Cambridge: Cambridge University Press, 2003), 4.

6. Cavell, *The Claim of Reason*, 31. Cited in Duck-Joo Kwak, "Skepticism and Education: In Search of Another Filial Tie of Philosophy and Education," *Educational Philosophy and Theory* 44 no. 5 (2012): 539.

7. Cavell, *The Claim of Reason*, 31.

8. Saito, "Philosophy as Education and Education as Philosophy," 351.

9. Stanley Cavell, *In Quest of the Ordinary: Lines of Skepticism and Romanticism* (Chicago and London: University of Chicago Press, 1988), 9. Cited in Eldridge, "Cavell on American Philosophy and the Idea of America," in *Stanley Cavell*, 180.

10. See Bernard Williams, "Saint-Just's Illusion," in *Making Sense of Humanity and Other Philosophical Papers 1982–1993* (Cambridge: Cambridge University Press, 1995), 135–50.

11. John Dewey, *Democracy and Education*, in *The Middle Works of John Dewey, 1899–1924*, 15 vols., electronic edition, ed. Larry Hickman (Carbondale and Edwardsville: Southern Illinois University Press, 2008), 9: 367.

12. Eldridge, "Cavell on American Philosophy and the Idea of America," 174.

13. See Stanley Cavell, *The Senses of Walden* (Chicago: University of Chicago Press, 1992); *In Quest of the Ordinary*; *The New Yet Unapproachable America: Lectures after Emerson after Wittgenstein* (Chicago: University of Chicago Press, 1988); *Conditions Handsome and Unhandsome: The Constitution of Emersonian Perfectionism* (Chicago: Chicago University Press, 1990).

14. Saito, "Philosophy as Education and Education as Philosophy," 351.

15. Fergus Kerr, *Immortal Longings: Versions of Transcending Humanity* (Notre Dame, IN: University of Notre Dame, 1997), 121.

16. Eldridge, "Cavell on American Philosophy and the Idea of America," 174.

17. Stanley Cavell, *A Pitch for Philosophy: Autobiographical Exercises* (Cambridge, MA; Harvard University Press, 1994), 4.

18. Eldridge, "Cavell on American Philosophy and the Idea of America," 180.

19. Naoko Saito, "Philosophy as Education and Education as Philosophy: Democracy and Education from Dewey to Cavell," *Journal of Philosophy of Education* 40 no. 3 (2006), 354.

20. Saito, "Philosophy as Education and Education as Philosophy," 354.

21. Cavell, *Conditions Handsome and Unhandsome*, 13.

22. John Dewey, *Experience and Nature*, in *The Later Works of John Dewey, 1925–1953*, 17 vols., electronic edition, ed. Larry Hickman (Carbondale and Edwardsville: Southern Illinois University Press, 2008), 1: 141.

23. I take the expression "guardians of meaning" from David T. Hansen's article "Creativity in Teaching and Building a Meaningful Life as a Teacher," *Journal of Aesthetic Education* 39 no. 2 (2005): 57–67.

24. For a selection of the literature in this field see Mona Baker, *Translation and Conflict: A Narrative Account* (London and New York: Routledge, 2006); Susan Basnett and Harish Trivedi, eds., *Post-Colonial Translation: Theory and Practice* (London and New York: Routledge, 1999); Michael Cronin, *Translation and Globalization* (London and New York: Routledge, 2003); Lisa Foran, ed., *Translation and Philosophy* (Oxford: Peter Lang, 2012); and Lawrence Venuti, ed., *The Translation Studies Reader* (London and New York: Routledge, 2000).

25. Venuti, *The Translation Studies Reader*, 5.

26. As with the later Wittgenstein, Dewey considers language to be in the service of communication and the creation of forms of life. See David A. Granger, *John Dewey, Robert Prisig, and the Art of Living: Revisioning Aesthetic Education* (London: Palgrave Macmillan, 2006), 20. Granger writes: "As noted earlier, Dewey's account of the structure and function of concepts is likewise compatible with Wittgenstein's. It also constitutes a rejection of the notion of fixed, a priori essences."

27. Iris Murdoch, *The Sovereignty of Good* (New York and London: Routledge, 1970), 33.

28. Ibid., 28.

29. Louise Glück, *Averno* (New York: Farrar, Straus and Giroux, 2006), 60.

30. Ibid.

31. Ibid., 61.

32. Ibid., 67.

33. Cora Diamond, "Losing Our Concepts," *Ethics* 98 (1988): 255–77.

34. See Stephen Mulhall, "Ethics in the Light of Wittgenstein," *Philosophical Papers* 31 no. 3 (November 2002): 316.

35. Dewey, *Democracy and Education,* in *Later Works,* 9: 9.

36. John Dewey's wife, Alice, wrote their children letters from China and Japan that were subsequently published. See Alice Dewey and John Dewey, *Letters from China and Japan* (Brazil: Griffo, 1920).

37. Dewey, *Experience and Nature*, in *Later Works*, 1: 132. The sacrament of transubstantiation, for those not familiar with Catholic theological doctrine, is the conversion of bread and wine into the body and blood of Jesus Christ or Eucharist, as it is sometimes referred to. The sacrament of transubstantiation is performed by an ordained clergy of the Church who consecrates the bread and wine, converting them into the body and blood of Jesus Christ. As there is no change in the outward appearance of the bread and wine, the conversion is considered to be metaphysical. Catholics consider the consecrated bread and wine sacred objects because Jesus Christ is literally present "in" them. The Eucharist is received and ingested by Catholic parish-

ioners in the form of Holy Communion. They participate in the original sacrifice of Jesus Christ's life for the forgiveness of our sins—his crucifixion and resurrection—by eating his body and blood in the form of bread and wine. As an act of divine grace, the sacrament of transubstantiation is mysterious—it happens without Catholics being able to give an account of how it happens—and inspires reverential piety.

38. Dewey, *Experience and Nature*, in *Later Works*, 1: 159.

39. Dewey, *How We Think*, in *Middle Works*, 6: 314.

40. Dewey, *The Public and Its Problems*, in *Later Works*, 2: 331.

41. Dewey, *Experience and Nature*, in *Later Works*, 1: 132.

42. Ibid. Thus, Dewey writes that "even the dumb pang of an ache achieves a significant existence when it can be designated and descanted upon; it ceases to be merely oppressive and becomes important; it gains importance, because it becomes representative; it has the dignity of an office" (1: 133).

43. Ibid., 1: 132.

44. Ibid., 1: 133.

45. John McDowell, *Mind and World* (Cambridge, MA: Harvard University Press, 1996), 39.

46. Dewey, *Experience and Nature*, in *Later Works*, 1: 159.

47. Ibid., 1: 158.

48. Ibid.

49. David T. Hansen, "Dewey's Book of the Moral Self," in *John Dewey and Our Educational Prospect: A Critical Engagement with Dewey's "Democracy and Education,"* ed. David T. Hansen (Albany: State University of New York Press, 2006), 93.

50. Dewey, *Experience and Nature*, in *Later Works*, 1: 159. He writes: "When the instrumental and final functions of communication live together in experience, there exists an intelligence which is the method and reward of the common life, a society worthy to command affection, admiration, and loyalty" (1: 160).

51. Ibid., 1: 179.

52. Ibid., 1: 158–59. It is being able to share meaning that saves us from isolation and desolation. It is in this sense that Dewey refers to shared experience as "the greatest of human goods" (1: 157).

53. Ibid., 1: 160.

54. Dewey, *Art as Experience,* in *Later Works*, 10: 158, 174.

55. Ibid., 10: 154.

56. Ibid., 10: 159.

57. Ibid., 10: 189.

58. Dewey, *How We Think*, in *Middle Works*, 6: 348.

59. Ibid., 6: 301.

60. Ibid., 6: 239.

61. Ibid., 6: 281.

62. Dewey, *Reconstruction in Philosophy*, in *Middle Works*, 12: 163.

63. Dewey, *How We Think*, in *Later Works*, 8: 283.

64. Ibid., 8: 278.

65. Ibid., 8: 277.

66. Ibid., 8: 278.

67. Dewey, *The Public and its Problems*, in *Later Works,* 2: 349.

68. Dewey, *How We Think*, in *Middle Works,* 6: 301. Adopting different terminology, Dewey distinguishes the *empirical* attitude or orientation from an *experimental* attitude or orientation. He argues that the empirical attitude is unreflective whereas the experimental attitude is imaginatively oriented toward future possibilities.

69. Ibid., 6: 287.

70. Ibid., 6: 349.

71. Ibid., 6: 281. Dewey refers to vagueness as "the aboriginal logical sin" from which "most bad intellectual consequences" follow (6: 282).

72. Ibid., 6: 348.

73. Dewey, *Experience and Nature*, in *Later Works*, 1: 141.

74. Glück, *Averno*, 61.
75. Dewey, *How We Think*, in *Later Works*, 8: 295.
76. Dewey, *Experience and Nature*, in *Later Works*, 1: 141.
77. Murdoch, *The Sovereignty of Good*, 23.
78. Dewey, *How We Think*, in *Middle Works*, 6: 287.
79. Ibid., 6: 349.
80. Dewey, *Experience and Nature*, in *Later Works*, 1: 158.
81. Dewey, *The Public and its Problems*, in *Later Works*, 2: 349.
82. Dewey, *How We Think*, in *Middle Works*, 6: 316.
83. Dewey, *Events and Meanings*, in *Middle Works*, 13: 276.
84. Ibid., 13: 277.
85. Ibid., 13: 279.
86. Saito writes: "In the eyes of Deweyans, Cavell's emphasis on reading and writing may look like an indulgence in literary and, hence 'apolitical' activities." In "Philosophy as Education and Education as Philosophy," 348.
87. Phillip W. Jackson, "How We Think We Think," *Teachers College Record* 114, no. 2 (2012), accessed January 4, 2013, http://www.tcrecord.org.
88. David T. Hansen, "John Dewey's Call for Meaning," *Education and Culture* 20 (2004): 14.
89. Ibid.
90. Stanley Cavell, "What's the Use of Calling Emerson a Pragmatist?" in *The Revival of Pragmatism: New Essays on Social Thought, Law, and Culture*, ed. Morris Dickson (Durham, NC, and London: Duke University Press, 1998), 78.
91. Ibid.
92. Vincent Colapietro, "The Question of Voice and the Limits of Pragmatism: Emerson, Dewey and Cavell," *Metaphilosophy* 35 no. 1–2 (2004): 181.
93. Ibid., 187.
94. See the oeuvre of Richard Rorty, and Richard J. Bernstein's book, *The Pragmatic Turn* (Malden, MA: Polity, 2010).

BIBLIOGRAPHY

Baker, Mona. *Translation and Conflict: A Narrative Account*. London and New York: Routledge, 2006.
Basnett, Susan, and Trivedi, Harish, eds. *Post-Colonial Translation: Theory and Practice*. London and New York: Routledge, 1999.
Bates, Stanley. "Stanley Cavell and Ethics." In *Stanley Cavell*, edited by Richard Eldridge, 15–47. Cambridge: Cambridge University Press, 2003.
Bernstein, Richard, *The Pragmatic Turn*, Malden, MA: Polity, 2010.
Biesta, Gert. "Pragmatism as a Pedagogy of Communicative Action." *Studies in Philosophy and Education* 13 (1994–1995): 273–90.
———. "Of All Affairs, Communication Is the Most Wonderful: The Communicative Turn in Dewey's Democracy and Education." In *John Dewey and Our Educational Prospect: A Critical Engagement with Dewey's "Democracy and Education,"* edited by David T. Hansen, 23–38. Albany: State University of New York Press, 2006.
Cavell, Stanley. *The Claim of Reason: Wittgenstein, Skepticism, Morality and Tragedy*. New York and Oxford: Oxford University Press, 1979.
———. *In Quest of the Ordinary: Lines of Skepticism and Romanticism*. Chicago and London: University of Chicago Press, 1988.
———. *The New Yet Unapproachable America: Lectures after Emerson after Wittgenstein*. Chicago: University of Chicago Press, 1988.
———. *Conditions Handsome and Unhandsome: The Constitution of Emersonian Perfectionism*. Chicago: Chicago University Press, 1990.
———. *The Senses of Walden*. Chicago: University of Chicago Press, 1992.

————. *A Pitch for Philosophy: Autobiographical Exercises*. Cambridge, MA: Harvard University Press, 1994.

————. "What's the Use of Calling Emerson a Pragmatist?" In *The Revival of Pragmatism: New Essays on Social Thought, Law, and Culture*, edited by Morris Dickson, 72–82. Durham, NC, and London: Duke University Press, 1998.

Colapietro, Vincent. "The Question of Voice and the Limits of Pragmatism: Emerson, Dewey and Cavell." *Metaphilosophy* 35, no. 1/2 (2004): 179–201.

Cronin, M. *Translation and Globalization*. London and New York: Routledge, 2003.

Dewey, Alice, and John Dewey. *Letters from China and Japan*. Brazil: Griffo, 1920.

Dewey, John. *The Later Works of John Dewey, 1925–1953*. 17 vols. Electronic edition. Edited by Larry Hickman. Carbondale and Edwardsville: Southern Illinois University Press, 2008.

————. *The Middle Works of John Dewey, 1899–1924*. 15 vols. Electronic edition. Edited by Larry Hickman. Carbondale and Edwardsville: Southern Illinois University Press, 2008.

Diamond, Cora. "Losing Our Concepts," *Ethics* 98 (1988): 255–77.

Eldridge, Richard. "Cavell on American Philosophy and the Idea of America." In *Stanley Cavell*, edited by Richard Eldridge, 172–89. Cambridge: Cambridge University Press, 2003.

Foran, Lisa, ed. *Translation and Philosophy*. Oxford: Peter Lang, 2012.

Glück, Louise. *Averno*. New York: Farrar, Straus and Giroux, 2006.

Granger, David A. *John Dewey, Robert Prisig, and the Art of Living: Revisioning Aesthetic Education*. London: Palgrave MacMillan, 2006.

Hansen, David T. "John Dewey's Call for Meaning." *Education and Culture* 20 (2004): 7–24.

————. "Creativity in Teaching and Building a Meaningful Life as a Teacher," *Journal of Aesthetic Education* 39, no. 2 (2005): 57–67.

————. "Dewey's Book of the Moral Self." In *John Dewey and Our Educational Prospect: A Critical Engagement with Dewey's "Democracy and Education,"* edited by David T. Hansen, 165–88. Albany: State University of New York Press, 2006.

Jackson, Phillip W. "How We Think We Think." *Teachers College Record* 114, no. 2 (2012). Accessed January 4, 2013, http://www.tcrecord.org.

Jakobson, R. "On Linguistic Aspects of Translation." In *The Translation Studies Reader*, second edition, edited by Lawrence Venuti, 138–43. London and New York: Routledge, 2004.

Kerr, Fergus. *Immortal Longings: Versions of Transcending Humanity*. Notre Dame, IN: University of Notre Dame, 1997.

Kestenbaum, Victor. "Dewey Paideia and Turbulence." *The Pluralist* 8, no. 1 (2013): 13–30.

Kwak, Duck-Joo. "Skepticism and Education: In Search of Another Filial Tie of Philosophy and Education." *Educational Philosophy and Theory* 44, no. 5 (2012): 535–45.

Laverty, Megan J. "Music as an Apprenticeship for Life: John Dewey on the Art of Living." In *Art's Teaching and Teaching's Art: Philosophical, Critical and Educational Musings*, edited by Tyson E. Lewis and Megan J Laverty, 123–36. Dordrecht: Springer, 2015.

McDowell, John. *Mind and World*. Cambridge, MA: Harvard University Press, 1996.

Mulhall, Stephen. *Stanley Cavell: Philosophy's Recounting of the Ordinary*. Oxford: Clarendon Press, 1994.

————. "Ethics in the Light of Wittgenstein." *Philosophical Papers* 31, no. 3 (November 2002), 316.

Murdoch, Iris. *The Sovereignty of Good*. New York and London: Routledge, 1970.

Putnam, Hilary. "Philosophy as the Education of Grownups—Stanley Cavell and Skepticism." In *Reading Cavell*, edited by Alice Crary and Sanford Shieh, 119–30. London and New York: Routledge, 2006.

Saito, Naoko. "Philosophy as Education and Education as Philosophy: Democracy and Education from Dewey to Cavell." *Journal of Philosophy of Education* 40, no. 3 (2006): 345–56.

Saito, Naoko, and Paul Standish. "What is the Problem with Problem-Solving? Language, Skepticism, and Pragmatism." *Contemporary Pragmatism* 6, no. 1 (2009): 153–67.

Saito, Naoko, and Paul Standish, eds. *Stanley Cavell and the Education of Grownups*. New York: Fordham University Press, 2012.

Shusterman, Richard. "Putnam and Cavell on the Ethics of Democracy." *Political Theory* 25, no. 2 (1997), 193–214.

Venutia, Lawrence, ed. *The Translation Studies Reader*. London and New York: Routledge, 2000.

Williams, Bernard. "Saint-Just's Illusion." In *Making Sense of Humanity and Other Philosophical Papers 1982–1993*, 135–50. Cambridge: Cambridge University Press, 1995.

Chapter Nine

The Strange in the Familiar

Education's Encounter with Untranslatables

Claudia W. Ruitenberg

"Undergoing the experience of translation means experiencing the strange in the familiar," writes Naoko Saito in this volume. Translation, here, is seen as occurring not only between languages, but also within a language, and between and within human lives, more generally. Indeed, who does not recognize the experience of translation when seeking to understand another person's experience, even if that person speaks the same language? Or of looking for the words to describe a highly technical conversation at work to a friend who does not work in the same field? Or even of trying to understand one's own thoughts and decisions of twenty, thirty years ago? As Saito puts it, our lives "are always being translated, transformed, and transcended, . . . they are always on the way, with a rift within them never to be filled."

However, in the promise of translation as a concept to think about aspects of our lives far beyond language and linguistic difference, it can be easy to forget that linguistic translation, that seemingly obvious level of translation, still has much to offer us that is not so obvious at all. Education, as the field of my particular interest, is rife with linguistic translations, both of spoken words and of written texts. Educators and educational scholars face translation especially but not exclusively in culturally diverse contexts. In this chapter, I want to call attention to a particular aspect of linguistic translation that offers an experience of the strange in the familiar: encounters with untranslatables. Of course, untranslatables are interesting as linguistic phenomena, and problematic in the economic sense of wanting to get on with things, but my interest here is how untranslatables are beneficial for helping us think about things that are broader than the untranslatables themselves. I will highlight three areas that untranslatables can help us think about: (1) They underscore the inadequacy of the Platonic assumption, persistent in some analytic philosophy circles, that concepts are universal and independent of the words that represent them; (2) They help us recast the question of concept validity in intercultural qualitative research; (3) They add nuance and complexity to the rhetoric of internationalization and intercultural education. Before I turn to these three areas, however, let me say a few words about the concept of the untranslatable itself.

THE UNTRANSLATABLE

There is a longstanding debate among philosophers and translation scholars about whether or not there are words and phrases that are truly untranslatable, in the sense that they defy all efforts at translation into another language. On the one hand, we can observe in everyday communication that no word or phrase renders us entirely speechless when seeking to convey it in a different language. For basic communication we can often manage with what Paul Ricoeur calls the "construction of the comparable."[1] Jacques Derrida concurs:

> If you give someone who is competent an entire book, filled with translator's notes, in order to explain everything that a phrase of two or three words can mean in its particular form . . . there is really no reason, in principle, for him to fail to render—without any remainder—the intentions, meaning, denotations, connotations and semantic overdeterminations, the formal effects of what is called the original.[2]

However, the fact that some words and phrases require such extensive "translator's notes" suggests that there is a difficulty here, something that makes the reader's or listener's encounter with the translated text quite different from the reader's or listener's encounter with the text in its original language. For this reason, Ricoeur writes that "there remains a final untranslatable that we discover through the construction of the comparable."[3] This remainder is the gap between the *experience* of the text in its original language and the experience of the translated text. Derrida addresses the aesthetic qualities of this experience, noting that the book of translator's notes is "not what is called a translation, a translation worthy of the name" because, while it may convey the signified(s) of the words or phrases in one language, it spectacularly fails to convey the signifier(s).[4]

   In recent work literary scholar Emily Apter calls attention to "the importance of non-translation, mistranslation, incomparability, and untranslatability."[5] She does so in the context of a discussion of literary translations, especially in the field of "world literature." The desire to produce work that is intelligible to a particular audience can lead to a "tendency to zoom over the speed bumps of untranslatability in the rush to cover ground,"[6] not just in those working on literary texts but also in those working on philosophical or research texts. Such "speed bumps of untranslatability" are moments when a word or phrase in the source language forces the translator to pause because no immediately obvious equivalent exists in the target language. As Barbara Cassin puts it in her introduction to the *Dictionary of Untranslatables* (to which Sandra Laugier, also an author in this volume, contributed several entries), untranslatables are "symptoms" of the differences between languages, those words or phrases that "one keeps on (not) translating."[7]

Apter is critical of the assumption of translatability, which suggests that, with enough effort, everything is translatable; "untranslatability," on that view, is a technical problem to be solved. The problem with the assumption of translatability is that it is built on a presupposition of "oneworldedness,"[8] the idea that the world and people's experiences in that world are fundamentally unified, and that only the contingency of linguistic dispersion keeps us from understanding one another. Literary translator Edith Grossman demonstrates this presupposition of oneworldedness when she writes that "translation . . . dedicates itself to denying and negating the impact of divine punishment for the construction of the Tower of Babel, or at least to overcoming its worst divisive effects."[9] Grossman is referring to the biblical story of a united people with one language, who wanted to build a tower that would reach into heaven. In order to diminish their power and punish them for their hubris, the story suggests, God scattered people across the earth and made them speak different languages. Even if we do not believe that the existence of many languages is the result of divine punishment, the story illustrates that there is often a sense of regret at the difficulties of understanding and being understood across linguistic difference.

By contrast, the view I want to posit is that translation can be used not only to repair cultural and linguistic gaps but also to call attention to them.[10] The purpose, in that case, is not to overcome these cultural and linguistic gaps as efficiently as possible, but rather to dwell in them and see what they can teach us. I agree with Apter, then, when she posits the untranslatable "as a linguistic form of creative failure with homeopathic uses."[11] In other words, while too much untranslatability leads to the breakdown of communication, some untranslatability is salutary. The untranslatable both demands and defies translation and, in the process, forces us to think about our constant conscious and unconscious acts of translation and how these assist or hinder "words in their becoming philosophical."[12]

THE UNTRANSLATABLE IN EDUCATIONAL THEORY

I am by no means the first or the only one to discuss the concept of the untranslatable in educational theory. For example, Lovisa Bergdahl takes the concept of the untranslatable as discussed by Walter Benjamin and Jacques Derrida and uses it as a lens to consider the ethical double-bind in the educational encounter with an Other who is fundamentally inaccessible to me. The impossible demand "translate me, don't translate me," that Derrida discusses in relation to the proper name, also pertains to the encounter with an Other, in which we are faced with "two imperatives of understanding and [at the same time] respecting the untranslatable."[13] Bergdahl considers such educational encounters in contexts with cultural and, especially, religious diversity.

Naoko Saito has discussed how American philosophers' treatment of the untranslatable can help us think differently about the challenges of cosmopolitanism.[14] Like Bergdahl, Saito is interested in the existential implications of moments of untranslatability in encounters between people of different cultural backgrounds. However, different from Bergdahl—and closer to my interests in this paper—Saito keeps such encounters with cultural difference closely connected to the languages and texts that typically mediate such encounters. For example, she recounts not only how John Dewey's visit to Japan in 1919 "proved to be a test-case in which he was caught out by a real gap in cross-cultural communication" but also how, in this gap, the untranslatability of the English word "democracy" into Japanese played a role.[15] Saito takes up Stanley Cavell's perspective of "philosophy as translation"; like Apter's literary perspective that I described above, philosophy as translation focuses on the salutary effects of encounters with untranslatables. The particular cosmopolitan benefit Saito is interested in is unsettling the taken-for-grantedness and assumed internal unity of one's home culture and language:

> In encountering the untranslatable, our familiar use of the *native* language is returned to us; the criteria we have so far employed are tested. In such moments, we are reminded of the way that our relationship to our (allegedly) native culture is itself already burdened by tensions, conflict and separation.[16]

I experienced such an unsettled return of my native language when working on the concept of hospitality in English and realizing that the literal meaning, "guest freedom," of the Dutch word for "hospitality," *gastvrijheid*, had escaped me in the years I had used this word in everyday Dutch.

A third recent example of a philosopher of education who has addressed the vicissitudes of translation in education is Paul Standish, and I am thinking in particular of his discussion of "social justice" in translation. Standish notes that "social justice" is frequently used in English-language educational discussions today—in pedagogy and curriculum as well as in policy and theory—but that this expression does not have a single straightforward correlate in Chinese or Japanese. Because of "policy borrowing" and the cachet for non-native English speakers of using English (or at least "Globish")[17] terms, "when social justice is the topic of research in Japan, the katakana *sosharu jasutisu* is sometimes used instead of the authentic *shakai seigi*."[18] Standish does not discuss it in those terms, but surely "social justice" is an untranslatable as it requires translator's notes to identify and bridge the gap between the respective connotations of *sosharu jasutisu* and *shakai seigi*. Standish critiques the monolingualism that pushes policy terms such as "social justice" ever more deeply into international discourses, and calls for conversation in a sense of the word that honors a turning and reversal. The question, then, is not how we can make non-native English speakers understand "social justice" but rather to call attention to the complex genealogy that has made "social justice" in English what it is.

Acknowledging and building on this work in educational scholarship, I want to dwell at greater length in and on untranslatables in education because I believe they can give us a deeper insight into some of the concrete difficulties in educating and studying across *linguistic* boundaries that are sometimes papered over by other discourses of building intercultural understanding. By focusing on linguistic untranslatables I want to resist the tendency to think of language as just a surface layer, indeed too superficial to spend too much attention on, merely a practical obstacle to get to the more significant barriers that stand in the way of intercultural understanding and collaboration. Although Saito notes (in this volume) that Cavell's notion of philosophy as translation "shows that translation is not simply an interaction between different language systems," I would argue we should not abandon attention to the linguistic aspects of translation too quickly. Translation is not just a metaphor, metonym, or other trope, and untranslatables are important reminders of the significance of language and its inseparability from the larger systems of concepts, assumptions, and values with which we interpret the world. An example of this can be seen in Graham Parkes's discussion of the Japanese aesthetic term *iki*, approximated by "urbane, plucky stylishness."[19] The untranslatability and cultural specificity of this word has historically— and, according to Parkes, mistakenly—been intertwined with the attribution of nationalism to Japanese thinkers of the Kyoto School.

THE LINGUISTIC INDEPENDENCE OF CONCEPTS

Let me turn now to the first area that I mentioned the untranslatable can help us think about: the Platonic assumption in some analytic philosophy of education that concepts are universal and independent of the words that represent them. Cassin describes this assumption as follows: "For a certain tendency in 'analytic philosophy' . . . philosophy relates only to a universal logic, identical in all times and all places. . . . Consequently, the language in which the concept finds its expression, in this case English, matters little."[20] The idea is that concepts are "out there" like Platonic forms that remain unaffected by the linguistic tools we use to handle them. This idea has influenced not just analytic philosophy in general, but also analytic philosophy of education. In reference to the work of the British philosophers of education R. S. Peters and Paul Hirst, Christopher Winch observes sharply: "Analytical philosophy of education, as it was practised in the 1950s and 1960s, sought to provide a universal conceptual analysis of *education* and related concepts by an examination of the way in which those concepts were employed within the English language of the time."[21] The sharpness of this observation lies in Winch's pinpointing the fact that analytic philosophers of that era claimed to conduct analyses of concepts that were held to be universal and transcendental, even though access to these concepts was channeled through the particularity of the English language. These philosophers of education were, apparently, unperturbed by the possibility that their use of the English language might give them some (culturally mediated) access to certain concepts, but got seriously in the way of access to other concepts that were not employed in the English language. In a footnote, Winch confirms: "Peters and Hirst make few references to languages other than English, with the exceptions of Greek and Latin."[22]

Peters and Hirst were likely the best-known proponents of the view that concepts could be considered as concepts, independent of the particular words a given language uses to refer to them, but they are not the only ones. More recently, Robin Barrow has reaffirmed his belief in both the possibility and necessity of analyzing concepts as such:

> An account of education, if it is really an account of what loosely we refer to as education, as opposed to an account of what we refer to as marriage or beauty, must be an account of something to do with the business of acquiring knowledge. Because it is a fact that that is broadly what the term means in the English language.[23]

Barrow indicates here that, in order for English speakers not to descend into complete incomprehensibility, any use of the word "education" must maintain reference to the concept "education," and this concept, whatever else it involves, minimally involves "the business of acquiring knowledge." It is interesting that, in distinguishing education from other concepts, Barrow chooses the English words "marriage" and "beauty" rather than, say, the German *Bildung* and the Dutch *vorming*, both of which are imperfect translations to and from the English "education." When Barrow writes that "that is broadly what the term means in the English language," he is referring to the meaning of the word in a particular language, not the essence of the concept. The difficulty is, of course, that if the English word "education" is a perfect match for the concept education but an imperfect match for the concept *Bildung*, and the German word *Bildung* is a perfect match for the concept *Bildung* but an imperfect match for the concept "education," and so forth, then it shows the thesis of the universality and linguistic independence of concepts—or what Cassin calls "a logical universalism indifferent to languages"[24]—to be rather tenuous.

Contra this logical universalism, then, I believe that it is worth attending to the "conceptual differences carried by the differences between languages,"[25] and that untranslatables force us to think about such conceptual differences. It so happens that "education" itself, and many words related to it, provides a nice example of an untranslatable that enters us into a realm of conceptual differences. Gert Biesta observes that "the word 'education' cannot be translated unambiguously with another word in, say, German or Dutch. In those languages there are conceptual distinctions—such as, in German, between *Erziehung*, *Unterricht* and *Bildung* or, in Dutch, between *opvoeding*, *onderwijs* [and] *vorming*—that cannot be easily translated into English."[26] This was quite clear when, in one of my graduate seminars, we discussed the German philosopher Hannah Arendt's essay "*Die Krise in der Erziehung*" using the English translation "The Crisis in Education." The graduate seminar included students from China, Latin America, the Middle East, and Canada. While the question raised in the essay, of the extent to which adults should predetermine children's future, is relevant in all contexts, the German term *Erziehung* raised significant challenges. Not only is there no direct, unproblematic English translation for *Erziehung*, the fact that English was an additional language for several of the students, who also sought a translation in their mother tongues of Mandarin, Spanish, Farsi, and so forth, compounded the challenge. How to make sense of the claim, in the English translation, "Since one cannot educate adults, . . ."[27] without attending to the gap between this translation and the German "*Da man Erwachsene nicht erziehen kann*"?[28] As Stefan Ramaekers and Judith Suissa point out: "The English translation of *Erziehung* as *education* might be slightly misleading if 'education' is taken in a narrow sense, i.e. as pertaining to the formal processes of education as schooling. However, *Erziehung* first and foremost applies to those informal processes, mostly within the family, by which parents bring up their children."[29] In English the claim that "one cannot educate adults" is quite contentious, especially in a university context that includes programs in "Adult Education," but the claim "*Da man Erwachsene nicht erziehen kann*" is less contentious. Taking the time to attend to this untranslatable, the conversation can turn to the larger constellations of assumptions that have revolved around educational practices in different places and at different times.

I should add that encountering an untranslatable like *Erziehung* is not the exception but the rule; it is rare to study a text that does not involve at least one untranslatable germane to the text's core argument, hence at least one concept of which the various shifts and slippages involved in translation are worth attending to. I agree with Cassin that "the universality of concepts is absorbed by the singularity of languages."[30] As a consequence, the singularity of the languages in which we conduct philosophy of education matters a great deal and should, itself, be the object of substantive philosophical inquiry.

Of course, it is not some novel phenomenon that many texts and concepts are encountered in translation. Rather, it is the nature of texts and concepts to travel, not to stay confined to their linguistic field (permeable as the boundaries of this field already are), regardless of the intentions of the author. When the translations return to the author, some may have undergone significant transformation. An example of this is the uptake in American philosophy and literary theory of Derrida's *deconstruction*. Roger Bell comments: "Cavell might have recognized the different registers of language through which Derrida constantly would hear his voice thrown, that ventriloquism. Derrida's deconstruction must be understood in its translation to especially American English."[31] When scholars in the United States speak of "Derrida's deconstruction," then, it is less clear whose deconstruction they are referring to, despite the appearance of a stable anchor in the author's name.

THE VALIDITY OF CONCEPTS IN QUALITATIVE RESEARCH

The question of translation and of the linguistic specificity of key concepts has, in empirical research, sometimes cropped up as a concern with concept (or construct) validity. For example, Robert Vallerand et al. discuss both the translation of a research instrument and the validation of this translated instrument in its new linguistic environment. When translating the *Echelle de Motivation en Education* into the Academic Motivation Scale, they sought to assess whether the English instrument measured English speakers' intrinsic motivation, extrinsic motivation, and amotivation toward postsecondary studies as validly and reliably as did the French instrument with French speakers. They developed the English-language Academic Motivation Scale after a "parallel back-translation"[32] and subjected this instrument to several statistical analyses to conclude that "preliminary support exists for the reliability and some elements of validity of the AMS."[33] They note that further research is needed to understand the effects of gender, culture, age, and socioeconomic background.

Elizabeth Peña provides a richer perspective on the complexities of seeking construct validity in cross-cultural research, in her case in the area of child development. Peña recognizes that in the translation of research instruments and procedures, "linguistic equivalence" is not enough to ensure validity in research results; "functional equivalence, cultural equivalence and metric equivalence" all have to be taken into account as well. [34] For example, in tests assessing the development of communication in children of different cultural backgrounds, linguistic equivalence alone will not produce valid test results if the relative frequency and familiarity of translated vocabulary items is not taken into account.

While I appreciate that, in cognitive-behavioral research, the translation of key constructs and research instruments matters and would be improved by taking into account the multiple types of equivalence that Peña discusses, I want to suggest that untranslatables are not just threats to validity but beneficial in interlinguistic empirical educational research. Untranslatables offer an opportunity for empirical researchers to question and rethink the appropriateness of both the word and concept originally selected in a research question or theoretical framework. [35] It is worth noting, for example, that Vallerand and his team sought to translate from French into English languages that are quite closely related. But what if they had sought to translate the *Echelle de Motivation en Education* into a language from a different language family, such as Finnish, or Mandarin, or Cree? Might "motivation" itself or one of the other central concepts have shown up as an untranslatable that was not just a hurdle to the cross-cultural validation of the research instrument, but an opportunity to rethink the assumptions that informed that core concept?

Pedro Pitarch's work on the translation of the Universal Declaration of Human Rights into Tzeltal, the Mayan language spoken by approximately four hundred thousand people in the state of Chiapas, in southeast Mexico, illustrates this well. Pitarch is well aware that "between more distant languages and cultures, the linguistic translation implies an intercultural translation." He asks: "if the principles of human rights are deeply linked to modern occidental culture, how does a non-Western culture translate these concepts into its own vocabulary and categories of thought?" [36] Pitarch attends to the gaps that remain between the English "laws" and the Tzeltal *mantalil*, as well as between the English "rights" and the Tzeltal *ich'el ta muk*, and explains how several of the translational challenges stem from the social and reciprocal conception of personhood in Tzeltal, which is quite different from the more individual conception of personhood that underpins Western texts such as the Declaration of Human Rights.

While Pitarch himself does not describe an empirical research project, his observations are significant for empirical researchers investigating how human rights are or can be taught in different places around the world. The cultural specificity and therefore untranslatability of core concepts in the Declaration of Human Rights pose not just a threat to the validity of research results but also an opportunity for more fundamental reflections on the assumption that individuals are and should be the basic units to which rights accrue, and how this assumption affects educational practices.

In this discussion of how cultural gaps between different language families affect empirical educational research, let me revisit also Saito's discussion of the absence of a Japanese equivalent for "democracy" encountered by Dewey on his visit to Japan. It is my understanding that there are at least three Japanese translations for the English "democracy": *minshu-shugi* for democracy as set of principles, *minshu-sei* for democracy as form of governance, and *demokurashi*, a loan word from English (like *sosharu jasutisu*) that is mostly associated with the form of governance and social system during the reign of emperor Taisho (1912–1926).[37] What would this mean for educational researchers today who want to do a comparative study of, say, "education for democratic citizenship" in the United States and Japan? How can the research question be operationalized in each context so that some comparable is construed and so that, at the same time, the researchers benefit from the gaps in comparability to discuss the fundamental differences in cultural assumptions about "democratic citizenship"?

THE RHETORIC OF INTERNATIONALIZATION AND INTERCULTURAL EDUCATION

Let me attend to the third area in which I have mentioned encounters with untranslatables as salutary. Many universities today have declared the explicit aim of becoming more international and intercultural. University strategic plans show how internationalization and interculturalization are imagined. For example, the strategic plan *Place and Promise* of the university where I work, the University of British Columbia, contains sections on "International Engagement" and "Intercultural Understanding." In the latter, one of the strategic goals is to "increase awareness and experience of the benefits of intercultural learning and developing intercultural fluency."

The literature on internationalization and interculturalization in higher education acknowledges several challenges these processes pose.[38] For instance, true internationalization does not just mean the successful recruitment of more international students, who are then exposed to a curriculum with an unchanged national focus. Internationalization must also involve curriculum change, the recruitment of international faculty, and the encouragement of international learning opportunities for students and faculty through exchange programs or research collaborations. In other words, internationalization and interculturalization should amount not to the assimilation of international students and faculty into an unchanged university, but require genuine opportunities for two-way international encounters. Tellingly, UBC uses as the epigraph for the abovementioned section on International Engagement a line from the American writer Lillian Smith: "No journey carries one far unless, as it extends into the world around us, it goes an equal distance into the world within."

Discussions of the linguistic challenges that result from internationalization and interculturalization typically focus on English proficiency requirements for students coming to North America, and second-language requirements for English speaking students who go abroad for research, service learning, or other international experiences.[39] However, when universities seek to internationalize more deeply, for example through curriculum change and fostering international research partnerships, other linguistic and cultural challenges can arise that involve *conceptual* translation and encounters with untranslatables.

I do not believe universities have grappled well with what it means to educate linguistically diverse groups of students. The ways in which we educate should change not just in response to students not being fluent in the dominant language of the institution but in response to students bringing languaged ways of thinking that give them a different access to the texts we read together and the concepts we seek to understand together. Sometimes, we may need to work with a Mandarin-speaking student who is reading Paulo Freire's *Pedagogy of the Oppressed* in English and trying to make sense of the conceptual schema.[40] Sometimes we have a Portuguese-speaking student who challenges the English translation of *Pedagogy of the Oppressed* because the limitations of English reduce the evocations and connotations of the Portuguese original.[41]

The untranslatable I would like to dwell on here at greater length is one that is used in several professional higher education programs such as nursing and teacher education in the United States, United Kingdom, and Canada, and that is the word "care." Note that these universities generally have strategic plans that involve statements about internationalization and intercultural understanding like the one I cited earlier and that, on top of that, nursing and teaching are professions that see ethnic diversity in the profession as desirable (not least because of the ethnic diversity of patients and students) and as playing an important role in the recertification of internationally trained nurses and teachers. It is reasonable to assume, then, that in teacher education and nursing programs that discuss the ethics of care or even see the ethics of care as the guiding framework for the program, there will be students for whom English is a second or additional language.

At the panel *Noddings' Inferno* at the Philosophy of Education Society Conference 2014, the Russian philosopher of education Alexander Sidorkin raised the question of what happens to the difference between *caring for* and *caring about*, so significant in Nel Noddings's ethics of care, when translating these terms into Russian, in which the "caring" in "caring about" and in "caring for" would not take the same verb, and the noun "care" has multiple Russian correlates. In my mother tongue, I encounter a similar phenomenon: while "caring for" in Dutch is *zorgen voor*, the closest to "caring about" would be *bezorgd zijn om*, which would be more commonly translated in English as "being concerned about."

In the *Dictionary of Untranslatables*, Catherine Audard notes: "The word 'care' has recently been used with increasing frequency in English philosophy, but its translation into other languages raises a problem for two reasons in particular. First, it is used to translate the Heideggerian term *Sorge* . . . and second, it appears in the expression 'the ethics of care.' . . . In both cases, it is impossible to translate 'care' into French."[42] The English noun "care" corresponds to at least three common French nouns: *soin*, *souci*, and *sollicitude*, each of which is more specific than the single English noun "care." How have translators addressed this impossibility when faced with the concrete task of translating an English-language text on the ethics of care into French? Hervé Maury translates key terms in Joan Tronto's chapter on care[43] as follows:

- caring about: *se soucier de*
- taking care of: *se charger de*
- care giving/receiving: *accorder/recevoir des soins.*[44]

Even without delving more deeply into the etymologies and trajectories of use of the various words, it is obvious that a discussion in English alone of the distinctions and connections between caring for and caring about is going to be quite a different discussion from one that takes into account the untranslatability of "care."[45] Even in Noddings's own reconsideration of her initial sharp distinction between caring for and caring about, she does not—at least not explicitly and visibly—take into account the untranslatability of "care," nor does she (explicitly and visibly) benefit from the defamiliarization that would result from deliberate and repeatedly thwarted attempts at translating this discussion out of the familiarity of English: "In many cases, we simply cannot care for because of distance or limited resources. We make a step in the right direction by caring about. But when we do this, we should also follow up by finding out *whether our caring-about eventuates in actual caring-for*."[46] When educators and educational scholars discuss whether it is possible and desirable to educate young people or professionals such as teachers and nurses to be capable of and disposed toward establishing and maintaining "caring relations," it matters whether these are relations of *soin*, *souci*, or *sollicitude*. When we ask what it might mean to see caring-about "eventuate" in caring-for, how does this question change when it concerns the "eventuation" of *se soucier de* in *accorder des soins*?

CONCLUSION

In this chapter I have wanted to highlight some of the ways in which challenges of linguistic translation are significant in educational practices and policies, especially in culturally diverse contexts. More specifically, I have focused on untranslatables as linguistic phenomena or what Candace Barrington calls "nodal points of incommensurability,"[47] that can point to places where "speaking across linguistic and cultural differences," or "intercultural understanding," requires attending to deeper differences in worldviews and conceptual schemas. Untranslatables confront educational scholars with the cultural situatedness of what it is possible for us to think and argue, and demand that we pause before engaging in "cross-cultural" dialogue. While there are many untranslatables in educational philosophy worth thinking about as such (care, *Erziehung*, *Bildung*, social justice, democracy, etc.), the more general point I want to make is that these can and should prompt us to attend more carefully to the conceptual challenges of teaching and learning across multiple linguistic gaps. In educational settings we experience again and again that we cannot take for granted that we speak from a common ground, from some shared set of understandings not of highly technical terms but of concepts fundamental to the presuppositions of a text, or perhaps an entire course or program of studies. The particularities of language and the demands of linguistic translation are, on this view, not merely a superficial layer to pass through to get to the more significant concerns of educating persons across cultural differences. Instead, they are a layer worth dwelling in and attending to because language, translation, and untranslatables are inextricably connected with these cultural differences.

NOTES

1. Paul Ricoeur, *On Translation*, trans. Eileen Brennan (London: Routledge, 2006), 37.

2. Jacques Derrida, "What Is a 'Relevant' Translation?" trans. Lawrence Venuti, *Critical Inquiry* 27, no. 2 (2001): 179.

3. Ricoeur, *On Translation*, 38.

4. Derrida, "What Is a 'Relevant' Translation?" 179.

5. Emily Apter, *Against World Literature: On the Politics of Untranslatability* (London: Verso, 2013), 4. The remainder of this section borrows from the theoretical framework used in Claudia W. Ruitenberg, Autumn Knowlton, and Gang Li, "The Productive Difficulty of Untranslatables in Qualitative Research," *Language and Intercultural Communication* 16, no. 4 (2016): 610–26, doi:10.1080/14708477.2016.1189559.

6. Apter, *Against World Literature*, 3.

7. Barbara Cassin, "Introduction," trans. Michael Wood, in *Dictionary of Untranslatables: A Philosophical Lexicon*, ed. Barbara Cassin (Princeton: Princeton University Press, 2014), xvii.

8. Apter, *Against World Literature*, 8.

9. Edith Grossman, *Why Translation Matters* (New Haven, CT: Yale University Press, 2010), 17.

10. See also Claudia W. Ruitenberg, "Distance and Defamiliarisation: Translation as Philosophical Method," *Journal of Philosophy of Education* 43, no. 3 (2009): 421–35.

11. Apter, *Against World Literature*, 20.

12. Emily Apter, "Preface," in Cassin, ed., *Dictionary of Untranslatables*, viii.

13. Lovisa Bergdahl, "Lost in Translation: On the Untranslatable and Its Ethical Implications for Religious Pluralism," *Journal of Philosophy of Education* 43, no. 1 (2009): 38.

14. A 2014 symposium in the journal *Educational Theory* also takes up questions of cosmopolitanism in relation to translation.

15. Naoko Saito, "Is Thoreau More Cosmopolitan than Dewey?" *The Pluralist* 7, no. 3 (2012): 73.

16. Ibid., 83.

17. Cassin defines "Globish" as "a language of pure communication, which serves for ordering coffee from Tamanrasset to Peking and to make submissions to Brussels by proposing issues and deliverables in the framework of a programme of 'governance' in a knowledge-based economy": Barbara Cassin, "Untranslatables and Their Translations," trans. Andrew Goffey, *Transeuropéennes: Revue Internationale de Pensée Critique* (2009): 2–3. Standish comments, "It is English of this functional but culturally anodyne kind that has become the world language": Paul Standish, "Social Justice in Translation: Subjectivity, Identity, and Occidentalism," in *Educational Studies in Japan: International Yearbook, Vol. 6* (Tokyo: Japanese Educational Research Association, 2011), 73.

18. Ibid., 74. See also Tatsuru Akimoto, "Social Justice in an Era of Globalization: Must and Can It Be the Focus of Social Welfare Policies? Japan as a Case Study," in *The Routledge International Handbook of Social Justice*, ed. Michael Reisch (Abingdon, UK: Routledge, 2014), 48–60.

19. Graham Parkes, "The Definite Internationalism of the Kyoto School: Changing Attitudes in the Contemporary Academy," in *Repoliticising the Kyoto School as Philosophy*, ed. Christopher Goto-Jones (Abingdon, UK: Routledge, 2008), 166.

20. Cassin, "Introduction," xviii.

21. Christopher Winch, "On the Shoulders of Giants," in *Grey Wisdom? Philosophical Reflections on Conformity and Opposition Between Generations,* ed. Roel van Goor and Ernst Mulder (Amsterdam: Amsterdam University Press, 2006), 55.

22. Ibid.

23. Robin Barrow, "'Or What's a Heaven For?' The Importance of Aims in Education," in *The Aims of Education*, ed. Roger Marples (London: Routledge, 1999), 21.

24. Cassin, "Introduction," xix.

25. Peter Osborne cited in Apter, *Against World Literature,* 32.

26. Gert Biesta, "Philosophy of Education for the Public Good: Five Challenges and an Agenda," *Educational Philosophy and Theory* 44, no. 6 (2012): 592.

27. Hannah Arendt, "The Crisis in Education," in *Between Past and Future* (New York: Penguin, 1968), 177.

28. Hannah Arendt, "Die Krise in der Erziehung," in *Zwischen Vergangenheit und Zukunft: Übungen in Politisches Denken* (München: Piper, 1994), 258.

29. Stefan Ramaekers and Judith Suissa, *The Claims of Parenting: Reasons, Responsibility and Society* (Dordrecht, the Netherlands: Springer, 2012), 136.

30. Cassin, "Introduction," xix.

31. Roger V. Bell, *Sounding the Abyss: Readings Between Cavell and Derrida* (Lanham, MD: Lexington, 2004), 212–13.

32. "Back translation first involves translating the scale from the original to the target language by a bilingual individual. This translation is then translated back to the original language by another bilingual individual without the use of the original scale. . . . The parallel

back translation procedure necessitates the use of two independent back translation sequences": Robert J. Vallerand et al., "The Academic Motivation Scale: A Measure of Intrinsic, Extrinsic, and Amotivation in Education," *Educational and Psychological Measurement* 52, no. 4 (1992): 1009.

33. Ibid., 1016.

34. Elizabeth D. Peña, "Lost in Translation: Methodological Considerations in Cross-Cultural Research," *Child Development* 78, no. 4 (2007): 1256.

35. For more on the value of untranslatables for qualitative research, see Ruitenberg, Knowlton, and Li, "The Productive Difficulty of Untranslatables."

36. Pedro Pitarch, "The Labyrinth of Translation: A Tzeltal Version of the Universal Declaration of Human Rights," in *Human Rights in the Maya Region: Global Politics, Cultural Contentions, and Moral Engagements*, ed. Pedro Pitarch, Shannon Speed, and Xochitl L. Solano (Durham, NC: Duke University Press, 2008), 91.

37. Kiichi Tachibana, "Is Taisho Demokurashi the same as Taisho Democracy?" In *Japan's Multi-Layered Democracy*, ed. Sigal B. Galanti, Nissim Otmazgin, and Alon Levkowitz (Lanham, MD: Lexington, 2015).

38. See, for example, Fazal Rizvi, "Internationalization of Curriculum: A Critical Perspective," in *SAGE Handbook of Research in International Education*, ed. Mary Hayden, Jack Levy, and Jeff Thompson (London: SAGE, 2007), 390–403.

39. See, for example, Philip G. Altbach and Jane Knight, "The Internationalization of Higher Education: Motivations and Realities," *Journal of Studies in International Education* 11, no. 3–4 (2007).

40. Paulo Freire, *Pedagogy of the Oppressed*, trans. Myra Bergman Ramos (New York: Continuum, 2000).

41. Myra Bergman Ramos's English translation of the dedication at the beginning of the book reads: "To the oppressed, and to those who suffer with them and fight at their side." In the original Portuguese, this dedication reads: "*Aos esfarrapados do mundo e aos que neles se descobrem e, assim descobrindo-se, com eles sofrem, mas, sobretudo, com eles lutam.*" While elsewhere in the book Freire uses *oprimidos* (oppressed), in the dedication he uses *esfarrapados*, which means "tattered" or "ragged." There is a connection to Marx's (German) term *Lumpenproletariat*, which refers to the most downtrodden layer of the working class. The *Lumpen* in this term also means tattered or ragged clothing. I am indebted to David Romero for pointing out the gap between "oppressed" and *esfarrapados*.

42. Catherine Audard, "Care," trans. Steven Rendall, in Cassin, ed., *Dictionary of Untranslatables*, 125.

43. Joan C. Tronto, *Moral Boundaries: A Political Argument for an Ethic of Care* (New York: Routledge, 1993).

44. Joan C. Tronto, "Du Care," trans. Hervé Maury, *Revue Du MAUSS* 32, no. 2 (2008): 248–50.

45. When I say "English alone" it is not without an awareness of the impossibility of any language operating on its own; see Derrida, *Monolingualism of the Other or the Prosthesis of Origin*, trans. Patrick Mensah (Stanford, CA: Stanford University Press, 1998). Here I simply intend to mark the difference between a conversation about "care" in which languages other than English are at the forefront of interlocutors' consciousness, and one in which they remain, as it were, hidden in the shadows.

46. Nel Noddings, "Review of *Fruits of Sorrow: Framing Our Attention to Suffering* by Elizabeth V. Spelman," *Hypatia* 13, no. 2 (1998): 162–63, emphasis added.

47. Candace Barrington, "Traveling Chaucer: Comparative Translation and Cosmopolitan Humanism," *Educational Theory* 64 no. 5 (2014): 470.

BIBLIOGRAPHY

Akimoto, Tatsuru. "Social Justice in an Era of Globalization: Must and Can It Be the Focus of Social Welfare Policies? Japan as a Case Study." In *The Routledge International Handbook of Social Justice*, edited by Michael Reisch, 48–60. Abingdon, UK: Routledge, 2014.

Altbach, Philip G., and Jane Knight. "The Internationalization of Higher Education: Motivations and Realities." *Journal of Studies in International Education* 11, no. 3–4 (2007): 290–305.

Apter, Emily. *Against World Literature: On the Politics of Untranslatability*. London: Verso, 2013.

———. "Preface." In *Dictionary of Untranslatables: A Philosophical Lexicon*, edited by Barbara Cassin, vii–xv. Princeton, NJ: Princeton University Press, 2014.

Arendt, Hannah. "The Crisis in Education." In *Between Past and Future*, 173–96. New York: Penguin, 1968.

———. "Die Krise in der Erziehung." In *Zwischen Vergangenheit und Zukunft: Übungen in Politisches Denken*, 255–76. München, Germany: Piper, 1994.

Audard, Catherine. "Care," translated by Steven Rendall. In *Dictionary of Untranslatables: A Philosophical Lexicon*, edited by Barbara Cassin, 125–26. Princeton, NJ: Princeton University Press, 2014.

Barrington, Candace. "Traveling Chaucer: Comparative Translation and Cosmopolitan Humanism." *Educational Theory* 64, no. 5 (2014): 463–77.

Barrow, Robin. "'Or What's a Heaven For?' The Importance of Aims in Education." In *The Aims of Education*, edited by Roger Marples, 14–22. London: Routledge, 1999.

Bell, Roger V. *Sounding the Abyss: Readings Between Cavell and Derrida*. Lanham, MD: Lexington, 2004.

Bergdahl, Lovisa. "Lost in Translation: On the Untranslatable and Its Ethical Implications for Religious Pluralism." *Journal of Philosophy of Education* 43, no. 1 (2009): 21–44.

Biesta, Gert. "Philosophy of Education for the Public Good: Five Challenges and an Agenda." *Educational Philosophy and Theory* 44, no. 6 (2012): 581–93.

Cassin, Barbara. "Untranslatables and Their Translations," translated by Andrew Goffey. *Transeuropéennes: Revue Internationale de Pensée Critique* (2009). Retrieved from http://www.transeuropeennes.eu/en/articles/83.

———. "Introduction," translated by Michael Wood. In *Dictionary of Untranslatables: A Philosophical Lexicon*, edited by Barbara Cassin, xvii–xx. Princeton, NJ: Princeton University Press, 2014.

Derrida, Jacques. *Monolingualism of the Other or the Prosthesis of Origin*. Translated by Patrick Mensah. Stanford, CA: Stanford University Press, 1998.

———. "What Is a 'Relevant' Translation?" translated by Lawrence Venuti. *Critical Inquiry* 27, no. 2 (2001): 174–200.

Freire, Paulo. *Pedagogy of the Oppressed*. Translated by Myra Bergman Ramos. New York: Continuum, 2000.

Grossman, Edith. *Why Translation Matters*. New Haven, CT: Yale University Press, 2010.

Noddings, Nel. "Review of *Fruits of Sorrow: Framing Our Attention to Suffering* by Elizabeth V. Spelman." *Hypatia* 13, no. 2 (1998): 162–64.

Parkes, Graham. "The Definite Internationalism of the Kyoto School: Changing Attitudes in the Contemporary Academy." In *Repoliticising the Kyoto School as Philosophy*, edited by Christopher Goto-Jones, 161–82. Abingdon, UK: Routledge, 2008.

Peña, Elizabeth D. "Lost in Translation: Methodological Considerations in Cross-Cultural Research." *Child Development* 78, no. 4 (2007): 1255–64.

Pitarch, Pedro. "The Labyrinth of Translation: A Tzeltal Version of the Universal Declaration of Human Rights." In *Human Rights in the Maya Region: Global Politics, Cultural Contentions, and Moral Engagements*, edited by Pedro Pitarch, Shannon Speed, and Xochitl L. Solano, 91–121. Durham, NC: Duke University Press, 2008.

Ramaekers, Stefan, and Judith Suissa. *The Claims of Parenting: Reasons, Responsibility and Society*. Dordrecht, the Netherlands: Springer, 2012.

Ricoeur, Paul. *On Translation*. Translated by Eileen Brennan. London: Routledge, 2006.

Rizvi, Fazal. "Internationalization of Curriculum: A Critical Perspective." In *SAGE Handbook of Research in International Education*, edited by Mary Hayden, Jack Levy, and Jeff Thompson, 390–403. London: SAGE, 2007.

Ruitenberg, Claudia W. "Distance and Defamiliarisation: Translation as Philosophical Method." *Journal of Philosophy of Education* 43, no. 3 (2009): 421–35.

Ruitenberg, Claudia W., Autumn Knowlton, and Gang Li. "The Productive Difficulty of Untranslatables in Qualitative Research." *Language and Intercultural Communication* 16, no. 4 (2016): 610–26. doi:10.1080/14708477.2016.1189559.

Saito, Naoko. "Is Thoreau More Cosmopolitan than Dewey?" *The Pluralist* 7, no. 3 (2012): 71–85.

Standish, Paul. "Social Justice in Translation: Subjectivity, Identity, and Occidentalism." In *Educational Studies in Japan: International Yearbook*, vol. 6: 69–79. Tokyo: Japanese Educational Research Association, 2011.

Tachibana, Kiichi. "Is Taisho Demokurashi the same as Taisho Democracy?" In *Japan's Multi-Layered Democracy*, edited by Sigal B. Galanti, Nissim Otmazgin, and Alon Levkowitz, 37–51. Lanham, MD: Lexington, 2015.

Tronto, Joan C. *Moral Boundaries: A Political Argument for an Ethic of Care.* New York: Routledge, 1993.

———. "Du Care." Translated by Hervé Maury. *Revue Du MAUSS* 32, no. 2 (2008): 243–65.

Vallerand, Robert J., Luc G. Pelletier, Marc R. Blais, Nathalie M. Brière, Caroline Senécal, and Evelyne F. Vallières. "The Academic Motivation Scale: A Measure of Intrinsic, Extrinsic, and Amotivation in Education." *Educational and Psychological Measurement* 52, no. 4 (1992): 1003–17.

Winch, Christopher. "On the Shoulders of Giants." In *Grey Wisdom? Philosophical Reflections on Conformity and Opposition Between Generations,* edited by Roel van Goor and Ernst Mulder, 53–74. Amsterdam: Amsterdam University Press, 2006.

Chapter Ten

Immigrancy of the Self, Continuing Education

Recollection in Stanley Cavell's Little Did I Know *and Terrence Malick's* The Tree of Life

Naoko Saito

We commonly do not remember that it is, after all, always the first person that is speaking . . . I, on my side, require of every writer, first or last, a simple and sincere account of his own life, and not merely what he has heard of other men's lives; some such account as he would send to his kindred from a distant land.

—Henry David Thoreau, *Walden*[1]

Blanchot tells us that the bearing of stars no longer holds for us. There is now no sidereal orientation. There is still the alternation of day and night, hence the dawn that Emerson and Thoreau and Nietzsche propose for our orientation, or renewal. But that first light of life itself requires renewal.

—Stanley Cavell, *Little Did I Know*[2]

INTRODUCTION: AUTOBIOGRAPHICAL WRITING, RELIVING THE PAST IN THE PRESENT

In *Walden* Henry David Thoreau provides a first-person account of the period of nearly two years that he lived in the woods beside Walden Pond. It is an "account of his own life." The text combines a narrative of what is past and ongoing reflection on this, here and now—here as he writes, and here as we read. "The present," he writes, "was my next experiment" (*Walden*, 57): what it is to be present—temporally, spatially—is the subject of his experiment in the woods. What he writes, he announces, is not "an ode to dejection" (ibid.) (for Coleridge had already done that), but a wakening call for "an infinite expectation of the dawn" (*Walden*, 61). He writes to "improve the nick of time, and notch it on [his] stick too; to stand on the meeting of two eternities, the past and future which is precisely the present moment" (*Walden*, 11). Recollection in *Walden* is not mere retrospection: The past is relived now, amid his writing of this book. *Walden* raises philosophical questions—about the nature of recollection in autobiography, about remembering without nostalgia, about living in the present with the prospect of an unknown future, the present still to come. How can one be sincere in recounting one's life? How can such an account count with others?

Narrative trends in educational research and practice are richly promising in various respects, but they are apt, as Paul Smeyers, Richard Smith, and Paul Standish have shown,[3] to degenerate into neat objectifications, surveyed and presented under the clear view of the knowing subject. Life histories can fixate the subject in a schema of unity and linearity. The self is taken to be the legitimate and reliable "author" of the life story, and authenticity of voice is tacitly assumed. But in this self-conscious reflexivity, the authentic self is romanticized and sentimentalized. In the circumscribed territory of the subject, the very fact that the "author cannot fully contain herself in the writing," the "elusiveness of the first person perspective," is obliterated.[4] What is obscured is the "otherness of words to the author or reader," the "impossibility of the recovery of childhood,"[5] the "non-integrity of the self," and "the need for self-interruption."[6]

It is in the light of this that this chapter explores an alternative space for *education through recollection* based upon Cavell's "philosophy as autobiography."[7] This is an idea closely related to his idea of philosophy as translation—translation that involves human transformation as an integral component of his ordinary language philosophy. Cavell himself enacts this in his own recollection, *Little Did I Know* (2010). In his own autobiographical exercises, Cavell's preoccupation is with "finding my voice" (*Pitch*, 37). The idea of blending philosophy with autobiography is provocative and may be scandalous to some. But it reveals the way that recollection requires a radical reconfiguration not only of the human subject but also of time and language, crossing borders. It exacts a human transformation, a necessary, continuing education. To show the distinctiveness of Cavell's philosophy as autobiography, I shall explore some contrasts between *Little Did I Know* and Terrence Malick's film, *The Tree of Life* (2011). Despite the ground they clearly share, they turn out to diverge. Recollection lays the way, I shall argue, for a kind of onward transcendence, as part of the continuing education of grownups.

LITTLE DID I KNOW

[W]hat is the right to speak for oneself? . . . I shall just note here my conviction that had I not spent those weeks in Tougaloo I would not have claimed the right several years later to speak for Thoreau's *Walden*. And if I had not recognized *Walden* as a work of philosophy claiming to speak for me, I would not have felt bound, or been interested, to claim the right to speak for it. . . . I have been accustomed to think of my right to speak as the capacity to become responsible for my words, for their being always ahead of me, of each of us, intentional and at the same time inevitably and perpetually beyond intention. Here I am thinking of the matter as my right so speak of my death, of what it is on which my life is staked. (*Little*, 433)

My bargain with myself from the beginning has been to write here of the past essentially from memory, and to articulate memories, however unpromising in appearance, whenever I could, with some idea of how just these events and images have led to, or shaped, a reasonable life nevertheless also devoted to a certain ambition for philosophical writing, or what is meant as such. (*Little*, 516)

Disclosing events from his own past in amazing detail, and demonstrating in the process what he understands to be at stake in "philosophical autobiographies,"[8] Cavell's book is written in the Emersonian conviction that "our experience stands to be lost to us if we do not 'word' it."[9] Everyone's life is in part constructed by recollections of the past, but Cavell wants to see this as, in his case, intimately connected with what philosophy is: So philosophy in part involves a recovery and reappraisal of the past, not to make some kind of final statement or assessment, but in an ongoing project. Not only does he claim this, but Cavell also puts it into practice himself, in his own writing. "Thoreau's claim to philosophy," he writes, "is said to be a function of his claims of writing, as to awaken the voice."[10] Cavell's lifelong endeavor within philosophy is to restore a form of "autobiographical expression" (*Contesting*, 200). Institutionalized philosophy, with its fated arrogance, has brought about a denial of the other—a disparagement or neglect of the common and the ordinary, and, hence, of that distinctively American voice found in Ralph Waldo Emerson and Thoreau. Cavell's autobiographical self-searching is simultaneously the assiduous process of "philosophy's self-criticism" (*Little*, 500). His act of writing this book, and the very fact that this book has been published exemplifies what has in effect been a lifelong commitment to "replac[ing] philosophy."[11] The interrelated meanings this phrase carries deserve attention. First, philosophy as autobiography is not simply a matter of personal narrative; rather it involves attesting to an Emersonian idea of "representativeness" (*Pitch*, 11), such that, in the experience of the writer, "the deeper he dives into his privatest, secretest presentiment, to his wonder he finds this is the most acceptable, most public, and universally true."[12] This, Cavell wants to say, is fundamental to our relation to language itself:

> From the root of speech, in each utterance of revelation and confrontation, two paths spring: that of the responsibilities of implication; and that of the rights of desire. It will seem to some that the former is the path of philosophy, the latter that of something or other else, perhaps psychoanalysis. In an imperfect world the paths will not reliably coincide, but to show them both open is something I want of philosophy.[13]

Little Did I Know enacts and illustrates this distinctive way of connecting the private and the public, the personal and the universal, with the hope that the author's own privatest voice can eventually be most public.

Cavell's autobiographical writing embodies the Emersonian theme of achieving neutrality. Neutrality is gained through "onward thinking," by "the self as on a path" (*Little*, 499). A "proof" of universality, if any, can only be given through a projecting of our words, testing them in the responses of others. This involves "the education of humans, of making language mine, of finding my voice" (*Pitch*, 37). And voice necessarily involves tone, and so this is also a question of "the tone of philosophy and about my right to take that tone" (*Pitch*, 3). A striking tone that permeates *Little Did I Know* is that of *shame*.[14] Emulating Thoreau's practice of "unblushingly publish[ing his] guilt" (*Walden*, 40; *Senses*, 47), *Little Did I Know* is a philosopher's courageous experiment in "turning philosophically critical discourse into clinical discourse" (*Pitch*, 8).

Many episodes in the book seem on the surface to refer to matters of mere accident, and yet, as the story unfolds, the casual becomes causal. "Telling the accidental anonymous, in a sense posthumous days of my life is the making of philosophy" (*Little*, 5). Occasionally things are mundane: But then the moment of inspiration visits the reader, a moment that comes as a surprise and with a striking sense of "the ordinariness of the extraordinary" (*Little*, 374). The text, strangely mixing the insignificant and the significant, is not written in conventional autobiographical style—in which the focus is given retrospectively to an inner, true self.[15] Uncertain about himself as a child and as a youth, and even now as an adult, Cavell writes this autobiography in his early eighties, still in the process, as it were, of the salvation of his soul. *Little Did I Know* is the recollection of his past with the poignant sense of a "metamorphosis so traumatic as to be tantamount to death and rebirth."[16] There is a clinical impetus running through the book, the "therapeutic impulse" of ancient philosophy—"leading the soul up and out of a cave or deeper into a dark wood, in both cases eventually toward light" (*Little*, 514). William Rothman claims this therapeutic drive constitutes Cavell's echoing of Emerson's question, "Where do we find ourselves?" and of the Emersonian perfectionist quest for the unattained but attainable self.[17]

The structure of *Little Did I Know* deserves attention. On the one hand, it is chronological in tracking his life sequentially, from childhood to adulthood. On the other, it is written in the form of journal, with Cavell making daily, dated entries. Rothman identifies this as a "double time scheme."[18] Recollection for Cavell is not simply an exercise of memory, an exercise that becomes "routine as perception, conventional, unquestioned, serving merely to recall, not to reconsider" (*Little*, 518). When Cavell says that he wishes "to articulate memories," he does not mean to write with certainty and clarity about what happened in the past or about who he was: The project is one neither of securing his identity nor of affirming the correctness of his memory. The present self and the past self, childhood and adulthood, call upon each other—as if to be in dialogue at present, to project the self both toward past and toward future, for "liberation" (*Little*, 518). This is a process of "becoming what you are" by recounting your past—in the spirit of the Emerson who says: "I simply experiment, an endless seeker with no Past on my back" (*Emerson*, 260). There is no guarantee of continuity of identity as is typically presumed in autobiography. The prevailing tone of the text is rather of "disruption" (*Little*, 522), uncertainty and precariousness. In Rothman's words, this is a "path through uncharted territory."[19] And yet it is written to prove something, not for argument but for "*conviction*" (*Little*, 344).

Provocative and unique as Cavell's philosophical autobiography is, there are some challenging issues to be further addressed. The first concerns the paradoxical claim that the personal voice of the "I" can become representative voice of the human. The second regards *time*. What does it mean to narrate one's past *now*, and how can this be done without nostalgia, on the one hand, and the preoccupation, on the other hand—in stances that may vary from the maudlin to the heroically robust—with the finitude posed by death? What is the sense of reliving the past in the present? In what sense can the past be there in the now? The third point in *Little Did I Know* has to do with its structure: its strange mixture of contingency and necessity, of discontinuities and coherence, and of groundlessness and the sense of perfection. In this paradoxical structure, what does it mean to *find* ourselves by writing autobiography? Rothman points out that the writing of an autobiography leads Cavell "to where he longs to be," and at the same time, to "a place we have never been."[20] What kind of place would that be?

THE TREE OF LIFE

I never take up a film again that I care about unless I feel that I have something new to convey in considering it, which is part of my claim that the films I have studied, and the limited hundreds of others I imagine they rhyme with, domestic or foreign, are inexhaustible in ways not entirely unlike the great work of the human spirit in philosophy and literature and the comparable great arts. (*Little*, 494)

As a narrative film, *The Tree of Life*[21] illustrates certain aspects of Cavell's philosophy as autobiography and helps us find answers to challenging questions concerning the recollection of one's past. Film is one of the art forms in response to which Cavell addresses and performs the task of replacing philosophy. In *The World Viewed* (1971),[22] he refers to the French film critic André Bazin and addresses the question, "What happens to reality when it is projected and screened"? (*World*, 16). Film especially is the medium in relation to which Cavell addresses his abiding theme of remarriage with the world. Film exercises "its own power to establish connection with reality— by permitting us presentness to ourselves, apart from which there is no hope for a world" (*World*, 23). In particular, the following are the dimensions in which film and philosophy meet in Cavell's ordinary language philosophy. They implicitly indicate how his idea of translation as discussed in chapter 1 of this book plays a crucial role in the connection between film and philosophy. First and foremost, both film and philosophy are concerned with how we re-see the world (*World*, 22). In film what is revealed is "the world as world" (*World*, 157), while at the same time, in the technical effects of discontinuity, the changing frames of the film and varying camera techniques work to "deny the coherence of the world" (*World*, 160). It is a medium through which to translate the world: There is no world without translation. In this the viewer is called upon for his "perfect attention" (*World*, 25). Second, for Cavell, film and philosophy can both address the skeptical question concerning subjectivity, "our terror of ourselves in isolation" (*World*, 22, 160). The way of response is not by knowledge but in *acknowledgment*— "acknowledgment of that endless present of self" to the world (*World*, 22). This is the state of the self's repossession of itself through exhibition and revelation, and of its "conviction in reality" (ibid.).[23] Third, film and philosophy can be special media to convey the unsayable, beyond the limits of language (*World*, 152). The technique of the film captures the "ineffable," the obscure sense of the unsayable (*World*, 148). This has relevance to the realism of the obscure as a crucial component of philosophy as translation. Translation involves us in the "inexhaustible" possibilities of language. Cavell connects this with what, in *Philosophical Investigations*, Ludwig Wittgenstein calls a "physiognomy"—a concept that Cavell relates in turn to Wittgenstein's extensive exploration of "seeing as" in the later stages of that work. Cavell takes "seeing as" to be of immense importance in the understanding of art and of what film does (*World*, 157).

   The Tree of Life illustrates such a coalition between film and philosophy. Malick was Cavell's student at Harvard. As Rothman (who also studied film and philosophy with Cavell) points out, despite a difference in medium, there are striking similarities between *The Tree of Life* and *Little Did I Know* in that they both address the theme of remarriage with the world.[24] Robert Sinnerbrink reinterprets *The Tree of Life* through a Bazinian "cinematic belief" in film's power to restore our "belief in reality."[25] Pointing out the connection between Bazin's realism and its influence on Cavell's film theories, Sinnerbrink uses *The Tree of Life* as his "case study" for Bazinian belief.[26]

The Tree of Life is a narrative film, a story of recollection by Jack O'Brien, a middle-aged man who now works in Los Angeles, whose childhood is seen through a series of flashback. Yet the identity of this narrator is disrupted, discontinuous, and unstable. *The Tree of Life* addresses the question of what it means for the present self to relive its past. Rothman claims that Malick "eschews conventional continuity editing" with jump cuts, and that a "voice-over" technique makes it possible to make the "film's 'present'" its past, while at the same time making it feel like the future.[27] Present time in the film is situated between an aboriginal time when the Cosmos was created and an eschatological "end of time."[28] This is dramatically depicted in the film in the last scene, when the present (adult) Jack passes through a quasi-religious gate, rescuing his soul.

The memories recounted in *The Tree of Life* are of Jack's family life in Texas with his father, mother, and two brothers, the time of Jack's childhood and adolescence. The discontinuous and disrupted scenes go back and forth between past and present. In the film, the past intensifies its meaning by being recounted now by the adult Jack. The unrecoverable past of childhood is redeemed in the present. The fragmented moments in the film have the effect of asking the viewer to (re)thread the meaning and find coherence, paying particular attention to those moments. The tragic dimension of the film revolves around the family's loss of one of Jack's younger brothers at the age of nineteen (in the war). The loss is symbolized by a repeated voice-over, "Where are you?" Jack's therapeutic search is also entangled with his struggle between his rigorous father and suffering mother—evoking the image of Cavell's childhood in a tension between his parents. As another motif, the story revolves around Jack's, his mother's, and his father's struggle between two ways of life—the way of Nature and the way of Grace. This is portrayed in the film with reference to Job's trial on earth in the Bible— "Where were you when I laid the foundation of the earth? . . . When the morning stars sang together, and all the sons of God shouted for joy?"[29] After a struggle and suffering, the ending of the film culminates in Jack's remarriage with the world.

Despite this indubitable parallel structure and theme, "the sheer extent of coincidence, hence of significant difference" (*Philosophy*, 217)[30] between *The Tree of Life* and *Little Did I Know* is to be gradually exhibited. First is the concept of time and the relationship between past and present. Sinnerbrink describes the duration of time as "ahistorical" time in which the present being experienced is "unique" and "singular."[31] Likewise Rothman highlights this "now" as the "never-to-be-repeated moment," with a poignant sense of the "perfect moment" in "precious memory."[32] Furthermore, between the next world (after entering the heavenly gate) and the current world, and between past, present, and future, Rothman says, "there is a distinction without a difference."[33] Past and present are as if they were fused. In either reading, despite the emphasis on the uniqueness of the present moment, there remains a nostalgic sense toward the past and the dramatization of the ending: The present moment is inevitably to be assimilated into two ending points—an aboriginal time and an eschatological end of time.

The second indication of divergence is concerned with the place where Jack (and his mother and his father) are to find themselves. In the ending scene Jack finds himself when he passes through a symbolic gate into another world. Sinnerbrink associates this place with Martin Heidegger on being and Emerson on "one big soul."[34] This involves an issue concerning how the salvation of one's soul takes place in recollection. Sinnerbrink describes Jack's passage toward rebirth as "spiritual reconciliation through love" and "spiritual transcendence."[35] The path is "teleological."[36] Does this coincide with Cavell's Emerson, an endless seeker with no "Past" on his back?

These interrelated points entail a potential danger of assimilating this film (and a certain use of the film) into that dominant tendency of narrative education: the romanticization of an authentic self, a quest for unity and harmony, the exaggeration of the retrospective, nostalgic tendency of autobiography. Is there not any other way toward recollection?

ONGOING TRANSCENDENCE, CONTINUING EDUCATION

> Man postpones or remembers; he does not live in the present, but with reverted eye laments the past, or heedless of the riches that surround him, stands on tiptoe to foresee the future. He cannot be happy and strong until he too lives with nature in the present, above time. (*Emerson*, 143)

> Nostalgia is an inability to open the past to the future, as if the strangers who will replace you will never find what you have found. (*Philosophy*, 218)

The point of juxtaposing *The Tree of Life* and *Little Did I Know* is not simply to make a comparison, showing their common ground or differences. Rather the point is, in Cavell's words (in his contrasting of Thoreau to Heidegger), "mutual assessment"—to elucidate one's uniqueness by mirroring each other (*Philosophy*, 217). After going through *The Tree of Life*, the distinctive aspects of *Little Did I Know* are now foregrounded.

In Cavell's *Little Did I Know*, it is true that the present is a "precious moment" and is in a sense "ahistorical." In *Little Did I Know*, however, the weight of the present moment cannot be contained between two end points of past and future or defined in those terms. In its strong present tense, the present does not serve our nostalgia toward the past or the eschatological end of time. Rather, and more in tune with Thoreau's evocation of standing tiptoe on the meeting of two eternities, the text of *Little Did I Know* is being written, with the production of our words here and now, to "improve the nick of time"—to keep translating his own language. The present tense moves us ahead, not in the Heideggerian anticipation of death, but in "anticipating the dawning of a new day, a new time, an always earlier or original time" (*Philosophy*, 217). Recollection in this sense is in service to the work of mourning, and to "letting the past go" (ibid.). This accompanies the poignant sense of ourselves crossing borders, of our identities in translation.

Cavell's writing of autobiography is more process-oriented, even *a*teleological, than the kind of narrative evoked by *The Tree of Life*. This is Cavell's Emersonian idea of "finding as founding" (*America*, 77), an art of sojourning—"living each day everywhere and nowhere, as a task and an event" (*Philosophy*, 229). Cavell's Emerson resists teleological salvation; it contests tears. The therapy of philosophy is conducted in Emerson's experimental spirit. In "discontinuous encirclings,"[37] Cavell presents this forward movement, echoing Emerson's idea of the "Flying Perfect" (*Emerson*, 252)—this evanescent moment that constantly betrays our grasp, and yet at the same time, awaits our expression. The continuity of one's life is created from within discontinuity, and this is a kind of continuity without "foolish consistency" (*Emerson*, 138). The self is always to be found, to be attained. The salvation of one's soul in Cavell's recollection is brought about only by the power of one's own words in conviction. We are continually to be redeemed by words, to undergo rebirth. Translation as human transformation is derived from and internal to language itself.

Returning home is an ongoing event, and paradoxically you can find home only by leaving, in *abandonment* (*Philosophy*, 229; *Senses,* 137), in "preparations for departure, adventure, futurity" (*Philosophy*, 225). The place you have never been to is this ordinary, the familiar place where we are now. Yet going through the recounting of the past, the ordinary is never the same; and at the same time, it is the realization of the same ordinary with its intimacy already lost, the revivification of the sense of the familiar in strangeness. The work of recollection is a strange mixture of negativity (loss) and affirmation (rebirth). We relive the past to leave it, to re-create the present. *Little Did I Know* is marked by multiple moments in the past when the voice, "I stand here for humanity" (*Little*, 538), resounds in conviction. Cavell, who is writing this book in his early eighties, is still in the process of finding as founding. We continue education not to know about ourselves, but to realize the little we knew.

To continue education through philosophical autobiography is to keep returning to the ordinary, and yet with strangeness. We adults require continuing education in dialogue with the voice of the childhood within and without ourselves: We require "philosophy as the education of grown-ups" (*Little*, 9).[38] Growing up means to learn to be divided, to be separated from home. Writing recollection, one learns the "essential immigrancy of the human" (*Philosophy*, 229), with no final destination. And yet, there is *a* direction in such education. Toward the end of *Little Did I Know*, in referring to Emerson's phrase, "Hitch your wagon to a star," Cavell indicates that the Emersonian way of transcendence is to invoke a power that is "not that of leading but of being drawn." The direction of action is not "aiming high" or "thinking big," but "receiving high, accepting high" in the ordinary (*Little*, 533). Our education requires recollection for our ongoing onward transcendence as "[t]here is more day to dawn. The sun is but a morning star" (*Walden*, 223).

NOTES

An earlier version of this chapter was presented at the fifteenth Biennial Meeting of the International Network of Philosophers of Education, University of Warsaw, August 18, 2016. The author was the program chair for this meeting, the theme of which was "Philosophy as Education and the Understanding of Other Cultures."

1. Henry David Thoreau, *Walden and Resistance to Civil Government*, ed. William Rossi (New York: W. W. Norton & Company, 1992), 3; hereafter cited as *"Walden."*

2. Stanley Cavell, *Little Did I Know: Excerpts from Memory* (Cambridge, MA: Belknap Press of Harvard University Press, 2010), 529; hereafter cited as *"Little."*

3. Paul Smeyers, Richard Smith, and Paul Standish, *The Therapy of Education: Philosophy, Happiness and Personal Growth* (New York: Palgrave, 2007).

4. Ibid., 64.

5. Ibid., 70.

6. Ibid., 103.

7. Stanley Cavell, *A Pitch of Philosophy: Autobiographical Exercises* (Cambridge, MA: Harvard University Press, 1994), 44; hereafter cited as *"Pitch."*

8. Stanley Cavell, *Contesting Tears: The Hollywood Melodrama of the Unknown Woman* (Chicago: University of Chicago Press, 1996), 3; hereafter cited as *"Contesting."*

9. Ibid.

10. Stanley Cavell, *This New Yet Unapproachable America: Lectures after Emerson after Wittgenstein* (Albuquerque, NM: Living Batch Press, 1989), 117; hereafter cited as *"America".*

11. Stanley Cavell, *The Senses of Walden* (Chicago: University of Chicago Press, 1992), 130; hereafter cited as *"Senses."*

12. Ralph Waldo Emerson, *The Essential Writings of Ralph Waldo Emerson*. ed. Brooks Atkinson (New York: The Modern Library, 2000), 53–54; hereafter cited as *"Emerson."*

13. Stanley Cavell, *Philosophy the Day after Tomorrow* (Cambridge, MA: Belknap Press of Harvard University Press, 2005), 185; hereafter cited as *"Philosophy."*

14. "[A] text such as Emerson's 'Self-Reliance' is virtually a study of shame" (Stanley Cavell, *Conditions Handsome and Unhandsome: The Constitution of Emersonian Perfectionism* [Chicago: University of Chicago Press, 1990], 47).

15. Cavell refers to Marcel Proust here (*Little*, 31).

16. William Rothman, "Precious Memories in Philosophy and Film: Stanley Cavell's *Little Did I Know* and Terrence Malick's *The Tree of Life*," paper presented at the "International Workshop in Honor of Stanley Cavell," l'Université Paris–Sorbonne, July 10, 2015.

17. Ibid.

18. Ibid.

19. Ibid.

20. Ibid.

21. *The Tree of Life* (2011), written and directed by Terrence Malick, starring Brad Pitt, Sean Penn, and Jessica Chastain.

22. Stanley Cavell, *The World Viewed: Reflections on the Ontology of Film*, enlarged ed. (Cambridge, MA: Harvard University Press, 1971); hereafter cited as "*World*."

23. This is the state in which "the self exhibit[s] itself without the self's intervention" (*World*, 159).

24. William Rothman, "Seeing the Light in *The Tree of Life*" (unpublished).

25. Robert Sinnerbrink, "Cinematic Belief: Bazinian Cinephilia and Malick's *The Tree of Life*," *Angelaki: Journal of Theoretical Humanities* 17, no. 4 (December 2012), 96.

26. Ibid.

27. Rothman, "Seeing the Light."

28. Sinnerbrink, "Cinematic Belief," 105.

29. Job 38: 4, 7.

30. In fact, when Cavell uses these words, he is writing of the relation between his own work and that of Levinas.

31. Sinnerbrink, "Cinematic Belief," 100, 101.

32. Rothman, "Seeing the Light."

33. Ibid.

34. Sinnerbrink, "Cinematic Belief," 103.

35. Ibid., 108, 109.

36. Ibid., 111.

37. Cavell, *Conditions Handsome and Unhandsome*, xxxiv.

38. Stanley Cavell, *The Claim of Reason: Wittgenstein, Skepticism, Morality, and Tragedy* (Oxford: Oxford University Press, 1979), 125.

BIBLIOGRAPHY

Cavell, Stanley. *The World Viewed: Reflections on the Ontology of Film*. Enlarged edition. Cambridge, MA: Harvard University Press, 1971.

———. *The Claim of Reason: Wittgenstein, Skepticism, Morality, and Tragedy*. Oxford: Oxford University Press, 1979.

———. *This New Yet Unapproachable America: Lectures after Emerson after Wittgenstein*. Albuquerque, NM: Living Batch Press, 1989.

———. *Conditions Handsome and Unhandsome: The Constitution of Emersonian Perfectionism*. Chicago: University of Chicago Press, 1990.

———. *The Senses of Walden*. Chicago: University of Chicago Press, 1992.

———. *A Pitch of Philosophy: Autobiographical Exercises*. Cambridge, MA: Harvard University Press, 1994.

———. *Contesting Tears: The Hollywood Melodrama of the Unknown Woman*. Chicago: University of Chicago Press, 1996.

———. *Philosophy the Day after Tomorrow*. Cambridge, MA: Belknap Press of Harvard University Press, 2005.

———. *Little Did I Know: Excerpts from Memory*. Cambridge, MA: Belknap Press of Harvard University Press, 2010.

Emerson, Ralph Waldo. *The Essential Writings of Ralph Waldo Emerson*. Edited by Brooks Atkinson. New York: Modern Library, 2000.

Rothman, William. "Precious Memories in Philosophy and Film: Stanley Cavell's *Little Did I Know* and Terrence Malick's *The Tree of Life*." Paper presented at the "International Workshop in Honor of Stanley Cavell," l'Université Paris–Sorbonne, July 10, 2015.

———. "Seeing the Light in *The Tree of Life*." Unpublished.

Sinnerbrink, Robert. "Cinematic Belief: Bazinian Cinephilia and Malick's *The Tree of Life*." *Angelaki: Journal of Theoretical Humanities* 17, no. 4 (December 2012): 95–117.

Smeyers, Paul, Richard Smith, and Paul Standish. *The Therapy of Education: Philosophy, Happiness and Personal Growth*. New York: Palgrave, 2007.

Thoreau, Henry David. *Walden and Resistance to Civil Government*. Edited by William Rossi. New York: W. W. Norton & Company, 1992.

The Tree of Life. Directed by Terrence Malick. Los Angeles: Fox Searchlight Pictures, 2011.

Chapter Eleven

The Philosophy of Pawnbroking

Paul Standish

Be not too tame neither, but let your own discretion be your tutor: Suit the
action to the word, the word to the action; with this special observance, that
you o'erstep not the modesty of nature; for anything so overdone is from the
purpose of playing, whose end, both at the first and now, was and is, to hold,
as 'twere, the mirror up to nature; to show virtue her own feature, scorn her
own image, and time his form and the very age and body of the pressure.
　　—Shakespeare, *Hamlet*[1]

In a passage in the middle of *Little Did I Know*, recalling his early years
studying philosophy at UCLA, Cavell remembers the high hopes he had held
for the study of logic. He imagined that he would be able to "translate or
transpose" the sometimes incomprehensible texts he was otherwise assigned
into the terms of this "wonderful symbolism."[2] In fact, rather than reading
the English texts, he would devote himself to the mastery of logic until he
was equal to the task of complete translation. The teaching assistant on the
course informed him that "when logic got really interesting and powerful it
left natural language quite behind, which was too hopelessly vague and ambiguous to serve as a medium of serious philosophical analysis."[3] But the
unqualified pleasure this excited in the teaching assistant found a more
mixed reaction in Cavell—of deflation and disappointment of a kind but also
of "exhilaration at the prospect of eternally recurrent confusion and controversy over unfathomable perplexities."[4] The choice that seemed to be presenting itself was between what Cavell wanted to understand and what was
truly understandable. And for a time it seemed that philosophy could not
provide what he wanted.

　　The idea that logic is foundational to thought or that it subtends natural
language, with the complementary assumption that the latter offers only a
pale shadow of the precision that the former provides, might be seen as

philosophy's myth of an original language, a language before Babel. The directness and precision of such a language entails that it is without ambiguity. Logic has no puns. And in a sense, in its ideal fit with reason, it is *sans pareil*: There is nothing comparable into which it could be translated. While there are, of course, different notations, the ideal of logic is of a language without translation. In fact, it would be more accurate to say that it is not a language at all. None of this is necessarily to deny the power and importance of logic, but it is to illustrate the need to conceive of it and to place it differently. The ideal is a part of the myth that Ludwig Wittgenstein seeks to overcome. Far from being the foundation of reason, the most that could be said, so he comes to insist, is that logic is constructed out of ordinary language. It is the unqualified faith of the teaching assistant that needs to be deflated.

The trajectory of Wittgenstein's thought, from picture theory to meaning as use, turns intermittently toward the nature of the signs that human beings use, word and gesture. He ponders the physiognomy of a word. He wonders how it is that words function as they do: "Every sign *by itself* seems dead. *What* gives it life?—In use it is *alive*. Is life breathed into it there?—Or is the *use* its life?" Wittgenstein is drawn for a moment, so it seems, by the animistic phrasing that use "breathes" life into the sign but quickly modifies this with the thought that the use *is* its life—though this is still expressed as a rhetorical question. He wonders about the nature of gestures too: "The gesture—we should like to say—*tries* to portray, but cannot do it."[5] The negative thought here, which seems to afflict Wittgenstein's interlocutor, is that gestures and words alike are doomed to a kind of inadequacy, existing only in a precarious relation to the achieving of understanding, the grasp of inner meaning. The trace of a more positive thought is to be found, by contrast, in the idea that it is not exactly the purpose of words or gestures to "portray," as if there must be some other mental operation with which they correspond, for the meaning is already there in their use.

> If it is asked: "How do sentences manage to represent?"—the answer might be: "Don't you know? You certainly see it, when you use them." For nothing is concealed.
>
> How do sentences do it?—Don't you know? For nothing is hidden.
>
> But given this answer: "But you know how sentences do it, for nothing is concealed" one would like to retort "Yes, but it all goes by so quick, and I should like to see it as it were laid open to view." (*Investigations*, §435)

Wittgenstein then immediately refers to that dead-end in philosophy where the difficulty seems to consist in "our having to describe phenomena that are hard to get hold of, the present experience that slips quickly by, or something of the kind. Where we find ordinary language too crude."[6] Philosophy, then, in some of its phases encourages the all-too-human thought that reality lies, as it were, just outside our ordinary grasp, that something lies hidden beneath the surface of our experience and language. The teaching assistant committed to the power of logic seems to suppress the tonality of this experience (a tonality without which Wittgenstein's thoughts in the above lines could scarcely be conveyed), and it is this perhaps that so quickly disillusioned Cavell.

In an interview with Katherine Dunlop and Scott Shuchart in 1997, Cornel West makes the following remark:

> All the philosophers of darkness, I think, very much like the artists of darkness, are going to be relevant for the twenty-first century. Paul Celan's poetry is going to be central in the next century, Kafka central, Hardy central, the Schellings and Schopenhauers. Not because their conclusions are convincing, but [by] the nature of their wrestling. There's a sense in which in analytic philosophy we overlook the tonality of the philosopher, and the Schellings and Schopenhauers and Kierkegaards will come back because of their tonality.[7]

Yet the logician in our example is likely to see the question of tone as irrelevant to the real business of philosophy. Tone is, after all, a literary matter, no more than an aspect of rhetorical form. By contrast, the prose style appropriate to philosophy is inspired by the model of logic, and tonelessness is what it seeks. This becomes the rigor of philosophy. As Richard Rorty tells us in *Philosophy and the Mirror of Nature*, William James expressed despair regarding "the grey-plaster temperament of our young PhDs, boring each other at seminaries, writing those direful reports of literature in the *Philosophical Review* and elsewhere, fed on 'books of reference' and never confounding 'Aesthetik' with 'Erkenntnistheorie.'"[8] Rorty goes on to suggest that the "spirit of playfulness" that could be found at the turn of the twentieth century, the credit for which he attributes, *inter alia*, to James and F. H. Bradley, was "nipped in the bud"[9]—and this especially as a result of the efforts of Bertrand Russell and Edmund Husserl. Toward the end of the century, *Philosophy and the Mirror of Nature* set out what seemed a liberating account of the state to which philosophy had come: the "epistemological turn" taken by René Descartes—himself, ironically, anything but a toneless philosopher—had inaugurated the characteristic self-understanding of many of those practicing the subject over the next four centuries, especially those thinking of themselves as philosophers by profession. The sense of liberation aroused by Rorty's book was in part the product of its tone. Rorty displayed an inside knowledge of the discipline but also the confidence to reflect on it in a way that deflated its pumped-up, overly masculine style and unmasked its metaphysical presuppositions.

The book's reliance on its signature image of the mirror deserves some attention. "The picture which holds traditional philosophy captive," Rorty writes, "is of the mind as a great mirror, containing various representations—

some accurate, some not—and capable of being studied by pure, non-empirical methods."[10] Toward the end of the book, in a chapter entitled "Philosophy Without Mirrors," he presses still more insistently the implications of the image:

> The notion of an unclouded Mirror of Nature is the notion of a mirror which would be indistinguishable from what was mirrored, and thus would not be a mirror at all. The notion of a human being whose mind is such an unclouded mirror, and who knows this, is the image, Sartre says, of God. Such a being does not confront something alien which makes it necessary for him to choose an attitude toward, or a description of, it. He would have no need and no ability to choose actions or descriptions. He can be called "God" if we think of the advantages of this situation, or a "mere machine" if we think of the disadvantages.[11]

The implications of the imagery of the mirror have their greatest salience in respect of two facets of thinking—in the prioritization of notions of representation and in the fantasy of transparency. Thinking of this kind in turn generates a series of oppositions, between nature and convention, and between philosophy and literature. When the appropriate tone for professionalized philosophy becomes the tonelessness of logic, this is an equitable outcome, to be sure, for those who are tone-deaf.

Many have found Rorty's characteristic idiom compelling in its description of the philosophical scene these past four hundred years and in its stolid defense of a controversial and unpopular position in the face of those who prefer to practice philosophy-as-usual. But I sense also in his tone, for all its urbane laid-back elegance and wit, something overly defended. Might this not be a barrier to the kind of exposure that philosophy in some of its most inspiring forms, and particularly in its American forms, has sometimes succeeded in making real? Rorty famously insists upon a division between one's public responsibility in respect of social justice and one's private irony—the latter occasioned by a sense of the provisionality of any vocabulary one takes to be final, of those points of view that are most basic to one's ways of seeing the world. Sensitivity to the provisionality of final vocabularies will require a kind of low-flame stoicism, an attractive, deflationary humility in the face of the fact that one's ways of seeing the world may change. Such a brake on one's taking oneself too seriously may then stabilize things so that one's energies can be better directed to those more social concerns.

But is it not sometimes the case that the refusal to take oneself too seriously ends up, ironically enough, shoring itself up within a form of language and thought characterized by the somewhat defended tone I have tried to identify—ends up, that is, in a failure to expose itself when most it matters? Humility in these matters would require rather more. Is it clear what taking oneself too seriously amounts to and how far this is to be condemned? When

Stanley Cavell, by contrast, bridles at the suggestion that one not take oneself too seriously, this cannot reasonably be a defense of egocentricity or an endorsement of vanity: It is rather an attempt to acknowledge a commitment to offer one's words, and to offer them seriously, to expose oneself in one's words, without which philosophy degenerates into a merely scholarly exercise, one form of which is the toneless tradition with which Rorty takes issue. "This is how I would say it. How would you? Does this ring true?"—these are questions advanced in finding sense that depend upon the speaker's sincerity in his or her words. Without this the words are nothing, just as without sincerity aesthetic judgment is void. Cavell draws attention to the fact that, in ordinary language philosophy's characteristic "what-we-say-when," the plural pronoun indicates that this is never a purely "subjective" matter, never merely a private judgment, for it is a seeking after objectivity, an affirmation of community. In the end my autonomy depends upon this seeking after meaning with others, and this radically resists the kind of separation of the public and the private upon which Rorty insists.

This is illustrated well later in *Little Did I Know* where Cavell recounts an episode that presses the point keenly in respect of exposure and vulnerability. Sometime in the early 1960s, Cavell asked his colleague Rogers Allbritton to read a recently published response to the first two papers he had put in print—"an unmitigatedly vicious attack," Cavell writes, "including the summary evaluation that the work my writing represented was . . . 'deleterious to the future of philosophy.'"[12] The next day Allbritton's words mixed reassurance with exasperation: "Well of course the response doesn't touch you. But it is you I do not understand. How could you possibly have left yourself so vulnerable to such ill will?"[13] Cavell's response was as follows:

> I see no alternative. And you of all people cannot expect any assertion to make itself invulnerable. So in my state of perfect gratitude to you I have to warn you of something. If I can find a way to write philosophy that I can believe in day after day I am going to go on doing it. The alternative I can see is to cultivate a private sense of the public world's intellectual vulgarity. However essential that may be it is not enough for me.[14]

No doubt we depend upon Cavell's testimony here, but without testimony what would autobiography be? Without it what would philosophy be? Cavell sees no alternative. In other words, there *can* be no retreat into privacy. That private irony is not an option means that one must be ready to deal in the currencies of this world. For what else is there? How else are we to account for ourselves? Those currencies may not exactly be a consolation, but they constitute the terms, the arena of exchange, and, let us say, the agora in which the possibilities of the human are played out. Sometimes they are counterfeit, but they cannot all be so all the time. Hamlet is concerned that the troupe of players should not overact, the possibility of which opens a

distinction between what, in suiting action to word and word to action, is
fitting and what is not. We are provoked to wondering, then, what it is, in
being overdone, in o'erstepping the modesty of nature, that is fake; what it is
that can count as serious speech; and what it is to act well.

In a multiply allusive passage, at the end of an essay entitled "Recounting
Gains, Showing Losses" in *In Quest of the Ordinary*, and in a manner that
cannot fail to allude in part to Rorty's text, but whose tonal differences can
scarcely be missed, Cavell reprises the image of the mirror but to markedly
different effect:

> Is the life of the world, supposing the world survives, a big responsibility? Its
> burden is not its size but its specificness. It is no bigger a burden than the
> responsibility for what Emerson and Thoreau might call the life of our words.
> We might think of the burden as holding, as it were, the mirror up to nature.
> Why assume just that Hamlet's picture urges us players to imitate, that is, copy
> or reproduce (human) nature? His concern over those who "imitated humanity
> so abominably" is not alone that we not imitate human beings badly but that
> we not become imitation members of the human species, abominations; as if to
> imitate, or represent—that is, to participate in—the species well is a condition
> of being human. Such is Shakespearean theatre's stake in the acting or playing
> of humans. Then Hamlet's picture of the mirror held up to nature asks us to see
> if the mirror as it were clouds, to determine whether nature is breathing (still,
> again)—asks us to be things affected by the question. [15]

While the mirror that clouds invokes the further Shakespearian connotation
of the death of Cordelia,[16] there is also the glimmer of a suggestion of
something more—of a journey, of being on the way, of an exodus guided by
night by a pillar of fire, by day by a pillar of cloud.[17] Responsibility for the
life of our words cannot be satisfied in terms of a pure representation; as
Rorty says, an unclouded mirror would not be a mirror at all. Cavell's words
prompt thoughts of nature that, if they are not quite animistic, at least imply
the breath of life: and the breath of life becomes no less than the human
voice, the voice that words the world.

More darkly the reactivation of the image harbors the thought that nature
may be in danger of being deadened at our hands, murdered, say, in dissec-
tion—perhaps by the dissections of philosophy. The earnest philosopher's
anxiety never to confound "Aesthetik" with "Erkenntnistheorie" meets Cavell's insistence that things are con-founded—that is, at least, that one cannot
be founded without the other, because our judgment that something is the
case, or our sense of an expression's use and aptness, depends upon a faculty
that is aesthetic: Aesthetic judgment will model the judgment upon which
ordinary language philosophy depends. It will model *a fortiori* the political
too.

There is, however, still more. The disconcerting proximity of "con-found-ing" to "confounding" intimates a disturbance at the heart of thought, albeit that it is this that renders it mobile. To see this is to have found one's way through a network of connections that might begin with the thought, which Cavell finds in Ralph Waldo Emerson's essay "Experience," that finding is founding.[18] This requires a finding together through the projection of our words, in an ongoing aspiration toward the common. But this is also a process through which we are confounded—that is, a process through which we are, to put it colloquially, messed up, a process to and by which we are, to put it eschatologically, damned—damned by the fixity of our words, by their too solid (and too sullied?) foundation, or by the consolidation, the fixation, of the "we." Cavell's artful coinage for these contrary movements is that this is a "deconfounding," where the force of the prefix is to undo both: It unsettles our tendencies toward consolidation, and it retrieves us from damnation. A good reading deconfounds, and this is the condition of human experience we need.

Philosophy and the Mirror of Nature was published in 1979, the same year as *The Claim of Reason*. Cavell's book is more difficult to penetrate and harder to place than Rorty's. Rorty provides an eloquent, descriptive account of the development of philosophy in modern times and of the ways that, in his view, this has gone wrong; Cavell's targets may seem similar, but his purpose is something other—more engaged, more disturbing, more original, more exposed—than the setting out of a thesis. The tonal contrasts evident in the passages quoted earlier relating to the mirror image say something of a difference regarding willingness for exposure, a difference regarding their background too. As a child, Rorty had served sandwiches at a party attended by John Dewey, was bounced on the knee of Sidney Hook, and "not infre-quently encountered a Robert Penn Warren or Allen Tate or A. Philip Randolph at the dinner table"—all this in a home where, in 1940, John Frank, a secretary of Trotsky's in flight from Stalin's assassins, was harbored as a houseguest.[19] Impressive formative years! As a teenager, and around the time Rorty was serving sandwiches, Cavell spent many of his out-of-school hours less glamorously, working in his father's pawnshop in Sacramento, California. But his account of aspects of this experience bears attention.

California law required at that time that pledges be held for six months, plus a one-month period of grace before they could be offered for sale. "Grace amazingly," Cavell comments, "is what the law actually called the additional period, and what the police called it."[20] One of his responsibilities was to fill out a form with details of the day's pledges and to take the page to the police station to be filed. Another was to remove expired pledges and to prepare them for sale. But his father directed him not to remove any pledge until it had been kept, not merely for the legal span of seven months, but for something approaching a year—and for a further six months if it was a wedding ring. Cavell reflects on this in the following lines:

> The concepts of grace and of redeeming are only beginning suggestions of the poetry of pawnbroking. Counting, especially counting up the monthly interest owed, upon redemption (I mean upon the pawner's returning with his ticket to redeem his pledge), was another of my responsibilities. Here we encounter certain opening suggestions of the philosophy of the concepts of pawnbroking. The concept of what we count, especially count as of interest or importance to us, is a matter fundamental to how I think of a motive to philosophy, fundamental to what I want philosophy to be responsive to and to illuminate. Something like the poetry and philosophy caught intermittently in the ideas of redemption and grace and interest and importance (or mattering or counting) was of explicit fascination to me before I stopped working in the pawnshop, the year I graduated high school.[21]

Now to anyone steeped in the discourse of professional philosophy, to speak of "the philosophy of pawnbroking" will surely seem indecorous. It is sufficient to shock the philosophically genteel. Yet Cavell's recounting of this experience and his subsequent inclination, even against the odds, as it were, to invoke a religious vocabulary testify to the importance of these matters for philosophy. Pawnbroking's key terms, not to mention its associations with shame, are here found to coincide with economies of counting and interest, words likewise open to a religious inflection. Some twenty-seven years after this teenage experience, in writing his short book *The Senses of Walden*,[22] Cavell is struck by the multiple associations of these words in Henry David Thoreau's text—associations of counting and recounting, and of what it is to give an account, no less than of what it is to account for oneself. What is the nature of pawnbroking's exchange? What alternative fable does it provide?

In learning to deal in the currencies of the world, in an economy that is something like education, you may find that their ready exchange and accumulation enables you to gain the whole world. You master the terms well. Everything is at your fingertips. And then perhaps you find that everything you touch turns to gold, including perhaps the pure gold of "Aesthetik" and "Erkenntnistheorie."[23] Yet could it be that learning is otherwise, such that your words gain interest of a different kind? Is it fanciful to see the pawnshop then as an allegory of our coming to ourselves—say, our becoming human? This would be to figure a different economy, other than that of the social contract, rending the veil of ignorance. Suppose that the price of coming to words is that I begin, that I must already have begun, by forfeiting something of myself—myself, that is, such as it was in its nondivided, unmediated, inarticulate, animal, Edenic state. Such forfeiture means that I am never above reproach. Acquiring this currency, I am not so much facilitated: I am circumscribed—defined by its terms' cutting and dividing of the world, compelled to submit to conformities they exact. It is with them that I enter the exchange of the world. But if I use my words well, they will accrue interest, and in time I may find that something can be redeemed. This would be to see the self as not given but needing continually to be redeemed: Call *this* my education. What has been pledged is not exactly myself, but it is that on which the development of my self depends. This would be to understand my becoming human as involving the sense of something already lost, where my being committed to words, being sentenced by them, and the entry into knowing they provide—words to the use of which we are fated, and by which we are confounded—constitute the inevitable, original sin.

Cavell uses the title "Counter-Philosophy and the Pawn of Voice" as the title for the second chapter of *A Pitch of Philosophy*,[24] though he says far less there directly about pawnbroking than this title might lead one to expect. It is as if something had already had to be given up; or as if there were something too recessive to be directly addressed.

Far from the equivalencies and representations of accustomed economies of thought, pawnbroking reverses expectations. The withdrawal of the thing releases the currency of the sign. That currency and the signs themselves are marked by a promise, such that their exchange involves more than a circle of satisfaction. Something remains, as withdrawn or in excess. In fact, there is no exchange without remainder, no perfect translation, and it was a fantasy ever to think otherwise. The literal monument remains. There is always more to be said.

And this turns again to the thought that entry into the human involves a severance that has already taken place.[25] In the closing paragraphs of the essay "Emerson, Coleridge, Kant (Terms as Conditions)," Cavell reprises a question left hanging as to how far *The Rime of the Ancient Mariner* is to be read as a version of or interpretation of the myth of the Fall. He recalls a dominant interpretation of it to be, as in Georg Hegel, that "the birth of knowledge is the origin of consciousness, hence self-consciousness, hence of guilt and shame, hence of human life as severed and estranged, from nature, from others, from itself. Hence the task of human life is of recovery, as of one's country, or health." Certainly thoughts close to these have been suggested in the pages above. But Cavell finds himself "winding up somewhat differently." What is this difference, and how is it to be interpreted? "The explicit temptation of Eden is to knowledge," Cavell writes, "which above all means: to a denial that, as we stand, we know." So this would be to figure this precondition of the human as other than what was described earlier as a "non-divided, unmediated, inarticulate, animal, Edenic state." The truly animal is not tempted by the possibility of knowledge, any more than the true god can be anxious about its lack. The truly animal is without language, and there could for the animal be no God that "called the light Day, and the darkness he called Night."[26] "There was no Eden," Cavell writes, "no place in which names are immune to skepticism."[27] Hence, if Babel can stand as a figure for the multiplicity of tongues, and, that is, for the necessity of translation, there was no language before Babel. Both the Eden myth and the allegorizing of pawnbroking point back to an impossible time, a time before debt and division: But, so the paradox remains, for the human being there was no such time although the human condition, and that of language itself, is such that it is as if this has already taken place. Derrida speaks of this in terms of the archi-trace. Cavell says more simply that there are no firsts.

The Fall is familiar enough as initiating shame at being naked. But Cavell emphasizes rather that it is fear that it is expressed ("I was afraid, because I was naked; and I hid myself"). Hence, he wishes to emphasize that "its sense of exposure upon the birth of knowledge pertains not only to one's vulnerability to knowledge, to being known, to the trauma of separation, but as well to the vulnerability of knowledge itself."[28] So, as it were in place of Eden, or in a translation of the very idea, it might be said that there is a realization that one has been living "within a circle or behind a line." Allusions respectively to Emerson's circle around which another can be drawn[29] and to Samuel Coleridge's mariner's crossing and return across a line[30] indicate the terms of our present condition. The allegory of pawnbroking points to the possibility of a redemption gained through the gaining of interest in currencies to which we are committed. It will, in words of Cavell attuned perhaps better to the modesty of nature, retrieve a relation to the ordinary that is, as eventual, already marked.[31]

NOTES

An earlier version of this chapter was presented at a day conference marking the publication of the French translation of *Little Did I Know*, organized by Sandra Laugier, translator of the book. My thanks to those present for their comments.

1. Hamlet's words to the traveling players, act 3, scene 2, ll. 17–25.
2. Stanley Cavell, *Little Did I Know: Excerpts from Memory* (Cambridge, MA: Belknap Press of Harvard University Press, 2010), 244.
3. Ibid.
4. Ibid.
5. Ludwig Wittgenstein, *Philosophical Investigations*, trans. G. E. M. Anscombe (Oxford: Blackwell, 1953), §434.
6. Ibid., §436.
7. Cornel West, in S. P. Upham, ed., *Philosophers in Conversation: Interviews from the Harvard Review of Philosophy* (New York: Routledge, 2002), 117.
8. William James, in Richard Rorty, *Philosophy and the Mirror of Nature, with an Introduction by M. Williams* (Princeton, NJ: Princeton University Press, 2009), 136.
9. In Rorty, *Mirror*, 166.
10. Rorty, *Mirror*, 12.
11. Ibid., 376.
12. Cavell, *Little*, 491.
13. Ibid., 492.
14. Ibid.

15. Stanley Cavell, *In Quest of the Ordinary: Lines of Skepticism and Romanticism* (Chicago: University of Chicago Press, 1988), 101.

16. "Lend me a looking-glass. / If that her breath will mist or stain the stone, / Why then, she lives," act 5, scene 3, ll. 275–77.

17. "And the LORD went before them by day in a pillar of a cloud, to lead them the way; and by night in a pillar of fire, to give them light; to go by day and night," Exodus 13: 21.

18. Ralph Waldo Emerson, *The Essential Writings of Ralph Waldo Emerson*, ed. Brooks Atkinson (New York: Modern Library, 2000).

19. See Christopher J. Voparil, "General Introduction," In C. J. Voparil and R. J. Bernstein, eds., *The Rorty Reader* (Oxford: Wiley-Blackwell, 2010), 5.

20. Cavell, *Little*, 115–16.

21. Ibid.

22. Stanley Cavell, *The Senses of Walden* (Chicago: The University of Chicago Press, 1992).

23. See also Cavell's speculation, late in *The Claim of Reason*, about a certain conception of "pure knowledge": "If there were a drama of pure knowledge, it seems that Faust must be its protagonist. But is Faust a tragic figure? Is he to be understood in terms of the life of skepticism? Skepticism has to do, after all, with the absolute *failure* of knowledge, whereas what Faust lived was the absolute *success* of knowledge. But apparently what he is to have discovered about this success is that it is not *humanly* satisfying. He is the Midas of knowledge" (Cavell, *The Claim*, 435).

24. Stanley Cavell, *A Pitch of Philosophy: Autobiographical Exercises* (Cambridge, MA: Harvard University Press, 1994).

25. Stanley Cavell, *In Quest*, 48–49.

26. Genesis 1: 5.

27. Cavell, *In Quest*, 49.

28. Ibid.

29. "Our life is an apprenticeship to the truth, that around every circle another can be drawn; that there is no end in nature, but every end is a beginning; that there is always another dawn risen on mid-noon, and under every deep a lower deep opens" (Emerson, "Circles," in *Essential Writings*).

30. Coleridge, *The Rime of the Ancient Mariner*. See my discussion in chapter 4 above.

31. Speaking of his inheritance of Wittgenstein and J. L. Austin, Cavell refers to their absolute devotion to the idea of the ordinary, notwithstanding the fact that they left this almost undiscussed: "They left it so that it's just simply obvious that if you consult how we ordinarily say things, judge things, you'll see that philosophy is in continuous conflict with this. How is it that we can do something like return words from their metaphysical to their ordinary use? How can words get away from being the ordinary things they are? And why should philosophy itself be disappointed in the ordinary and have to attack it? Attack it in its dimension called scepticism but also in its dimension called metaphysics? Metaphysics and scepticism go together in Wittgenstein. You metaphysicalize the idea of what it is to see an object then you create metaphysical objects called 'sense data' or 'objects as they are in themselves' and so on. And then you require what Wittgenstein calls a return to the ordinary. Austin doesn't speak of that, but I do. But I say this return is also to a place you've never been. So I say let's go, let's speak then of two ordinaries: the actual and the eventual" (Stanley Cavell and Paul Standish, "Stanley in Conversation with Paul Standish," *Journal of Philosophy of Education* 46, no. 2 [2012]: 167).

BIBLIOGRAPHY

Cavell, Stanley. *The Claim of Reason: Wittgenstein, Skepticism, Morality, and Tragedy*. Oxford: Oxford University Press, 1979.

———. *In Quest of the Ordinary: Lines of Skepticism and Romanticism*. Chicago: University of Chicago Press, 1988.

———. *The Senses of Walden* Chicago: University of Chicago Press, 1992.

———. *A Pitch of Philosophy: Autobiographical Exercises*. Cambridge, MA: Harvard University Press, 1994.

———. *Little Did I Know: Excerpts from Memory*. Cambridge, MA: Belknap Press of Harvard University Press, 2010.

Cavell, Stanley, and Paul Standish. "Stanley in Conversation with Paul Standish." *Journal of Philosophy of Education* 46, no. 2 (2012): 155–76.

Coleridge, Samuel Taylor. *The Rime of the Ancient Mariner*.

Emerson, Ralph Waldo. *The Essential Writings of Ralph Waldo Emerson*. Edited by Brooks Atkinson. New York: Modern Library, 2000.

Rorty, Richard. *Contingency, Irony, Solidarity*. Cambridge: Cambridge University Press, 1989.

———. "Truth without Correspondence to Reality." 1999. In *The Rorty Reader*, edited by C. J. Vosparil and R. J. Bernstein, 415–24. Oxford: Blackwell, 2010.

———. "Wittgenstein and the Linguistic Turn." In *Philosophy as Cultural Politics: Philosophical Papers, 4*. Cambridge: Cambridge University Press, 2007.

———. *Philosophy and the Mirror of Nature, with an Introduction by M. Williams*. Princeton, NJ: Princeton University Press, 2009.

———. "Trotsky and the Wild Orchids." In *The Rorty Reader*, edited by C. J. Voparil and R. J. Bernstein, 500–510. Oxford: Wiley-Blackwell, 2010.

Upham, S. P., ed. *Philosophers in Conversation: Interviews from the* Harvard Review of Philosophy. Foreword by T. Scanlon. New York: Routledge, 2002.

Voparil, Christopher J. "General Introduction." In *The Rorty Reader*, edited by C. J. Voparil and R. J. Bernstein, 1–52. Oxford: Wiley-Blackwell, 2010.

Williams, Michael. "Introduction to the Thirtieth-Anniversary Edition." In *Philosophy and the Mirror of Nature*, edited by R. Rorty. Princeton, NJ: Princeton University Press, 2009.

Wittgenstein, Ludwig. *Philosophical Investigations*. Translated by G. E. M. Anscombe. Oxford: Blackwell, 1953.

Index

About the Contributors

Vincent Colapietro is a liberal arts professor of philosophy and African American studies at Pennsylvania State University. One of his main areas of historical research is the pragmatist tradition, with special emphasis on Charles S. Peirce. A main focus of his systematic work is the articulation and application of a general theory of signs. Though devoted to developing a semiotic perspective rooted in Peirce's seminal work, Colapietro draws upon a number of authors and perspectives other than Peirce and pragmatism (including such authors as Bakhtin, Jakobson, and Bourdieu as well as such movements as phenomenology, hermeneutics, and deconstruction). He is the author of *Peirce's Approach to the Self: A Semiotic Perspective on Human Subjectivity* (1989), *A Glossary of Semiotics* (1993), and *Fateful Shapes of Human Freedom* (2003) as well as numerous essays. He has served as president of the Charles S. Peirce Society, the Metaphysical Society of America, and the Semiotic Society of America. At present, he is completing a book on pragmatism and psychoanalysis, while continuing his research on literary theory, intellectual history, and other topics.

Sandra Laugier is professor of philosophy at the University of Paris 1 Panthéon-Sorbonne, a senior fellow of the Institut Universitaire de France, and head of the Sorbonne Center for Contemporary Philosophy of the Institute for Legal and Philosophical Sciences (UMR 8103, CNRS-Paris 1). After studies at the Ecole Normale Supérieure (1980–1985) and at Harvard University (1983–1985), she received her PhD in philosophy in 1990 from the University of Paris 4 and her HDR (Habilitation) in 1997 at the University of Paris 1, was named professor at the University of Picardie Jules Verne (1998–2010), then junior fellow of the Institut Universitaire de France (1999–2004) before assuming her current position. Her interests are mostly in ordinary language philosophy (Wittgenstein, Austin, Cavell) and ethics (ethics of care, moral perfectionism, and environmental ethics). She has translated into French most of Stanley Cavell's work (including *The Claim of Reason, Pursuits of Happiness, Must We Mean What We Say?* and all his works on Emerson). She has directed several research programs including a major ANR (National Research Agency) program on the ethics of care (2007–2010) and is now deputy director of the Institute for Human and Social Science at the French CNRS. She was an invited professor at Johns Hopkins University (2008, 2009, 2011), and an invited lecturer at many universities (in Europe, and at the University of Chicago, UC–Berkeley, the New School for Social Research, University of Tokyo, and Doshisha University). She has published extensively (ten books, twenty-four edited works, many papers) on philosophy of language (Austin, Wittgenstein), North American philosophy (Emerson, Cavell), and moral philosophy in French, English, German, and Italian. Her most recent works include *Wittgenstein, Le mythe de l'inexpressivité* (2010), *Faut-il désobéir en démocratie?* (with A. Ogien, 2010), *La voix et la vertu. Variétés du perfectionnisme moral* (2011), *Tous vulnérables, le care, les animaux, l'environnement* (2012), *Face aux désastres: le care, la folie et les grandes détresses collectives* (with Veena Das, Stefania Pandolfo, and Anne Lovell, 2013), *Why We Need Ordinary Language Philosophy* (2013), *Le principe démocratie* (with A. Ogien, 2014), and *Recommencer la philosophie, Stanley Cavell et la philosophie en Amérique* (2014).

Megan J. Laverty is an associate professor of philosophy and education at Teachers College, Columbia University. She researches in philosophy of education, moral philosophy, and pre-college philosophy. Her recent books include *Art's Teachings, Teaching's Arts: Philosophical, Critical and Educational Musings* (2015), coedited with Tyson E. Lewis, and *In Community of Inquiry with Ann Margaret Sharp: Philosophy, Childhood and Education* (2017), coedited with Maughn Rollins Gregory. Laverty is the author of numerous articles and the book *Iris Murdoch's Ethics: A Consideration of her Romantic Vision* (2007).

Ian Munday is a lecturer in education at the University of Stirling. He teaches in the Initial Teacher Education, MRes, and Doctoral School programs. Ian's research activities testify to an engagement with philosophical issues in education, particularly those concerning teaching and learning. His publications have tended to focus on various approaches to performatives and performativities, and on demonstrating the significance of these ideas for education. The themes explored in these terms include race, gender, the construction of authority, and the language of schooling. Here, philosophical ideas are treated with regard to their relevance to the details of educational practice, covering such matters as teaching and learning, continuing professional development, and problem-solving. His more recent and forthcoming research focuses on theorizing "creativity" in education.

Sami Pihlström is professor of philosophy of religion at the Faculty of Theology, University of Helsinki, where he is also in charge of the "Contemporary Philosophy of Religion" research group within the Academy of Finland Centre of Excellence, "Reason and Religious Recognition." He was previously (2009–2015) the director of the Helsinki Collegium for Advanced Studies. He is the president of the Philosophical Society of Finland and is, among other things, a member of the Institut International de Philosophie. He has published widely on pragmatism, transcendental philosophy, metaphysics, ethics, and philosophy of religion. His recent books include *Pragmatic Pluralism and the Problem of God* (2013), *Taking Evil Seriously* (2014), *Death and Finitude* (2016), and *Kantian Antitheodicy* (with Sari Kivistö, 2016).

Claudia W. Ruitenberg is an associate professor of philosophy of education in the Department of Educational Studies at the University of British Columbia, Vancouver, Canada. She is the author of *Unlocking the World: Education in an Ethic of Hospitality* (2015), coeditor of *Education, Culture and Epistemological Diversity: Mapping a Disputed Terrain* (2012), and editor of *What Do Philosophers of Education Do (And How Do They Do It)?* (2010). Previous work on translation includes "Distance and Defamiliarisation: Translation as Philosophical Method" (*Journal of Philosophy of Education*, 2009) and "The Productive Difficulty of Untranslatables in Qualitative Research" (with Autumn Knowlton and Gang Li, *Language and Intercultural Communication*, 2016).

Naoko Saito is an associate professor at the Graduate School of Education, University of Kyoto. Her area of research is American philosophy and pragmatism and its implications for education. For many years she has been working as a mediator in cross-cultural settings, especially between Japan and Anglo-American cultures, and more recently European cultures. She was visiting fellow at the Institute of Education, London, from October 2010 to March 2011, and at Helsinki Collegium of Advanced Studies, University of Helsinki, from September 2014 to August 2015. She is a board member of the Society for the Advancement of American Philosophy, and was the program chair for the fifteenth biennial meeting of the International Network of the Philosophy of Education, University of Warsaw, August 17–20, 2016. She is currently running Kyoto University's international project, "Philosophy as Translation and Understanding Other Cultures" (2013–2017): http://www.educ.kyoto-u.ac.jp/nsaito/.

She is the author of *The Gleam of Light: Moral Perfectionism and Education in Dewey and Emerson* (2005), *Uchinaru Hikari to Kyoiku: Pragmatism no Sai-Kochiku* (*The Gleam of Light: Reconstruction in Pragmatism* [2009]), and *America Tetsugaku no Yoake* (*The Dawning of American Philosophy* [2017]), and coeditor (with Paul Standish) of the collections *Education and the Kyoto School of Philosophy* (2012), *Stanley Cavell and the Education of Grownups* (2012), and *Stanley Cavell and Philosophy as Translation: The Truth Is Translated* (2017). She is the translator of *The Senses of Walden* by Stanley Cavell (2005) and of *Beyond the Self: Wittgenstein, Heidegger, Levinas and the Limits of Language*, by Paul Standish (2012).

Paul Standish is a professor of philosophy of education and head of the University College London Centre for Philosophy of Education. His recent publications include *The Therapy of Education*, coauthored with Paul Smeyers and Richard Smith, and *The Philosophy of Nurse Education*, coedited with John Drummond. With Naoko Saito, he has coedited *Stanley Cavell and the Education of Grownups* and *Education and the Kyoto School of Philosophy: Pedagogy for Human Transformation* (2012). With SunInn Yun, he has coedited *Democracy and Education at 100* (2016). He is now associate editor and was editor (2001–2011) of the *Journal of Philosophy of Education*.

Joris Vlieghe is lecturer in philosophy of education at Liverpool Hope University. He obtained his PhD in 2010 with a dissertation on "The Democracy of the Flesh," in which he explored the role of corporeality in and for education. His current research deals with the impact of digitization (and more precisely the ubiquity of screens) on the meaning of education. As such he is interested in the way in which digital technologies affect dimensions that traditionally have been considered vital to education: transformation, emancipation, community, attention, literacy, formation/edification, and creativity. Central to this line of investigation is the question whether or not we still need schools in digital times.